THE CHILLING ~~~~~
A BRILLIANT YOUNG DOCTOR'S
MONSTROUSLY DEPRAVED PLOT TO
MURDER HIS EX-WIFE—TOLD BY THE
PROSECUTING ATTORNEY . . .

"HARROWING, FASCINATING, FIRST-RATE!"
—*Library Journal*

*"FROM TIME TO TIME A CRIME STORY GRIPS
AN ICY HAND ON THE SHOULDERS OF READERS
WHO REALIZE THEY COULD AS EASILY HAVE
BEEN THE VICTIM IN THE BOOK THEY'RE
HOLDING* . . . Such a story is told by William
Randolph Stevens in *Deadly Intentions*, a book about
a woman who came to learn that the brilliant
young doctor she married posed the gravest danger
to both herself and their infant son . . . a chilling
portrayal of a modern Jekyll-Hyde, made all the
more compelling because the story is true."
—*San Francisco Chronicle*

Deadly Intentions

Deadly
Intentions

William Randolph Stevens

A SIGNET BOOK

SIGNET
Published by the Penguin Group
Penguin Books USA Inc., 375 Hudson Street,
New York, New York 10014, U.S.A.
Penguin Books Ltd, 27 Wrights Lane,
London W8 5TZ, England
Penguin Books Australia Ltd, Ringwood,
Victoria, Australia
Penguin Books Canada Ltd, 10 Alcorn Avenue,
Toronto, Ontario, Canada M4V 3B2
Penguin Books (N.Z.) Ltd, 182–190 Wairau Road,
Auckland 10, New Zealand

Penguin Books Ltd, Registered Offices:
Harmondsworth, Middlesex, England

Published by Signet, an imprint of New American Library,
a division of Penguin Books USA Inc.

This is an authorized reprint of a hardcover edition published by
Congdon & Weed, Inc. The hardcover edition was published simultaneously
in Canada by Thomas Nelson & Sons Limited

First Signet Printing, October, 1983
16   15   14   13   12   11   10

 REGISTERED TRADEMARK—MARCA REGISTRADA

Printed in the United States of America

To Christina and her parents

Contents

The Ominous Passenger

GENE ZARR was ready for a break, ready to get off his feet a while. He glanced at his watch: he had been standing for two hours, and it would be another thirty-five minutes before he could leave the American Airlines counter in the Tucson airport. There were at least a dozen people in the line in front of his counter, and more were coming. The next American Airlines departure was scheduled for 11:55 A.M. After its passengers were checked in and the plane had left for Dallas, Zarr would get his break.

As the next passenger stepped forward, Zarr noticed his massive arms and chest, even though they were covered by a baggy, long-sleeve sweater. A weight lifter, thought Zarr. Then he saw the man's pants. They also were baggy, several sizes too large, but the man wore no belt; the pants seemed to be held up by safety pins. In his years with the airline, Zarr had seen his share of odd ducks, but this one was a lulu.

"I want to change my flight," the man said, handing Zarr a ticket. "I want to leave on the next available flight to Dallas." The ticket he handed over identified him as Mr. A. Donald Vester, scheduled to leave Tucson for Dallas the following night. Zarr began preparing a new ticket. As he punched information into the console, the computer recorded the time on the ticket—11:24 A.M., 6 December 1977.

"Mr. Vester," Zarr said, "changing from a night flight to a day flight is going to increase the cost of your ticket." As he spoke, Zarr noticed that the man was wearing a wig. It didn't quite fit, and the style was also peculiar: black stringy hair that almost reached his shoulders.

Zarr did not allow himself more than a glance. How a passenger dressed wasn't any of his business. But there was

.nething else—Zarr could sense it. The man was extremely nervous. Not the usual nervousness of a hesitant passenger; this was something more than that. The way he spoke, the way he kept looking from side to side, the taut expression on his face, his ill-fitting wig and clothing—they all told Zarr the same thing: watch this guy. In a matter of seconds, Zarr had gone from curiosity to suspicion.

He would pay the extra ticket cost in cash, Vester said, reaching into a pocket for his wallet. As he did so, Zarr saw the man's bicep *wrinkle*. It wasn't just the sweater; it was, somehow, the man's arm, his muscle, that had wrinkled. Zarr knew then that something was surely *wrong*. The passenger had to be checked, or questioned, or something, before he was allowed to board the aircraft.

Before Zarr could decide exactly how to proceed, Vester said, "I want to check my bag as luggage. I don't want to carry it." And, with that, he shifted his coat to his other arm, revealing the briefcase he was holding.

Zarr hadn't seen the case before. Vester had draped his coat in such a way that the briefcase had been concealed. As the case was handed over to him, Zarr noticed that the handle was broken; one of its ends was not attached to the case. For that reason he taped the luggage identification strap to the side of the case instead of circling the handle with it.

As he worked, Zarr was thinking furiously. The passenger had no other luggage. Why was Vester causing himself a thirty-minute delay in Dallas by checking a small bag that he could easily carry aboard the plane? Then the peculiar passenger was talking to him again.

"I need to get something out of it; I need to have it back," he said urgently. Zarr returned the bag without comment, and Vester began to walk away, saying, "I'll be right back."

Zarr knew this was his chance. Something was up, he was almost certain. He told the other agents at the counter that he would be gone for a minute. They were too busy checking in passengers to notice the worried expression on his face.

There was really only one thing he could do—report what he had just seen, and report it quickly. As he walked to his supervisor's office, he considered the most obvious possibility: the man could be a hijacker with some kind of explosive in the case. In the eleven years he had worked as an agent for

American, no other passenger had ever alarmed him as mu... as the one he had just seen.

Gene Weber, Zarr's supervisor, often gauged the seriousness of a problem by considering who was bringing it to him. Security training had made the newer agents, and even some of the older ones, a little jittery. They reported anything out of the ordinary. But Zarr rarely came to Weber. And so, without ever laying eyes on A. Donald Vester, Weber knew there was cause for concern.

He and Zarr quickly settled on a strategy. For the sake of the eighty passengers to Dallas, they had to find out if Vester was carrying anything dangerous, on his person or in his bag. And, in case he wasn't, they had to do it without causing an incident. Weber's solution required one simple falsehood. When Vester returned with the case, Zarr was to tell him that it was now too late to check the bag onto the 11:55 Dallas flight; the case would have to be carried aboard the aircraft. This would force Vester to take the briefcase through airport security, where the X-ray machines and magnetometers would reveal whether it held anything menacing.

Gene Zarr returned to the counter. There was a tightness in his chest, a slight quickness in his breathing. His fatigue was completely forgotten. Several minutes passed. He checked tickets, took luggage, answered questions, but his mind was on Mr. Donald Vester. He found himself getting impatient and then anxious. The man had been gone for almost ten minutes. That was plenty of time for him to have removed something from the case and returned. Where was he? Another minute went by, and then another.

The counter began to clear. Most of the passengers had checked in and gone down the concourse to board the waiting aircraft. A few people were still being helped by other agents, but there was no one in front of Zarr. He glanced around, hoping to spot Vester, and suddenly there he was, not more than twenty feet away, walking directly toward Zarr, briefcase in hand.

With a jolt, Zarr's heartbeat speeded up. As Vester covered the short distance to the counter, Zarr realized why he hadn't seen him sooner: Vester had put on the coat that he had been carrying. Zarr took a good look at him now, as he approached, and realized that the coat emphasized a strange contrast between Vester's head and body. They weren't in proportion.

.e coat made it more noticeable that Vester's head and neck were too small for his torso.

Zarr tried to settle down and act normally. He wasn't used to lying and hoped he could do it without giving himself away.

As the passenger lifted the bag to hand it over the counter, he said something, but Zarr didn't hear him. He was concentrating too hard on his own lines.

"I'm sorry, sir," he said as casually as he could. "You're too late to check your luggage, we've closed it down for this flight. You'll have to carry it aboard."

Vester's face registered shock. "I don't want to take it aboard; I want to check it." His voice sounded desperate.

Zarr didn't budge. "I'm sorry, sir, but that's impossible. Luggage has been closed; we can't put any more through."

"But I don't want to carry it. I want to check it," Vester's voice shook slightly, and Zarr thought his hands did too.

"I'm sorry, there isn't anything I can do. But if you take it down to the departure gate they'll check it for you."

With a great show of annoyance, Vester took back his briefcase and walked off in the direction of the departure gate. Zarr drew a deep breath and felt his shoulder muscles relax. In less than a minute Vester would reach the security checkpoint.

Michelle Griggs was on duty at the security gate on the B concourse. With her long blond hair and fine features, she was a striking woman, and no businessman who went through the gate ever minded when she inspected his briefcase.

Bag in hand, A. Donald Vester walked up to her and said curtly, "The people at the ticket counter told me my bag could be checked at the departure gate."

Without commenting, Griggs took the briefcase, and before Vester could react, she placed it on the small conveyor belt. Vester stared in dismay as his case moved slowly toward the X-ray machine.

"If you're carrying it to the gate, it still has to be examined," Griggs explained, leaning forward to stare at the small monitor of her machine. As the case passed under the X ray, the machine projected the contents on the screen in various shades of gray. She was quickly able to identify some of them—a pair of pliers and some tools—but there was a boxlike object that she could not identify. As Vester stood watching intently, she stopped the conveyor belt and ran it backward to put the case through again. Again the X ray displayed what it could, but Griggs still could not identify all the shadowy gray outlines she was seeing. She moved to the other side of the machine and grabbed the case as it emerged.

"I'm having trouble with this. What have you got in there?" As she asked the question, she realized that the passenger was wearing a wig.

"Just some stuff. Just tools, a knife and money."

"Well, I can't make them out. You'll have to open this up so I can see what you have."

Seeing that there was some problem, Officer Frank DeMercy of the airport police stepped forward.

"But I can't open the case, I don't have a key for it," Vester told them.

"The briefcase can't be taken aboard the aircraft unless the contents are examined," DeMercy said firmly. "You'll have to open it." This sort of minor confrontation with passengers was routine for DeMercy, and his suspicions were not aroused. But then, he and Michelle Griggs had not seen this passenger's baggy pants, now concealed beneath his coat, or his nervousness when Gene Zarr had told him he would have to carry the case through the security checkpoint.

"But I don't have the key; I can't open it," Vester objected.

"In that case, you'll have to return to the ticket counter and send the bag as checked luggage," DeMercy advised, totally unaware that the last thing Gene Zarr wanted was to see this particular passenger again.

When Vester reappeared at the check-in counter, Zarr knew his intuition had been right.

"They won't let me carry it to the plane," Vester said. "They say I have to open it if I want to carry it on, and I can't. I don't have the key."

Zarr didn't believe him. Just a few minutes before, after all, the man had taken back his bag in order to remove something he needed. But Zarr did not challenge him. "Why don't you leave the bag with me here at the counter," he said calmly, "and you go back to the security checkpoint and wait for me. I'll be right there."

This time, without protesting or making a face, Vester walked away, leaving the briefcase on the counter. Satisfied that Vester was following his instructions, Zarr grabbed the

⸱e by its broken handle and hurried again to Weber. Together they walked, almost ran, to confront Vester at the checkpoint.

Several people were gathered at the magnetometer, waiting to pass through.

"Which one is he?" asked Weber.

"He isn't here," Zarr answered, scanning the group again to be sure. But there was no mistake—Vester wasn't among them. "Maybe he's gone on down to the gate," Zarr suggested. Leaving the briefcase on Griggs' counter, in front of the X-ray machine, the two men hurried off again. Griggs looked up and recognized the case by the broken handle and the identification strap taped to its side.

A minute later Zarr and Weber reached gate B-5 and spotted Vester. He was standing in a dwindling line of passengers showing their boarding passes before getting on the aircraft. Weber went directly to the point.

"Mr. Vester, I do not intend to let that case of yours aboard the aircraft unless the contents are checked and found to be safe."

"But I don't want to carry it into the cabin; I want to check it as baggage."

"That doesn't matter any more, it doesn't make any difference how you want to send it. It isn't getting aboard at all until you've shown us the contents."

"But I can't do that. I don't have the key."

"Well, Mr. Vester, I've been told that you checked the case once, and then took it back to get something out of it, and that you were away from the counter for at least five or ten minutes. I think you can open it. I think you just don't want to."

"I can't open it, I told you. I lost the key. And I need that case with me. I have to have it in Dallas."

Weber caught the mistake instantly. If Vester needed the case in Dallas, why had he abandoned it at the ticket counter and tried to board without it? Weber's decision to prevent the bag from going aboard was now irreversible. His mind immediately shifted to the next question: did he have sufficient reason to deny Vester himself the right to board the aircraft? He was not drunk, he was not causing a disturbance, and he had passed security. His luggage hadn't, but he had. Weber had to let him board.

As if sensing his advantage, Vester began to complain loudly about being denied his own luggage. "This plane is about to leave and I need that briefcase." As if to underline the urgency of his situation, the final departure announcement came over the loudspeaker. Two other Dallas passengers still waiting to board regarded this confrontation curiously. Weber had to reach a solution, and quickly.

"Okay, Mr. Vester, here's what I'll do," he said. "Upstairs in the security office we have a collection of keys, probably a hundred or more. One of them is bound to open the case. With your permission, I'll take the case up there and have a police officer watch while I check the contents. If there's no hazardous material in the case, I'll send it to you on the next American flight to Dallas. That would be a flight arriving in Dallas sometime early this evening. But I'll need your permission."

Vester assented. "Okay, but I need that bag in Dallas."

Weber asked Vester for his luggage receipt stub and when it was produced he wrote "V.S." and the number "384" on it: voluntary separation, flight 384, the next plane to Dallas.

Weber watched as Vester walked out to the plane. Second thoughts worked their way into his anxious mind. Was he taking a chance by letting Vester board? He wasn't at all comfortable with his decision as he strode up the concourse to his supervisor, George Boiko's, office. As Weber finished relating each event, starting with the peculiarities Zarr had noticed and ending with the agreement that he and Vester had just reached, Boiko stood up and, without a word, he and Weber departed for the security checkpoint where the briefcase was.

When they reached the checkpoint Michelle Griggs was already X-raying the briefcase, trying again to identify the rectangular object she had noticed earlier. Its shape and color—light gray—told her it was a metal box of some kind. Within the rectangular shape, however, the grayness on screen was not consistent. Some areas were much darker, and Griggs had been taught that the greater the density of a metal object, the darker it appeared on the screen. Therefore, she concluded, she was seeing metal objects inside the box, and they were heavier—darker—than the box itself. This wasn't new to her; she had seen metal over metal before, but usually she simply instructed the passenger to open his luggage so she could identify the object. This time she had to interpret what the machine showed her.

As she concentrated on the darker objects within the box, it suddenly came to her. The darker object was a gun. She could see the faint outline of the barrel and handle.

"It's a gun," she reported. "I can see it. It's a gun." The men standing behind her immediately leaned over her shoulders, trying to get a glimpse at the screen. She stepped back and let Boiko take her place. But his eyes were not trained; he could see the rectangular box and some tools, but the different shadings within the rectangle escaped him. It didn't matter. He trusted Griggs.

Boiko told Officer DeMercy to take the case downstairs to the baggage area. Then he instructed Officer Jim Kelch, who had just arrived, to call for the Sheriff's Office explosive ordinance detail. Weber had already gone to the security office for the keys. Minutes later he joined Boiko and DeMercy in the large, open baggage area.

On his knees, with Weber beside him, Boiko tried the first key with no success. He tried another and another. The seventh key fit. It turned easily in the lock and one latch snapped open. But not the second latch; no amount of twisting or turning would open that. The case would open slightly, on just one side, but no more than three-quarters of an inch, and that was with Boiko forcing the two sides apart. Peering into the space he'd created, he located the metal box. Then he froze. Near the box he saw something else—a piece of wire or string, he couldn't be sure which. It made no difference. For the first time it hit him: he was in danger. As a matter of routine he'd sent for the bomb dogs, but he hadn't really expected to find explosives in the case. Now, moving slowly and very cautiously, he placed the case on the floor, then started backing away.

"Someone get a bomb basket, go get a bomb basket and take this thing outside," he yelled to the security officers. "Everyone else get back, stay away from it." As he spoke, it occurred to him that everyone else was already much further away than he was, at least fifty feet. They were all staring at him solemnly as he shouted.

Officer Kelch had called the Pima County Sheriff's Office and requested the explosive ordinance detail. Then he called for the Tucson Police Department's bomb dogs. But Kelch was worried. Officer DeMercy, who had been stationed at the security checkpoint, had told Kelch the story as he'd remembered it: he and Griggs had stopped a passenger because of his carry-on luggage. The passenger had left the briefcase behind, then run down the concourse and boarded a flight which was now en route to Dallas–Fort Worth. When Michelle examined the case under the X-ray machine, she'd declared positively that there was a gun inside.

There were some errors in this version of the story, but even more important, from a legal standpoint, were the omissions. DeMercy had not been told that Vester originally wanted to check his briefcase as luggage, and that Zarr had more or less forced him to present it at the security checkpoint. Nor did he know that Weber and Vester had eventually agreed that security could open the briefcase and send it along on a later flight. On the basis of what he did know, Kelch decided to notify the Tucson office of the FBI. It was possible that a federal crime had been committed.

Kelch told Agent Don Hall the story as he knew it, adding that explosive ordinance and the bomb dogs had been sent for. Hall in turn called the United States Attorney's Office. If what Kelch said was true, the federal antihijacking laws had been violated, and he wanted permission to arrest this A. Donald Vester without a warrant when the plane landed in Dallas. An assistant U.S. attorney gave permission and then informed Hall that the Attorney's Office would immediately seek an arrest warrant.

The Sheriff's Office explosive ordinance detail, Sgt. Davey Reagor and Deputy Ron Harris arrived at the airport at least ten minutes before the two dog units. After Boiko and Weber briefed them, Reagor asked for the flight's destination and the actual flying time. He was told that flight 156 was due to arrive at Dallas–Fort Worth at 2:43 P.M., Dallas time, and that the actual flying time was one hour and forty-eight minutes.

Reagor glanced at his watch: 12:24 P.M. The plane had been in the air approximately thirty minutes. With the briefcase secured outside in the bomb basket, his first concern was the aircraft and its passengers. Were they still in danger even though the briefcase was not aboard?

Just because the passenger himself had passed through security without incident once he'd abandoned the briefcase,

Reagor knew better than to assume that Vester was harmless. As a security training exercise, Reagor had concealed several pounds of explosives on his person and walked undetected through the magnetometers of a security checkpoint. His purpose had been to demonstrate that security's equipment alone would not detect everything. Nonmetallic substances such as dynamite or plastic explosives, or combustibles in plastic containers, would not be picked up by either the magnetometer or the X-ray machine. Reagor knew how easily someone could smuggle dangerous material through security; he'd been successful the three times he'd tried.

As he went over the facts again and again, additional possibilities occurred to him. The passenger had originally tried to check his briefcase as luggage. That might mean he had intended to check the case aboard and then not board himself. The bomb would explode while the plane was in the air, with Vester himself safely on the ground, far from the airport. Reagor preferred the other possibility—that Griggs and Boiko were wrong: there was no gun in the box, and the wire or string Boiko had seen was harmless.

But that was just a hope, and the "potential for danger" was real. His next step was to examine the bomb basket and its contents.

Outside in the driveway he instructed Weber, Boiko, and several airport police officers to remain where they were, while he approached the bomb basket.

The basket was nothing more than a large fiber glass barrel about four feet high. There was no top or bottom, just a net inside that held objects off the ground, resting just below the upper rim of the barrel. If a bomb exploded, the basket would direct the impact up and down, rather than sideways.

Around Reagor's neck hung an electronic stethoscope. After studying the briefcase for a few seconds, he raised the stethoscope and placed the listening tubes to his ears. Then, carefully, he placed the cup against the briefcase. Nothing. Even at full amplification he heard nothing, neither the telltale humming sound nor the clocklike ticking.

But still he could not relax. The absence of sound could mean there was no bomb, but could just as easily mean the explosive had a silent detonator. Reagor decided to wait for the dogs before he proceeded further. He hoped Zitto would show up; Zitto was the only dog he could count on.

Zitto had been lying on the floor when the telephone rang. He'd watched hopefully as Jim Richards had answered, listened, and hung up. The moment Richards had grabbed the collar and leash from their hook, the big shepherd had sprung to his feet. They were going to do what Zitto liked to do more than anything. Racing through traffic, Jim Richards and Zitto arrived forty-five minutes past noon.

Butch Weadock and his dog Archie had also been called out, and had arrived just seconds before Richards. Archie, Weadock's dog, did not have Zitto's experience; he had been "on the street" less than a year. Reagor would rely mainly on Zitto.

A small crowd of six or seven people watched from a safe distance as Richards slipped another collar over his dog's head. The leather collar was a signal to the dog: the game is starting, go to full alert. Zitto responded as he always did; ears erect and forward, tail rigid, he put his head down and began the short repeating breaths that would reveal the thing he sought, if it was there. Zitto was capable of detecting by smell the slightest quantity of twenty-one different types of nitrate-based explosives.

Richards did not lead the dog immediately to the bomb basket. Instead he walked Zitto to an adjacent wall, then turned and moved backward slowly toward the bomb basket. As he walked, Richards controlled Zitto's attention by pointing at different objects, while repeating over and over a series of questions: "What's that? What's this? What's this, boy? Zitto, check here." Zitto worked the area inch by inch, his nose constantly sniffing, his body tense with concentration.

Zitto reached the basket and began sniffing around its base, then up its sides. Then, in a slow, deliberate movement, he raised his front paws to the top of the barrel and used the rim to balance himself. Jim Richards stood just behind; he could see the briefcase in the basket. Zitto put his nose as close to it as he could get without touching it. He sniffed, then hopped back and sat down, immediately turning his head to look back at his master.

A wave of relief broke over the small crowd of onlookers as they watched the dog's reaction. Gene Weber and George Boiko exchanged weary glances, then smiled. The small crowd started laughing, talking, and breathing again. Two officers started forward. Richards shot them a quick glance, his message clear: "Be quiet, get back."

They stopped. No one moved. No one said a thing. They could see Richards's hands moving slowly up the leash to Zitto's collar, his grip as tight as he could make it. Sergeant Reagor understood why. Richards was making sure that Zitto couldn't jump up to the rim again—that movement might set it off the next time. For Zitto had told those who knew how to read his movements what they needed to know—that the case contained some type of explosive. A single bullet, perhaps, or a bomb that could shred an airplane and its passengers.

Now it was Archie's turn. Archie would be used to confirm Zitto's findings.

Together Butch Weadock and Archie worked their way down the wall very much as Zitto and Richards had, only more slowly. When they were within a few feet of the basket, Weadock placed his feet apart and set the weight of his body on his back foot. In that stance he could hold Archie back on his hind legs and keep his paws from touching the upper rim of the basket as Zitto's had.

The dog approached the basket, sniffed its base and sides, then raised up to smell the top. Butch held him back. Archie, on hind legs, strained his neck and body to get at the object in the basket. Butch slowly leaned forward, just enough to let Archie's muzzle reach the case. Archie held his position a second or two, then abruptly sat and turned his head toward his master.

It was conclusive. Reagor glanced at his watch again: 12:45 P.M. Now that he knew the case contained explosives, his thoughts returned to the passengers on the aircraft. For them, he was afraid, time was getting short. Vester might either be carrying a bomb, or have concealed another one aboard the airplane somewhere. Reagor knew that people who place explosives aboard aircraft generally set the detonators so the explosion occurs at the halfway point, or during the second half of the flight. Flight 156 would be halfway to Dallas in less than five minutes.

As soon as the captain had leveled the aircraft after takeoff, the four flight attendants prepared to serve lunch. It was almost noon and they had less than two hours to serve the entire plane.

Two attendants reached aisle 13 with the beverage cart, and asked the three people seated on the right if they wanted lunch. Before anyone else could answer, the man seated in the middle looked up and said, "I'm not in the right seat. I'm supposed to be in 9C. I don't belong here." He released his seat belt and stood up, then began to squeeze out into the aisle, which was blocked by the cart. As he did, he said to one of the attendants, "I've got to get to my seat." The attendant glanced over at her partner, who was close enough to have heard the remark, and they exchanged a look that spoke clearly: "What's his problem? What's the big deal?"

Without saying anything, the two attendants moved the cart back and allowed him to pass. As one of them watched him walk up the aisle she wondered why he was still wearing his overcoat, buttoned up to his chin.

Within an hour of takeoff, everyone who wanted to eat had been served, even the crew. The flight attendants would take a short break and then begin to collect the trays. The first part of the flight had been completely routine, almost monotonous. From the attendants' point of view the flight was progressing exactly as American Airlines had planned: uneventfully.

None of them paid particular attention to Dr. Noah Fredericks, a tall, distinguished-looking gentleman with gray hair and wire-rimmed glasses, seated in 8D. Dr. Fredericks was not enjoying the flight. He couldn't, considering what he'd seen at the airport just before departure, and what he was seeing now.

His attention was focused on the man in 9C, across the aisle from him and one row back. Dr. Fredericks had been directly behind him at the security checkpoint, when the X-ray machine revealed metallic objects in his briefcase. He had also been one of the two passengers still waiting to board when the airline officials had stopped the man at the gate for questioning. The doctor had heard them insist that the man's luggage was not going aboard unless he opened it for their inspection. He had seen the man's nervousness as he'd said he couldn't open the case, and had taken in the man's wig and odd clothing. But what had really disturbed Dr. Fredericks was when he heard one of the airline officials tell the man that they didn't believe he couldn't open the case.

Now, aboard the flight, Dr. Fredericks had seen the man switch seats after the plane was in the air, and then he'd watched him sit trancelike for almost the first half of the flight. Even during lunch the man had sat staring ahead, moving his arms slowly, mechanically. Dr. Fredericks tried to relax and read a medical journal, but he couldn't concentrate. In the end he decided to keep an eye on the man. He wasn't sure what good that would do, but at least it would make him feel a little better.

Reagor and Harris decided to open the briefcase. They agreed not to bother with the protective gear the Sheriff's Office recommended for dangerous situations. It took too long to put it on, and then it was too confining to work in. Besides, they had both heard the standard explosive ordinance training school joke: wearing the protective gear just guaranteed your wife an uninjured chest to bury.

Harris lay flat on the pavement, his head within a foot of the case, his feet pointing away. In his hand was a special flashlight: a narrow metal finger extended eight inches from the barrel, with a small light bulb at the end of the finger. Holding the light up to the case, Harris tried to see into the crack George Boiko had created by unlocking one latch. Through the crack they could see the wire and the metal box Boiko had reported but little else—possibly some clothing; they weren't sure.

Reagor knelt on one knee and tore off three strips of adhesive tape. With Harris holding the case upright, Reagor applied two parallel strips perpendicular to the handle across the case's opening. He left a little slack over the crack created by the open latch. The third strip was placed parallel to the first two, but with more slack, perhaps an inch more, over the crack. Then, with tape in place, he began very slowly to pry the second latch open.

Although Reagor was actually opening the case, both he and Harris were so close to the briefcase that they shared the danger equally. Both of them were afraid. These moments might very well be their last. But they expected the fear. That was the most important and the most difficult part of their work—learning to control the fear so it could not rob them of their skills just when they needed them most.

They had taught themselves to put the fear into a compartment of the mind and then to seal it off completely. Total and absolute concentration on the job was by far their best tool.

To maintain that concentration, the two men talked to each other continuously, discussing each step as it was taken. That kept their minds from wandering back to the sealed compartment.

"I'm pulling, I can feel it . . . it's giving away."

"I still can't tell what's next to the metal box; it's either wire or string."

"It's coming, it's coming."

"Take your time. Take your time, Dave. It could have a clothespin device. Give me a chance to get my light in there."

"It's coming."

"Easy, Dave, easy."

After long anxious minutes, the latch began to give way under Reagor's deliberate strength. If it were rigged, this was the time it would be most likely to explode, but Reagor did not slacken his steady pressure. Suddenly it gave way; only the three strips of adhesive tape kept the case from spilling wide open. As it was, the slack that Reagor had left in the tape allowed an opening of at most an inch more. Holding the case firmly in both hands, not daring to move, Reagor nodded to Harris, who moved in with the special flashlight. In its beam they could see one thing clearly. "The "wire" that had alarmed George Boiko wasn't wire at all; it was twine, and not attached to the metal box.

Reagor did not allow himself the feeling of relief. It was too soon to relax. He cut the first two pieces of tape and the case opened another inch, as far as the third tape would allow. Now Harris carefully insinuated the metallic flashlight probe into the case. It revealed tools, clothing, twine, and other objects—no hidden wires, nothing to indicate that the case could not be safely opened. The third piece of tape was then cut and the case opened very slowly. Visible for the first time was a plumber's plunger, glass cutters, masking tape, gloves, and a bulky white envelope. Inside they found, not a bomb, but an assortment of firecrackers.

Again Reagor resisted relief. The metal box was still the biggest unknown, and it was taped shut. Carefully Reagor lifted it from the case and placed it several feet away. He needed Zitto again. While the amount of nitrate in the firecrackers was small, it was enough to have triggered the dog's first reaction. In training Zitto had been known to react to an empty wrapper that had once contained explosives. The metal box would have to be checked separately.

Zitto approached it in the same manner as he had the briefcase: at his master's direction, working slowly from the adjoining wall, following commands. His demeanor was the same, on his toes, tense, tail out straight. When they came to the box he approached it slowly, placing his muzzle near it without touching. Then his ears shifted slightly forward, his tail went up, and he sat abruptly, turning his head for his reward.

Again Richards withdrew to safety with Zitto, and Reagor knelt in front of the box. With a small knife he severed the tape and cautiously lifted the lid. For the first time in an hour and a half, Reagor allowed himself to relax. He wanted to laugh, to shout, to let the euphoria flood in.

"Come on back, it's okay," he shouted to the spectators. "This guy is no bomber. You've got yourselves a burglar here."

The officers surged forward, curious to see what Zitto had alerted to inside the metal box. As they drew closer, Reagor withdrew from within the box a .32-caliber pistol with several extra rounds of ammunition, and held them aloft triumphantly. Zitto had reacted to the gunpowder inside the bullets.

There were other items in the box: a boy scout hunting knife, a ratchet screwdriver set with several changeable blades, and several more firecrackers. But the gun was enough for Officer Kelch. He immediately returned to the security office and phoned the local FBI office that a gun had in fact been found in the briefcase. Agent Don Sickles informed Kelch in return that the U.S. Attorney's Office had granted oral permission to arrest A. Donald Vester without a warrant when he deplaned in Dallas. The FBI was now seeking a warrant.

Kelch immediately dialed the number of the Dallas Department of Public Safety, the office responsible for security at the Dallas–Fort Worth airport. He gave them Officer DeMercy's erroneous account of what happened, and DeMercy's description of the passenger they were to arrest.

As Kelch finished his call to Texas, Reagor and DeMercy walked into the security office with the briefcase. As Kelch watched, the two officers began to inventory the briefcase's contents. Each article was removed from the case and described by one officer, while the other wrote down the description. One of the last items was a birth certificate in the name of Terry Lee Cordell. Neither officer could be certain if the spelling of the name was Cordell or Cardell. Kelch decided to check both names with the National Crime Information Center (NCIC) to see if there were any outstanding warrants in either name anywhere in the United States. He also decided to check the name A. Donald Vester at the same time. When all three names were punched into the computer, the computer answered: no outstanding warrants.

Kelch placed another call, this time to the FBI office at the Dallas–Fort Worth airport. He advised them that he had notified the Department of Public Safety of a possible hijacking incident involving American Airlines flight 156, and that DPS had the necessary information. He requested that they, too, arrest and detain the passenger upon his arrival.

The inventory of the briefcase was completed and double-checked by the time FBI Agent Sickles walked into the security office. All he needed for his federal charge was the loaded pistol. By taking it to the security gate in an attempt to board the Dallas flight, Vester had violated the federal antihijacking law. Sickles did not know that, in fact, Vester had done everything in his power *not* to carry the case—and gun—aboard. Sure that his case was good, Sickles took possession of the briefcase and its contents, and looked over a copy of the inventory.

One black attaché case, no brand name
One Iver Johnson, caliber .32 revolver, five shot
Nine rounds, caliber .32, Winchester
23 firecrackers (two brand name Flash Salute)
One pair men's trousers, Farah, no size listed
One boy scout hunting knife, blade length 4⅜ inches
Plumber's plunger with detachable handle
Two bottles containing unknown liquids
Three books of matches
One ratchet handle for screwdriver with two blades
One pair of pliers
One pair of brown cloth gloves
Two pairs of Flomax latex procedure gloves
One roll of masking tape
Homemade blackjack, 9 inches in length
One roll of brown string, 380 feet

One handwarmer
One combination lock
Two pen flashlights
One glass cutter
Five assorted keys
One adjustable wrench, 4 inches long
One green metal box
One tube of Super Glue
One bottle of Clinique makeup
One wool stocking cap, purple in color
One birth certificate for Terry Lee Cordell (Cardell),
   date of birth April 25, 1948
One Continental Airlines schedule, plus forty 13-cent
   postage stamps stuck to the schedule

Sickles checked the inventory against the contents of the briefcase. Many of the articles were clearly burglar's tools. The plunger, glass cutters, and Super Glue, for example, could be used to cut through a windowpane in such a way that the glass would not fall noisily to the floor after it was cut. The gloves, small flashlights, and other tools were all appropriate to a burglar.

Yet, as Agent Sickles prepared to interview all the Tucson airport witnesses, Sgt. Dave Reagor felt puzzled. A lot of the items—like the bottle of Clinique makeup—had no apparent use. One article in particular bothered Reagor—the boy scout knife. Both edges, the blade and the edge that normally would be blunt, were razor keen. The knife had been sharpened on both sides, surgically sharpened. Now why, thought Reagor, would a burglar do *that?*

Corporal Frank Ramirez of the Dallas–Fort Worth airport police had only a few minutes' notice to meet flight 156 from Tucson. The dispatcher's voice, tinny over his hand-held radio, had advised him that a passenger, Mr. Donald Vester, had tried to take a weapon aboard an aircraft in Tucson, Arizona, and had then boarded American flight 156, which was scheduled to arrive momentarily. Ramirez listened carefully to the passenger's description: a six-foot-tall caucasian; twenty-eight to thirty years old; wearing a black wig, a brown sweater, black horn-rimmed glasses, and a dark overcoat. Ramirez was to detain and hold him for a possible antihijacking offense.

Ramirez asked if the man was armed, but the dispatcher

didn't know. Ramirez didn't bother to ask the question that instantly came to mind: "Who let the aircraft take off with him aboard?" After acknowledging his instructions, he requested that the airport office of the FBI be notified. The dispatcher assured him that they were being contacted. Relieved to know he would have assistance, Ramirez walked to the nearest ceiling-mounted television screen that displayed the gate numbers and times for incoming and departing flights. Flight 156 was scheduled to arrive at gate 14 at 2:43 P.M.—by Ramirez's watch, in just another three minutes.

Alerted by Officer Kelch's call from Tucson, the airport FBI office notified one of their men to meet incoming American flight 156 to intercept someone who might have committed an offense. Sitting in his car near the Delta Airlines terminal, Special Agent Steven Rand held his radio and waited a few seconds for further instructions, but the dispatcher did not continue. Puzzled, he radioed for additional information, but was told that none was available at the moment.

Just as Rand finished talking to his dispatcher he was summoned by the second of the two radios in his car, this one turned to the frequencies of the Dallas–Fort Worth airport Department of Public Safety. The DPS dispatcher advised him to respond to gate 14, terminal B, American Airlines, for a possible antihijacking violation involving flight 156. Within minutes Rand was at the American Airlines terminal. At the security checkpoint he cut to the head of the line and dashed through the magnetometer. It buzzed a warning to the security personnel, but Rand simply held up his FBI credentials and kept on going.

In the concourse, he spotted several uniformed DPS officers but they knew even less than he did. Frank Ramirez, whom Rand had worked with in the past, joined the small group and together they hurried toward gate 14. The aircraft was clearly visible through the large, brown-tinted windows; it was just pulling into place at the gate.

At that moment both Rand and Ramirez were experiencing the same fear: that this passenger, who they had to assume was still armed, would get by them in the crowd. If he made it as far as the terminal, they would never find him. They had to stop him in the jetway, the covered bridge between the hatch of the plane and the concourse—but if they confronted him and he decided to use his weapon, they and the other passengers would be trapped without cover in the narrow corridor.

As the hatch door was swung open and secured, they took their final positions, unaware of what had happened aboard flight 156, approximately sixty miles out, just after the captain had begun his descent.

Dr. Fredericks had been trying, again, to read one of his journals. He was just becoming absorbed in an article when he realized the man in 9C was leaving his seat. Waiting several seconds until he felt he could look without being noticed, he turned in time to see the man go into a lavatory at the end of the aisle. Dr. Fredericks turned back to his journal and resumed reading. But his mind kept returning to the confrontation he'd witnessed at the airport, the man's wig, odd trousers, and nervous, almost trembling hands. Dr. Fredericks turned around again, just in time to see the strange passenger step out of the lavatory. But he looked so different the doctor almost didn't recognize him. The horn-rimmed glasses and long, stringy black wig were gone. Now the man had short, neatly cut brown hair, graying at the temples. He was still wearing the dark coat mysteriously buttoned up to his chin, but to a casual onlooker he looked perfectly normal.

Not wanting to be caught spying, Dr. Fredericks faced front again. But now he was genuinely alarmed. Checking his watch, he saw they would be landing in less than twenty minutes. He searched for a piece of paper, but could find only a napkin. That was going to have to do. Making an effort to write legibly, he composed a message to the captain.

Captain:
The man in seat 9C had trouble getting his bag through the security gate. I was immediately behind him when he was stopped because of his briefcase, which contained metallic objects. I witnessed at the gate (prior to boarding) that his case had been taken from him. Also, prior to boarding two American Airlines officers confronted him with a request for the key to the case. He said he had lost the key; whereupon, the officers informed him that they would forward the case on another flight, providing they could first open the case.

This man looked as though he was wearing two sets of pants and he was extremely nervous and had difficulty controlling his hands. He has just gone to the toilet and removed the wig! That is odd to say the least. Thought you should know.

                              Noah Fredericks, M.D. (seat 8D)

As soon as it was completed, he grabbed the first attendant to walk by and asked her to give the note to the captain. She took it and went to the attendant in first class for the cockpit key. Outside the cockpit she stopped and read the note through, then delivered it to the captain.

Capt. David Donaldson looked up from the note to ask the attendant if there had been any problems, any at all, with the passenger. She reported that there had been none; the whole flight had been routine. As the captain thought it over, he realized there was nothing he could do. The passenger had caused no trouble, and it was now time to begin the descent into Dallas. He scribbled a note of thanks to Dr. Fredericks and concentrated on reducing his airspeed to something under 250 knots.

The attendant delivered the captain's note to Dr. Fredericks. Then, wanting a closer look at the passenger, she stepped back to the next row and asked the man in 9C if she could remove the empty plastic cup from his tray. The man nodded yes, and did not look up. She had no choice but to take the cup and leave.

As soon as she was a few rows away, the man in 9C stood, moved into the aisle, and stepped back several rows. Then, unobtrusively, he slipped into a vacant seat on the opposite side of the aisle—his third seat since the flight had begun. Dr. Fredericks did not see this last-minute change. The captain had turned on the seat-belt sign, and everyone was preparing for landing.

Now seated several rows behind Dr. Fredericks, the passenger sat quietly during the remainder of the flight. In his lap was a bundle. It appeared to be nothing more than a long-sleeve gray workshirt, but clearly visible over the left breast pocket was a small white patch bordered in red, with the name Herman sewn in the center.

                    *   *   *

The first passengers to emerge from the plane walked briskly down the jetway completely unaware that they were being studied by an FBI agent and a corporal assigned to the airport DPS antipiracy unit. Rand stood at the hatch door, within a foot of the off-boarding passengers, while Ramirez stood further back at the bend of the jetway ramp, but not so far away that he couldn't see Rand.

After the first spate of deplaning passengers, no one appeared for almost a minute. Rand could see them in the cabin, all trying to do several things at once—put on their coats, collect their carry-on luggage, get out of each other's way. Finally they began to filter out, two or three at first, and then a constant stream. The first fifteen to twenty passengers were easily eliminated by height, weight, sex, or age.

Then came a passenger with graying brown hair, carrying a workshirt with the name Herman stitched on it. His height was right, so Rand studied him carefully. But nothing else in the description fit: the man did not wear glasses, the age seemed wrong, and the name should have been Donald, not Herman. In a matter of seconds Rand had eliminated him and was looking the next passenger over.

Frank Ramirez spotted the same man seconds later, as he came down the jetway. The height and age struck him as within the range of possibility, and the dark coat was right. But the man fitted Vester's description in only the most general way, and Ramirez quickly glanced at the next group coming down the ramp to see if anyone more likely was approaching. By the time Ramirez had checked out everyone else within range, the man with the workshirt was walking by. There just wasn't enough that fit the description, so Ramirez decided to let him pass. As the man continued toward the concourse Ramirez found himself taking one final look. Then he saw it.

Hair. Sticking out of one of the coat pockets was a small clump of black hair. Instantly Ramirez acted. Gluing his eyes to the man's hands, watching for the slightest movement, he took two steps forward and grabbed his arm.

"Excuse me, sir, I'm Officer Frank Ramirez, Department of Public Safety. I'd like to talk to you."

The man, who had previously avoided Ramirez's eyes, looked directly at him and replied calmly, "What is it, what's the matter?'' Holding his arm firmly, Ramirez led him to the side, a step or two away from the other passengers.

"Do you have any identification, sir?"

"No, I don't."

"Then would you tell me your name, please." Ramirez's eyes were scanning the man from head to foot—his face, his build, his clothes, his hands. Especially his hands, in case he had a gun.

"What's this about, what's the problem?"

"Would you tell me your name, sir?"

"Donald Vester. Why?"

Ramirez cautiously took the bundled-up workshirt from Vester and squeezed it. There was something soft and cushiony inside, but nothing hard that would suggest a weapon. Ramirez tossed it to the floor and called to Rand. To Vester he said, "I'm going to ask you to unbutton your coat and to put your hands on the wall, sir. Turn around and put your hands on the wall."

"But why, what's this all about? I haven't done anything."

"Just put your hands on the wall, sir."

When Vester did as he was told, Ramirez told him to spread his feet further apart, then began to pat him down. He started at the man's neck and shoulders, then felt along his arms, under them, then down his torso. Something wasn't right—the man's body felt too soft, almost boneless—but Ramirez's chief concern was finding concealed weapons. When he was certain the man had none, he turned him around.

"This is Mr. Vester, Steve," he said to Rand, who had come over. As he spoke, he pointed to the hair sticking up out of the passenger's pocket. "May I see your ticket, please," he said to Vester.

The passenger produced it from one of his pockets and handed it over. It was in the name of A. Donald Vester. Ramirez noted that and handed the ticket back.

Other passengers began to slow down and cluster in the jetway, watching curiously. It was time for Ramirez and Rand to move on with their suspect.

Behind the concourse walkway in the Dallas–Fort Worth airport, interspersed with restaurants, luggage areas, and waiting lobbies, are a series of small offices, one of which is used by the Department of Public Safety. Vester was escorted to that office. Windowless, furnished with a table, a few chairs, and a sink, the room was stark and uncomfortable.

Vester had come along quietly enough, but Rand nevertheless sensed something disturbing. He had the feeling that Vester might fly into a rage at any second. Maybe that was it: the man seemed calm, but his eyes were saying something else. When Ramirez left to phone in a report to his department, Rand decided to play it safe by bringing in the biggest DPS officer he could find, Bill Grigsby, six foot three and 230 pounds. Moments later Rand's regular partner, Agent Tom Porter, arrived.

Porter and Rand began their investigation by introducing themselves and showing their identification. Rand did most of the talking. He explained that they had received word from Tucson that a Mr. Donald Vester had tried to board an aircraft with a weapon in his possession. He paused, hoping that Vester would comment, but the passenger said nothing. Rand then explained that Vester would be detained until the matter was looked into, and they knew precisely what had happened. It was then that Vester spoke. He protested his detention and demanded to be released. Rand cut him off, making it quite clear that Vester was going to be held until they were certain what happened. He then read the suspect his rights from a card that he carried. When he had finished, he gave Vester the card and insisted that he read it back, out loud. The form read in its entirety, Rand asked if Vester wanted to answer his questions, and Vester replied indignantly that he would answer no questions without an attorney present.

Rand asked nothing further. He directed his attention to the workshirt, which Ramirez had left on the table. Unwrapping the bundle, he found a piece of foam rubber rolled up inside. It was quite large—twelve to eighteen inches wide, almost two feet long, and about two inches thick. Vester watched him impassively and offered no explanation.

Mentally summarizing the few facts on hand, Rand was not at all sure he knew what was going on. He didn't really know what had happened in Tucson. The man was being held for a possible antihijacking violation, but they had not found a weapon on him. The shirt he carried had the name Herman on it, and to top it all off, the man was decidedly weird, and had no intention of explaining what he was doing with Herman's shirt, a wig, and ridiculously baggy pants.

Porter was every bit as baffled as Rand. Looking for anything that might help, Porter had told Vester to stand up and empty out his pockets and wallet. Vester complied without comment. Among the things removed and placed on the table were a bottle of pills, a sheet of Ramada Inn stationery, a Hertz Rent-a-Car application, a key, a Texas map, a street map for the city of Tucson, a piece of note pad paper with the words "Acne Gel, Benzac," printed on it, and a handful of safety pins. Nothing to go on there.

Then Porter began going through the wallet. Now they had something. In spite of what he had told Ramirez, Donald Vester was carrying identification. In fact he was carrying two sets of I.D., in two different names. And neither of those names was A. Donald Vester.

Removing all the cards from the wallet, Porter and Rand separated the two sets of I.D. and examined them. A Maryland driver's license, a Social Security card, a library card, and a post office rental receipt were in the name "Terry Lee Cordell." A Master Charge card, a United States Public Health Services card, and a VISA card, were all in the name "Patrick Henry." On the Health Service card was a photograph of the man they had in custody, and identified him as Dr. Patrick G. Henry. Agents Rand and Porter were intrigued now, but more puzzled than ever.

Vester had been sitting passively, apparently unconcerned with what the agents might be finding in his wallet. Then, suddenly, he startled everyone in the small room. "I'll bet you think you've got some big-time criminal, don't you?" he exclaimed. "Why aren't you out doing something important?" And then, just as abruptly, he went back to staring quietly into space. To Rand it was as if Vester had tuned them in for a second, then immediately tuned them out again.

Looking for some hard information, he called his office and asked them to patch him through to the Tucson FBI. The agent he talked to in Tucson could tell him nothing new, except that Agent Sickles was at the Tucson airport and would be calling in soon. As Rand asked Tucson to have Sickles call him as soon as possible, he overheard Vester telling Porter that his name was indeed Patrick Henry and that he was a medical doctor.

"Then what's all this about?" Rand asked, pointing to the pile of identification in the name of Terry Lee Cordell.

"I found that stuff," the man replied. He paused and then went on, as if anticipating Rand's next quetion. "I find it expedient to keep them for my own personal reasons."

"And the wig?" asked Rand.

"I like to travel incognito."

Without pausing, Rand changed subjects. "Where's your luggage?" he asked, already knowing that none had been found in the baggage area, at least not in the name of Vester.

"It's in room 602 at the Ramada Inn on the Central Expressway in Dallas."

"What were you doing there?"

"I don't care to answer that question. Why are you holding me, anyway? You have no reason to."

Instead of answering, Rand dialed the Ramada Inn. Identifying himself as an FBI agent, he ascertained that Dr. Henry was indeed a guest there, and that the doctor's reservation had been made by a Mr. Russell Swigart, who was staying at the Hilton Inn in Dallas.

Now they were getting somewhere. Rand called the Hilton immediately and reached Swigart. After identifying himself he asked why Swigart had reserved a room for Dr. Henry at the Ramada Inn. Swigart explained that he represented Syntex Laboratories of Palo Alto, California. Every year, when the American Academy of Dermatology held its annual meeting, Syntex invited 250 third-year dermatology residents to attend the convention as guests. This year's meeting, continued Swigart, was now in progress at the Dallas Convention Center, and Dr. Henry, a senior resident at the University of Maryland Hospital in Baltimore, was a Syntex guest. Dr. Henry had specifically requested a single room, so Swigart had booked him into the Ramada Inn Central. Doctors who hadn't objected to double rooms were staying at the Hilton.

Rand thanked Swigart and hung up with a sigh. They had a lot more facts now, but no explanations for the wig, the false name of Vester, and the I.D. papers of Terry Lee Cordell. Was Dr. Patrick Henry a nut, an eccentric, or something else entirely? Hoping for an answer, he and Tom Porter began to systematically examine the papers they'd found on Dr. Henry's person. No sooner had they begun when the doctor addressed them.

"Can I take one of my pills?" he asked, gesturing toward the bottle he had removed from his pocket earlier.

Rand examined the bottle and then the seven pills it contained. The bottle was labeled "Sinequan," something he'd never heard of before.

"No," he said curtly to Dr. Henry and returned to the papers. Some of them, he noticed, had notes penciled on them. The handwriting was almost illegible, and the pencil marks were so light they were hard to detect, much less decipher. As Rand studied the papers, he sneaked a glance at Dr. Henry out of the corner of his eye.

Dr. Henry was perspiring. He didn't seem nervous, unlike most people Rand had seen arrested or questioned, and he wasn't shaking or stuttering. Yet his forehead and hair were damp, and several times he reached up to adjust the neck of his sweater.

Rand looked back at the papers on the table. On the sheet of Ramada Inn stationery he thought he saw some kind of itinerary outlined. As he held it up to study more closely Dr. Henry stirred.

"May I take off some of my clothing?"

"Sure, go ahead."

With that, Dr. Henry rose to his feet and stepped out of his baggy pants. Then he pulled the loose-fitting brown sweater over his head. At first the three officers were just amused. Then, as they got a good look, they exchanged disbelieving glances. Under the pants and sweater Dr. Henry wore a full length pair of waffle-weave thermal underwear, which explained why he had been sweating. But what had astonished them was not the long underwear but the cotton padding sewn onto it. The doctor's shoulder muscles, his biceps and triceps, his forearms, chest, hips, thighs, buttocks, and calves had all been enlarged with cotton padding. To Rand he looked like a football tackle dummy with a human head.

Dr. Henry stripped off the underwear and left it in a pile on the floor. Then he dressed again in the baggy sweater and pants and resumed his seat without ever changing expression. Instead of explaining what was going on, he simply stared off into space again. Porter looked at Rand and raised an inquiring eyebrow: Did you see what I just saw?

Rand stared at the pile of underwear, then at Dr. Henry, then back at the underwear. The padding had added the appearance of thirty-five or forty pounds to the doctor's build. If he had tucked the foam rubber he was carrying back into his waistband, that would have added another fifteen or twenty.

"All right," Rand said to Porter, "let's grab everything. His papers, his wallet, his underwear, everything. We'll take every single thing as evidence." He looked to Dr. Henry for a reaction, but there was none. The doctor sat remote and impassive, as if the bizarre clothing on the office floor no longer had anything to do with him.

The two agents had just begun to inventory the evidence when the phone rang. It was FBI Agent Sickles in Tucson. Rand greeted him enthusiastically. Now Sickles could fill them in on what had really happened at the Tucson airport, and they could tell him what they had discovered in the DPS office: the two sets of I.D., the foam rubber, and, of course, the elaborately padded underwear.

But Sickles was on another wavelength. Rand could tell from his voice that something was wrong; Sickles just didn't sound like an agent on the trail of a hijacker.

Rand's suspicions were quickly confirmed. Sickles reviewed what he had been told initially, via Officer Kelch: that the passenger had tried to take a briefcase through the security checkpoint; that a weapon had been discovered; and that the man had run on down the concourse and boarded the flight. Rand interrupted to say that he had heard roughly the same version from the airport DPS.

Sickles continued. He had seen the weapon that had been found in the briefcase, and had then thought he had a good case. But in the course of questioning the airport witnesses, he soon discovered major errors in that first account. The man originally wanted to check his case, not carry it on. It was a ticket agent, alarmed by the man's appearance and behavior, who had kept him from doing so. The man had insisted that he didn't want to carry his briefcase aboard, but the ticket agent and his supervisor had deliberately compelled him to carry it to the checkpoint. And finally he explained the agreement the passenger had reached with the American Airline supervisor—that the airline could open the case, then forward it to Dallas on a later flight.

Rand saw his case crumbling. Without a deliberate attempt

to take a weapon aboard an aircraft, all he had was some odd doctor in a padded outfit. He could just envision the lawsuits.

Sickles finally delivered the good news. The U.S. Attorney's Office in Tucson felt there was probable cause to make an arrest on lesser charges and therefore had authorized detention and arrest. So there would be no lawsuits. A warrant would still be forthcoming, not on hijacking charges but on a federal firearms violation involving interstate commerce. Everything would be turned over to the U.S. Attorney's Office in Tucson, Sickles said. Let them figure it all out.

Rand hung up. His own investigation was closed. He and Porter had jurisdiction under the federal antihijacking law, but that was not the law that had, in fact, been violated. Dr. Henry had failed to get the airline's permission to transport a weapon in his luggage. That was nothing more than a technical charge, enforced not by the FBI but by a federal agency called the Bureau of Alcohol, Tobacco, and Firearms. All he and Tom Porter had to do now was collect the evidence, inventory it, and take their prisoner to Fort Worth. The U.S. Attorney's Office would do the rest.

Their inventory completed, Rand and Porter drove Dr. Henry to Fort Worth and booked him into the Terrant County Jail. When they had told him why he was being arrested, Dr. Henry had remained silent. During the ride to jail his silence had continued. It was unnerving. Watching him in the rearview mirror, Rand was impressed by the man's ability to tune out. But the image of Dr. Henry as a tackle dummy came back to nag him. Why was a visiting dermatologist traveling incognito between Dallas and Tucson? If his only crime had been to overestimate the privacy of his luggage, why had he seen fit to transform his physical appearance beforehand?

Charles Wallace, an agent with the Bureau of Alcohol, Tobacco, and Firearms (ATF), fumed and cursed all the way back to his office. They'd dumped the whole mess on him, and he'd have to spend hours sorting it out and writing reports. Just thinking about it made him madder. He knew that even after all the paperwork was prepared, the case would never get to court. And if by some remote chance it did, the worst the guy would draw was a small fine. He'd never heard of anyone going to jail because he didn't tell the airlines he had a weapon in his luggage.

Wallace had just come from the U.S. Attorney's Office in Tucson, where he'd been told to report in order to take over the Patrick Henry case from the FBI. There he had been briefed by Agent Sickles on everything that had happened the day before at the Tucson and Dallas–Fort Worth airports. Sickles turned over the briefcase and all its contents, including the gun. He also reported to Wallace on the evidence that was still in Texas—the underwear, I.D., and so on.

Wallace left the Attorney's Office and immediately filed the warrant charging Dr. Patrick Gerald Henry with a violation of Title 18, United States Code, Section 922 (e). Now he was back in his own office, knee deep in someone else's mess. Why had this Patrick Henry been arrested in the first place? Wallace knew from experience that airport security people usually kept their cool. If they stopped someone for carrying a weapon, they tried to determine whether the person had intended to commit an act of air piracy, or any other crime. If it seemed clear that no crime was intended, they would explain the law, give the person a warning, then release him or her without filing any charges. At most, the person might be charged with a misdemeanor for carrying a concealed weapon. But this man had been arrested and even jailed. Wallace couldn't understand it.

Perhaps ATF in Texas could enlighten him. He had a message on his desk from ATF Agent Jerry Lloyd, who had said he would wait in Fort Worth for a return call. Wallace dialed the number immediately.

When he got Lloyd, Wallace informed him that he had just obtained a warrant, and told him on what charges Dr. Henry should be arraigned in Texas. For his part, Lloyd said that the FBI had given him all the evidence they'd seized at the airport, and that he would be sending it on to Tucson.

"Have you got it right there in front of you?" Wallace asked.

"I sure do."

"Could you describe the items for me?"

"I can try," Lloyd replied. "There's a lot of them." He began to run down the list, with Wallace taking notes and saying nothing. In due course he got to the Hertz car rental application, which he described as having "some scribbling" on it. When he said the same thing about the Ramada Inn stationery, Wallace interrupted. "Read me what you've got," he said.

But Lloyd had the same problem Rand had had the day before. The scrawled pencil marks were hard to spot and harder to read.

"The writing doesn't make much sense," he told Wallace. "It's just words and numbers and phrases. But if you want, I'll give it a try. All this I'm gonna read is written up like a list, but not in very neat order or anything. Ready?

"First thing: 'dean up' or 'clean up,' I can't tell which. 'Tucket. Umb. Suit etc. Pants. Paper. Pluzer' or 'pluigr,' I can't be sure."

Wallace scanned the items he had taken out of the briefcase. "Jerry, could it be plunger?"

Lloyd looked at the scrawl again. "Yeah, it could," he agreed. Then he went on. "The next part is really confusing: '9:05 331-TU. 10:15. Tu car? cab-U.' "

Wallace's earlier irritation was gone, replaced by curiosity.

"Tu would be Tucson," he guessed. "The rest could be times, or schedule. Keep going."

Lloyd continued. " 'Prepare self; carry extras; case lights; feed dogs; activity; ck 1403 key; inside; neighborhood; routes; phone; changing place.' "

Lloyd stopped and told Wallace that the next part was written in larger script. " 'In 1409; select window; tape; plunger; thru-open; find T; M T; out front; or rm window.' "

As Lloyd was reading the last series, Wallace stood up, cradled the phone between his ear and shoulder, and began sorting through the briefcase. "Wait a minute, Jerry, wait a minute. . . . There's a roll of tape in here, a plunger, and a goddamn glass cutter. I'll be damned. . . . Why the hell was a Baltimore doctor, at a convention in Dallas—a *dermatology* convention, for God's sake—in Tucson, Arizona, with this kind of breaking-and-entering equipment?"

Lloyd had no answer. The two men continued going down the list: " '1:00 Route; 1:15 change; 1:20 wrap suit box; 1:30 call cab mail; 2:15 airport—chg flt; 12:00 Out Tu-D; 5:30 D.' " Both agents guessed that the last part was a schedule for leaving Tucson and returning to Dallas.

Then, without waiting for Wallace to ask, Lloyd went back to the notes that mentioned "T." What was T? "Find T," the note said. Then, "M T." They both concluded the note meant that Henry would go through a window with the glass cutters and plunger, then find T and M T, whatever that was. "Maybe T stands for Terry," Lloyd suggested suddenly. "Terry Lee Cordell, the guy whose I.D. Henry was carrying."

Wallace agreed that was possible, then asked Lloyd to go on reading. Lloyd turned over the sheet of stationery and read off a series of words that made no sense to either of them: " 'Oil; stain; 5 batteries C; cutters; string; meat; box.' "

Lloyd stopped again and explained that next to the word "box" was a picture of a box, with its length, width, and height marked 1, 2, 3. Then he continued.

Under the box was written "P.O.-camera +." Under the word camera was written, "umbr + wallet"; then the words "record: Main A genetic; Main B-Dermitt on HLA;—Katy on HG." Then the word "or"; then "Main C Immunology."

Matching this new list with items in the briefcase, Wallace came up with glass cutters, twine, an umbrella, and the green metal box that had held the gun and boy scout knife. The other items listed were a mystery to both of them.

"Okay, let's go on," said Lloyd. "Next is a yellow and white Hertz rental application with some numbers on it: 6240503, and then 6238175."

"Hey, back up a minute," said Wallace. "Can you give those to me slower?"

Lloyd complied. The second time he heard the numbers Wallace was certain. They were Tucson telephone numbers; he recognized the prefixes.

"Okay, what else?" he asked Lloyd.

"That's it for the Hertz application," Lloyd said. "Let me give you the numbers on the VISA and Master Charge cards."

But Lloyd hadn't caught everything. There was more writing on the Hertz application, some of it penciled so lightly it was barely visible, some of it scratched into the colored part of the folder with a sharp pointed object. These notes would not be discovered till much later.

Wallace and Lloyd wrapped up their conversation.

"I'm curious as hell to see what all this looks like," Wallace confessed. "I just can't visualize it. Will you send me everything as soon as you can?" Lloyd promised he would, and they hung up with the promise to keep each other advised.

Wallace stared down at the notes on his desk. He was no

longer bored with the case he'd inherited. Clearly there was more to it than some weird, eccentric doctor traveling around using different names. Dr. Henry had disguised himself physically, written cryptic notes to himself, and refused to answer any questions without an attorney present. The doctor was hiding something. To find out what, Wallace would have to dig.

Grabbing the telephone he dialed Mountain Bell Telephone security. After identifying himself, he asked them to check the two numbers that had been scrawled on the Hertz form. If they were, as he had guessed, Tucson telephone numbers, he also wanted the name and address corresponding to each number. The woman at Telephone security took the numbers and said she would call back with the information. That was routine procedure; she would call him back at the ATF office as a means of confirming his identity.

Wallace placed another call, this time to the Master Charge security office in Phoenix. Identifying himself again, he gave them Dr. Henry's Master Charge number and said he wanted information about that account. He got the reply he expected— someone would call him back.

As he hung up, a call from Telephone Security came in on the other line; 624-0503 was the number of the Broadway Boulevard Kindergarten and PreSchool at 1403 East Broadway Boulevard and 623-8175 was the number of a Mr. William Bellios at 1409 East Broadway.

At first Wallace was disappointed. Bellios. The name meant nothing to him. Then it clicked. Paging through his notes he found it. "In 1409; select window; tape; plunger; thru-open; find T; M T." Bellios's address, 1409, was the same as the number on Henry's list.

Before he could think it all through, Master Charge security returned his call.

"What information were you looking for concerning that account, Mr. Wallace?" asked the security official.

Wallace's reply was simple: "Anything."

There wasn't much to tell, the woman said. Just the date the account was opened, and the names of the people authorized to use the card: Dr. Patrick G. Henry and Mrs. Christina Bellios Henry.

Bingo—Bellios. Wallace checked the spelling; it was the

same as that of William Bellios, the name the phone company had given him.

"So that's why the flight from Dallas to Tucson," Wallace thought: a wife or, more likely, an ex-wife . . . Christina Bellios Henry, probably living at 1409 East Broadway. For a moment Agent Wallace was pleased with himself and his detective work. Then the meaning of what he had discovered sank in. The gun. The knife. The elaborate disguise. Selecting a window. Through the window with glass cutters, the plunger guaranteeing a silent entry. And then, Christina Bellios Henry.

In less than thirty seconds Agent Wallace was in the office of his supervisor, Lyman Schaffer, laying out what he had just learned. Wallace had brought his overcoat with him; Schaffer grabbed his and they rushed to the ATF garage. In Wallace's car they raced for 1409 East Broadway, located exactly a mile and a half from their office in downtown Tucson.

Even with heavy traffic, Wallace and Schaffer made the trip in less than five minutes. They were giving it their best shot, but neither man could pretend to be optimistic. "Let's face it," said Wallace, "we're too late. We're going to find a body there."

They screeched to a halt in front of a modest stucco house, trimmed in brick. Running up the walk, Wallace knocked frantically on the front door. The two men waited a long minute, then knocked again. There was no reply. Wallace knocked harder. Still no reply. Wallace was positive now about what they were going to find. He'd never worked a homicide before, he thought grimly, or seen anyone who'd been murdered. There wasn't much of that in the ATF line of duty. He remembered the scout knife he'd seen in the briefcase, surgically sharpened on both sides, and dreaded what he might see inside.

From next door both agents could hear what sounded like children playing. They left the porch of 1409 and stalked around to the space between the two houses. Beyond a small wooden fence they could see five or six children in the next backyard and a woman supervising them. Hoping that she might have seen or heard something, the agents opened the gate and strode into the yard.

"Can I help you?" the woman asked, coming toward them.

"Yes, ma'am," Wallace answered. "We're looking for the woman who lives in 1409, next door."

"You're looking for me, then," said the woman. "I'm Christina Henry."

PART ONE

Pat and Christina 1967–1974

"WELL, this is a hell of a place to leave me hanging," I said. "What happened?"

It was nearly two o'clock on the afternoon of December 12, 1977. For the last ten minutes, Agent Wallace had been relating what had happened at the Tucson and Dallas airports on the sixth of December, six days before, and what notes had been found on the doctor's person when he had been arrested. I was chief prosecutor for Pima County, and Wallace was turning over to me the material on Dr. Patrick Henry. He had brought the briefcase with him, and had laid its contents out in front of me, along with the notes Agent Jerry Lloyd had forwarded to him from Dallas. Coming around to my side of the desk, he had taken me through the penciled jottings, explaining his own interpretation: that it was a plan for breaking into the house at 1409 East Broadway and murdering someone inside. He had stopped at that point to catch his breath.

"What happened?" I repeated. If a homicide had been committed in my jurisdiction, I sure didn't want to be hearing about it for the first time from a federal agent.

"That's the point—nothing happened," Agent Wallace said. "No one was dead. But I can't figure out why."

Now he really had me curious. With a glance at my old friend Bates Butler, a United States attorney who had brought Wallace to my office, I leaned back and concentrated on Wallace's account of the conversation between him and Christina Henry.

"Miz Henry, do you know a Dr. Patrick Henry?"

"Yes, that's my husband—my ex-husband; we're divorced. He lives in Maryland, in Baltimore. He's a doctor there."

"Could you tell me, ma'am, when you saw him last?"

She looked startled, and thought a moment before she answered. "I think I saw him yesterday. I'm not sure, but I'd almost swear it was him."

"Where did you see him? Where was he?" Wallace was speaking softly and slowly, so as not to alarm her, but he could see that Mrs. Henry was becoming agitated.

"I saw him right over there, on the sidewalk. On the other side of the street." She pointed across the street that ran next to the yard in which they were standing. "I'd swear it was him, but he looked different—much heavier, and with longer hair than my husband." She paused, trying to visualize what she had seen. "He was wearing a cap pulled way down, and a dark coat. The cap fit his head tight, and his hair was long and black, kind of stringy. But even with the way he looked, I thought it was Pat."

"Miz Henry, did anything else happen?"

The words were barely out of his mouth when she exclaimed, "The call! I got a call! It was later, though. Later in the morning." Her voice was rising and she was talking faster in her excitement. "The phone rang around 9:30, sometime near then, and it was Pat, I know it was. It was him. I know his voice even though he was trying to disguise it." Wallace and Schaffer could see her trying to recall what had happened. She was thinking and speaking at the same time.

"Yes, it was around 9:30, I remember. And he said he wanted information about the school. That was it. I run a nursery school here, and he said he wanted to meet me there and see what I had to offer. Those were his words: 'I want to see what you have to offer.' I knew it was Pat, but he gave some other name."

She paused, thinking. "I wrote it down. I have it. I can find it. I'll be right back," and she hurried into the house. Wallace and Schaffer exchanged glances.

"Here it is. I've got it." She was talking to them as she came out the back door. "Tim LaShanta, that's the name he gave me." She handed a small piece of paper to Wallace. Penciled on it was the name she had just told them.

Wallace was curious. Christina Henry lived next door, at 1409, yet she and the children were in the yard next door, and it was into that house that she'd gone to retrieve the message.

"Ma'am, whose house is this? Who lives here at this address?"

"It's not a private house any more, it's my school. There is where I run the nursery." Without pausing, she continued. "He used to live here. My husband, my ex-husband, used to live in this house. That's how we met. He was going to medical school and he rented a room from our neighbor here."

After she had hung up on "Tim LaShanta," she had called her lawyer and asked him to make a note of the fact that Dr. Henry had called. They had been divorced in 1975, she explained, and since that time had been involved in hearings to determine who would have custody of their son, Stevie.

"That's Stevie over there," she said, pointing out a little blond boy playing with the others. "I assumed that was why Pat was calling with a fake name—to get information about the nursery school that he could use against me in court."

Wallace's heart sank at the mention of divorce. If Dr. Henry had come to Tucson in disguise simply to snoop on his ex-wife, a lot of agents had wasted a lot of time. Fishing at random now, he asked Mrs. Henry the address of the school.

"1403 East Broadway," she replied.

Another piece of the puzzle slid into place. The second telephone number Dr. Henry had noted on the Ramada Inn stationery had been traced by Telephone security to 1403 East Broadway.

Wallace was certain that more was at issue here than custody skullduggery. Yet he didn't know enough to be able to make a statement to Mrs. Henry. Aware that he had to give some explanation for all his questions, he finally said, "Miz Henry, we're looking into an incident that involves your ex-husband. It has something to do with him taking a weapon—a pistol—aboard an airplane. He was arrested yesterday in Dallas; I don't know too much more than that."

"He was arrested?"

"Yes, ma'am, and as soon as I know more I'll get back in touch with you. Thank you for your help."

Christina Henry let him go without asking any further questions. She looked as if she was thinking about something.

There were plenty of questions she might have asked, Wallace thought as they drove back to the office. Lyman Schaffer verbalized the first: "What the hell was that guy doing out there with a gun?'' In his own mind Wallace asked the other two.

Dr. Henry had written in his notes, "find T. M T." Who, or what, was "T"? And why had Dr. Henry worn his disguise on the airplane? He had been disguised when Mrs. Henry saw him on the street; the knitted cap, the extra weight, the stringy hair all jibed with what Agent Lloyd in Texas had told Wallace. But if the doctor hadn't committed any crime in Tucson, why had he continued wearing the disguise on the way back to Dallas?

As soon as they arrived back at the federal building, Wallace went for the briefcase. The answers had to be inside.

He sorted through the items, studying each one, trying to figure out how they related to "find T. M T." The contents inventory mentioned keys, five of them. Wallace went through the case and collected them. They weren't together, but were interspersed with the other items. He examined each one as he found it, but the only one he could make anything of was a Volkswagen key. It reminded him of something he'd just seen—a Volkswagen parked in the alley behind 1409.

It was worth a try. Collecting the keys, he picked up the pistol that had been found inside the briefcase at the airport, told Schaffer where he was going, and hurried to his car. With his pride slightly damaged from his first trip, he was more determined than ever to find out what was really going on.

When he arrived for the second time, Christina Henry had been joined by her father, William Bellios. Christina introduced them.

"Ma'am, I have something I'd like you to look at, and tell me if you can identify it." As Wallace spoke he held up the pistol.

Before Mrs. Henry could answer, her father spoke in heavily accented English. "That is my pistol. I know it anywhere. It was given to me in 1939 by my brother, George, in Akron, Ohio. I know that pistol anywhere. I have that pistol almost forty years, then I give to Pat. I give it to him before they are married. I never buy bullets for it. Never shoot it."

Wallace said nothing. Turning to Mrs. Henry, he asked about the Volkswagen parked in the alley. She answered that it was her car. He handed her the Volkswagen key from Dr. Henry's briefcase and asked her to try it. She walked back and got into the VW. The engine whined for a second, then turned over.

Still saying no more than he had to, Wallace took the rest of the keys out of his pocket and handed them to Mrs. Henry. He asked her to check them against all the locks in the school and the residence at 1409. Mrs. Henry and her father exchanged glances, but neither asked a question. Wallace followed as they walked over to the school.

The first key she tried turned the lock on the back door. The second opened the front. Three of the five keys were now explained.

The three of them then walked next door to 1409. Wallace would have bet a hundred dollars that neither of the remaining two keys would fit the locks of that house. He was proved right.

Wallace's suspicion was confirmed. The notes had mentioned the number 1409 and then selecting a window and using a plunger and tape to get through it. There was a glass cutter in the briefcase, but no keys that fit 1409. All the physical evidence added up to the same thing: Dr. Henry didn't have a key to Mrs. Henry's house; he had been planning to get in through a window.

The pieces were falling into place. But who was "T"? Without explaining, Wallace asked Mrs. Henry if her little boy had a name or nickname that started with a T.

She couldn't think of one. She called him Stevie. When he was an infant he had been called Paddy. Her parents were Greek, she explained, but she could not think of any Greek names or nicknames that began with T.

William Bellios walked over to where they were standing. He hadn't heard Wallace's question and therefore wasn't sure what they were talking about. For that matter, he wasn't certain why this government officer was asking so many questions anyway. Turning to his daughter, he said, "Tina, what is this all about?"

Wallace felt the elation hit him. He had it. He had been correct from the start. "T" was Dr. Henry's ex-wife. And with the gun and the knife, "M" had to be "murder." "Find Tina. Murder Tina."

Wallace stood thinking for a few seconds, then made a decision. He *had* to warn them. Turning to Mr. Bellios, he said, "I think her ex-husband came here to eliminate her."

"You mean kill her?" asked Mr. Bellios, his voice rising in shock. Wallace didn't answer. He was looking at Mrs. Henry. Her hands had flown to her mouth and the color had drained out of her face. Her father turned and clutched her arm; Wallace thought the old man was trembling.

As he drove back to the office he thought about their reactions. Both of them had been frightened, all right. What seemed strange was that neither had been skeptical. Neither had said, "I don't believe it," or "Oh, that's impossible." Maybe they had been too surprised. Or maybe it was just the opposite. Maybe they hadn't been surprised at all.

Five days later Wallace received the evidence taken from Dr. Henry in Dallas. For the first time he saw for himself the sheet of Ramada Inn stationery and the penciled notes he'd come to think of as the "murder plan." There were also a series of times jotted down. After studying all the evidence closely, he was positive he was right.

The plan was simple enough. It called for Dr. Henry to leave Dallas at 9:05 P.M. on the fifth of December and arrive in Tucson at ten-fifteen Tucson time later that night. He would go to 1403 East Broadway, get inside the nursery school with his keys, and make his preparations. That done, he would get into 1409 through a window, then find Tina and kill her. Then he would return to the airport and fly back to Dallas, arriving there at 5:30 in the morning. He would be back at the medical conference early enough not to be missed.

Bates Butler was sitting back enjoying my reaction. As the chief prosecutor in my office, and as supervisor of all felony prosecutions, I'd observed tens of thousands of cases, but never one quite like the case being presented to me now.

"Sounds like Agatha Christie," I said.

"Or Columbo," agreed Bates. It was difficult to believe that someone, a physician at that, would go to such bizarre lengths—the disguise, the various identity papers, the coded plan. Yet Wallace had the evidence, and it was right in front of me.

But the topper was that, in spite of all his elaborate preparations, Dr. Henry hadn't done anything. He hadn't shot his ex-wife; hadn't even come near her. Until the next day, she hadn't been entirely sure it was him she had seen across the street. There didn't seem to be any way we could prosecute him.

Yet we had to try. I didn't see any alternative. Christina Henry's life had very definitely been in danger, and the evidence indicated that she was in danger still. As Agent Wallace had noted, Dr. Henry had very carefully kept his disguise, his notes, his tools, and his weapons. If he had changed his mind about killing his ex-wife, why had he held onto everything? If he had simply been prevented from carrying out the murder, it was very likely he was planning to try again.

Dr. Henry had to have violated some law. In the back of my mind a memory was stirring. In law school I had studied a group of cases dealing with "the crime of attempted murder." Under the law, if a person begins to commit a crime, that is, if he or she commits a series of "overt acts," and then is prevented from finishing the job, the person may be prosecuted for the attempt—in this case, attempted murder. It wasn't always necessary for the person to have tried to perform the actual murder itself, so long as he or she had performed acts toward that end. While I wasn't sure we could establish the chain of "overt acts" necessary for prosecution, we had to try. It was clear that Christina Henry's safety depended on it.

Knowing that I was going to prosecute, I was already thinking about my investigation team. I wanted Agent Wallace to be on it. He had had the brains to piece out Dr. Henry's plan and the initiative to follow up on what he had deduced. Were it not for him, no one would have known what Dr. Henry had intended to do in Tucson.

Instead of asking for Wallace directly, I asked Bates Butler if my investigation would have the cooperation of federal authorities. When he said yes, already guessing what I had in mind, I requested that Wallace remain on the case.

I gave Agent Wallace his first assignment immediately: to set up an interview with Christina Henry. We had no time to waste. On December 7, almost a week earlier, Dr. Patrick Henry had been released without bond from the Terrant County Jail and permitted to return to Maryland.

Christina Henry could not have been more different from what I had expected. There was something very old-fashioned about her, as if she belonged to another generation entirely.

When Wallace introduced us, she greeted me with unusual politeness and respect. She seemed almost awed at being in our presence.

Her appearance went along with her modest demeanor. Every one of her features—her hair, her face, her figure, everything—was attractive, and yet she herself wasn't. The total effect was one of plainness. She wore a dark wool skirt that came just below her knees, a beige blouse that tied in a bow at her neck, and wire-rimmed glasses that didn't sit right on her nose. She looked like a spinster schoolteacher.

Wallace had already cautioned Mrs. Henry and her parents that there might not be enough evidence to justify the state's taking the case. Although he didn't tell Mrs. Henry so, he himself believed there wouldn't be. Agent Jerry Lloyd in Dallas later told me that Wallace had called him after our first meeting.

"They've got the damndest law you ever heard of," Wallace had laughed. "A one-man conspiracy law. He can agree with himself to commit murder, start out to do it, and then not do it, and it can still be a crime. Can you believe this stuff? They'll never make a case, not in a million years."

Christina Henry obviously hoped we could. She burst into speech, desperate to convince me that her ex-husband was perfectly capable of murdering her, and that her life was still in danger. She was talking as fast as she could, leaping from subject to subject, frantic that I would not understand her danger.

When she paused for a second, I jumped in. I understood her danger all too well. But what we really needed to help put our case together, I told her, was the history of her relationship with Dr. Henry, from the time they met until the present. We needed to know of any incidents that showed his feelings toward her, what he was really like. We needed to know everything about Christina's life with him.

Nodding her head, Mrs. Henry quietly composed herself. After a few moments she began. Her story, as I first heard it, was not told chronologically or tidily; she couldn't help skipping backward and forward through the years. But her memory for detail was exceptional, even concerning events and conversations five or six years in the past. Later, when I reviewed and rearranged my notes, I saw that she had really told me a complete story, one with a beginning, a middle, and an end.

Christina Bellios sat at the dining-room table, trying to write thank-you notes. Her mother had suggested she do them now, because there would be even less time for such chores after the wedding. She still had a half dozen left and the wedding was only hours away. But she couldn't keep her mind on the job.

That afternoon she would cross a bridge that she could cross only once in her life. She looked down the table at her father. William Bellios had lived the first half of his life in Greece. Now he was an American, but he and his wife Athena had raised their two daughters in the Greek tradition. Christina and her sister Karen spoke Greek as fluently as they spoke English. They had gone to the same public school as their friends on the block, but after school they spent a few more hours in Greek school, learning the history, customs, songs, and dances of Greece. On Greek holidays both girls dressed up in the velvet robe and hat of Queen Amalios who had led her people's uprising against the Turks. And the daughters had learned the unspoken customs too: the husband was the indisputable head of the household. It was his responsibility to protect and provide for his wife and children; in return they respected and obeyed him.

Now that Christina was to be married, she knew it would be the same for her. As the daughter of William and Athena Bellios, as a fervent believer in the Greek Orthodox faith, Christina knew it was her duty to live up to the vows she would take that afternoon in God's house. The family honor demanded it. Although Christina had been born in America, she felt as bound as her father to the traditions he had been brought up in three thousand miles away, in the tiny, rocky village of his birth.

In the rugged limestone hills of southern Greece lies the village of Tziba. It is small, no more than eighty families, living in seventy houses. It was here, in 1905, that William Bellios, then called Vasilios, was born.

In the spring and summer, Tziba is as quaint and charming as many other Mediterranean villages. But in winter the quaint village becomes desolate, its poverty all too apparent. In December 1905, when Vasilios Bellios was born, the village was dying. The farmers brought in from the fields barely enough to feed their families. The people ate what they raised; usually nothing was left to trade in the market for shoes, clothing, or new farm equipment. Yet sometimes these trades had to be made, and then the family would go hungry.

It was not that people didn't work hard; they did, from first dawn until no light was left in the evening. The fault was with the soil. Like the streets of Tziba, the land had been used for hundreds of years, and it was tired. Like the people, it was hopelessly poor.

In the face of this desperation, the villagers turned to God. The simple, humble church was the finest building in town. On Sundays, every man, woman, and child in the village came to liturgy. Their faith comforted them and enabled them to struggle onward each day.

The villagers' second source of strength was their pride in being Greek. On cold winter nights, Vasily, his brother, and sisters would sit in front of the fireplace and ask their father to tell them the stories once again. And Nicholas Bellios would proudly oblige. Most of his stories were episodes in the Greeks' long struggle to drive the Turks from their land. The stories were endless, as was the children's delight in hearing them. But there was a purpose to the telling: to light the fires of Greek pride until they burned brightly enough within each child to last the child's lifetime, no matter how far he or she might stray from the village. Ironically, because the fields of Tziba could no longer feed its people, most of the children would eventually have to leave. Some would stay close by, in larger villages and towns; other would move to Athens or the other cities. And still others would be divided among the four corners of the earth. Vasily Bellios was to be one of these.

Vasily's mother had a cousin in Athens, Mr. Chacopolous, who came to visit several times a year. Vasily had seen him many times before. But on one visit he saw him as he had not seen him before. Mr. Chacopolous was different from the men in the village. As the owner of a large wholesale and retail grocery in Athens, he was his own man, not a slave tied to a few acres of poor farmland. Mr. Chacopolous could be or do whatever he wanted, and so could his children.

After Mr. Chacopolous's visit, Vasily went to his father and told him it was time—time for him to leave the family, time for him to go to the city and begin working. The day he left Vasily embraced his parents and promised to come home at Christmas and Easter if he could. Then he began the walk to Tripolis, where he would catch the train to Athens. He was eight years old.

Vasily lived in Mr. Chacopolous's house. During the day he worked in a nearby market; in the evenings he went to school. When he was nineteen he joined the army. Two years after his discharge he had saved enough to open his own small grocery.

His family was proud of him, but Vasily was restless. He worked long hours, spent no money on luxuries, and lived in a room at the back of his store. Yet at the end of every month he had earned no more than the equivalent of two or three American dollars. More than anything he wanted to better his situation, but he could see no way to do so. Then, when he was twenty-two, his half brother from America came to Tziba.

Christos Bellios was Nicholas's son by his first wife. When Chris and his brother George were little boys, their mother had died and her brothers, who had emigrated years before to America, sent for the two boys. Nicholas had not seen his eldest son for eighteen years.

Christos arrived from Tripolis in a taxi, an event which caused a stir in the village. As his father and brother embraced, Vasily could see the joy in his father's eyes. After all the years of separation their love for each other was as strong as ever. But Vasily was seeing more than the love between a father and a son, much more.

Chris and his brother George lived in a different world from Tziba, or even Athens. Chris had graduated from university, and then gone to law school. Now the brothers owned several successful businesses, and Chris had returned not just to see his family but to build his father a new house, a large well-furnished home that would have cost a village farmer his life's savings.

In the months following Chris's visit, Vasily dwelt on the memory of his brother. Chris's life would never have been possible in Greece, mired as the country was in poverty and political unrest. Vasily would always be faithul to his family

and Greece—as Chris was—but he now knew he would have
to leave.

In 1933 Chris and George sent for him. He sailed from
Piraeus along with several hundred Greek and Italian immi-
grants. Those aboard the ship brought with them few material
things. Although America was still gripped by the Depression,
they knew that soon life would be far better than anything
they had known before. They did bring with them what they
needed most: their religion, their culture, their heritage. Although they would become Americans, their traditions would
always make a bridge to home.

Christina put down her fountain pen. Her father had spread
the newspaper flat on the table and was checking the sports
scores.

"Papa," she began. He looked up inquiringly, and she
wondered how to express what she felt. When she went on
she spoke in Greek, as they often did at home. "I hope I'm
doing right by getting married," she said. "I know how I feel
about Pat now, but I don't know what it will be like when
we're married. How can I be sure it's the right thing to do?"

"Tina, no one ever knows for sure," said William Bellios.
"Your mother and I certainly didn't. We met through the
koumbari, the matchmaker. It was back in Ohio, in Akron,
when I first came to this country. I saw your mother in
church one Sunday and asked the *koumbari* if I could meet
her. The first time we drank tea together, her whole family
was there. After that it was always her mother, or one of her
aunts. We didn't know each other very well when we got
married, but I had a good feeling about her. And by the time
you were born, I knew I loved her. And she loved me. We've
worked hard, and we've had a good life together."

The familiar story of her parents' courtship reassured her a
little. Though she was not yet in love with Pat, she did have a
special feeling for him, and she was sure he loved her. As a
doctor, he would someday be able to take good care of her
and their children; that was important. Her mother had not
known much more than that about William before her wedding.

She and Pat had even met in a traditional way: through a
widowed neighbor who was a close friend of the family. But
not much else about her courtship had been traditional. . . .

Mrs. Kempf had been gardening in her yard next door

when Christina stopped to chat. A widow who had lost her two sons as well as her husband, Mrs. Kempf led a lonely life, and all the Bellioses went out of their way to visit with her when they had the chance.

Mrs. Kempf's house, 1403 East Broadway, was very much like the Bellios's at 1409. Both were small, modest buildings facing the street. Behind the Bellios house, however, at the far end of the back yard, William had built two small guest houses—one-room apartments, really—for Christina and Karen. They gave the girls, who were both in college a quiet place to study, and gave the whole family more privacy. The family would meet in the main house for meals and in the evenings.

Mrs. Kempf had no guest houses, but she had added an extra room to the back of her house. Now, with her family gone, she paid her mortgage by renting the room out to University of Arizona students. Christina knew there was someone living there now, but she had never met or even seen him.

"And how about school, Christina? How is it going?" Mrs. Kempf asked.

"Fine. I really like it," Christina said. "Except for physics. I just don't seem to be able to get it, and I have to pass it to graduate. There's a test tomorrow and I'll probably be out here studying until midnight. Not that it will do much good, probably."

"Well, maybe Pat, my tenant, could help. He's a first-year medical student; he must've passed physics, don't you think?"

"Sure, I guess," Christina agreed, moving backward toward the guest house as she spoke. She really had to get down to serious studying.

By the time she closed the door behind her she had already forgotten about Mrs. Kempf's medical student. But the more Mrs. Kempf thought about it, the better the idea seemed. Her tenant was tall, handsome in a boyish way, with brown hair and light blue eyes. He was quiet and polite. And if he really did understand physics, so much the better.

Christina was in the main house later that afternoon when the doorbell rang. On the steps was a tall, good-looking young man who seemed nervous.

"Hi," he said. "If you're Christina, Mrs. Kempf sent me over to help you study for your physics test."

Surprised and a little embarrassed, Christina laughed and said, "I am Christina—and I accept."

As she stepped back to invite him in, he said, "My name is Patrick Henry—and no jokes, please; I've heard them all."

They sat down at the dining-room table and he looked through her textbook and lab notes to get a sense of what level she was studying. Then she asked a few questions, and he explained some of the general principles she had trouble understanding. But he seemed to feel awkward, and so did Christina. After about an hour he suddenly looked at his watch and said, "Uh-oh, I'd better get going. I've got a quiz tomorrow myself that I've got to get up for."

Relieved that he had found an excuse to leave, Christina walked him to the door quickly. "Listen, thanks for taking the time to do this," she said. "You really have helped a lot."

When he was gone, she went back to studying and didn't think about him again. He was good-looking and smart, but she had quickly pegged him as a couple of years younger than she was, which automatically eliminated him as a possible boyfriend.

Had Christina been interested in him, she would have been disappointed. She had never glimpsed Pat before his visit and she didn't see him much afterward. According to Mrs. Kempf, he got up early, bicycled to school, then studied in his room from late afternoon until past midnight. He and Christina bumped into each other a few times, but exchanged no more than a wave or a few pleasantries.

In the spring of 1968 Christina graduated and started looking for a job. A local television station was looking for a kindergarten teacher to host a daily children's show called "Romper Room." Christina had no experience as a teacher, but she had majored in education so she interviewed for the job. She was hired two hours after the interview. The producer of the show told her she was perfect—tall and good-looking, but soft and gentle with the children they had introduced her to.

When Christina started work she continued living in the little apartment behind her parents' house. A Greek girl from her father's village only left home when she married. On weekends she also taught children in the Sunday school program at Saint Demetrious Greek Orthodox Church. She liked teaching so much that after a year she left "Romper Room" and started teaching kindergarten in a real school. Karen was still in college, living in the other little apartment, so the family stayed close. It was Christina's mother who brought Patrick Henry back into their lives.

Athena felt sorry for him. Her life was so full and contented, she couldn't help noticing how dreary Pat's was. Aside from going to class, he hardly ever left his room. His parents visited him once a week but they never stayed long. Athena was home all day herself; she knew what went on.

And she knew what to do. The young man needed someone to pay attention to him, to bring him out a little bit. He was a nice young man, but bashful. Between that and his studies, it was no wonder he seemed not to have many friends. According to Mrs. Kempf, Pat ate only one meal a day. Occasionally it was something his mother brought, but usually it was a TV dinner. He ate so many, said Mrs. Kempf, that he bought them wholesale, several weeks' supply at one time. Hearing this, Athena decided to invite him to dinner.

At first it was just once a month or so. Then Athena saw that Christina and Pat liked each other. Christina was seeing other young men, and Pat never actually asked her out, but they seemed to feel comfortable with each other. Pat talked to Christina more than anyone else at the dinner table, and she seemed to be able to draw him out instinctively.

Christina's sister Karen felt differently about their guest. She had disliked him instinctively.

"Mother, don't you think he's a little strange?" Christina heard her sister ask one day. "Does he ever leave the house? Does he ever see any friends?"

"Karen, have you no respect?" her mother replied. "Pat is studying medicine. His father is paying a lot of money for him to go to school, and Pat takes that seriously. He works hard, not like a lot of boys his age."

Athena began to invite him to dinner more often, and Christina was sometimes embarrassed by the way her sister would challenge Pat, and disagree with whatever he was saying.

Christina sometimes disagreed too, but usually she didn't say so. Despite her education she was sure Pat was much smarter than she was. Besides, she and Karen had different attitudes toward life. They looked a good deal alike, both tall, close to five feet seven, with dark hair and eyes and light olive complexions. And they had both been sheltered by their parents—not spoiled, just protected from unpleasantness and discord. But Karen was much more outspoken than Christina. Perhaps it was because she had gone to college four years later than her sister, when the women's movement was starting to make itself heard. Whatever the reason, she was independent and analytical where Christina was conservative and accepting. It was not a difference that caused problems between them—except when Pat was at the dinner table.

The next two years were busy for both sisters.

Karen got her B.A. and was admitted to a master's degree program. She taught school during the day and went to graduate classes at night. Christina continued with her kindergarten teaching and began going steady with a young man who had started his own small company. He was already a successful businessman, and seemed destined to become more so. But when he asked her to marry him, she refused. She just didn't feel about him the way she thought she should. Meanwhile, Patrick Henry finished his second and third years of medical school and Mrs. Bellios went on cooking a little extra.

The courtship began during Pat's last year in medical school. He still studied long hours, but somehow he now managed to make time in the evening to see Christina. Since he was strapped for money, he couldn't afford expensive dates, so they found other things to do. They went to free plays and concerts at the university or to an occasional movie, and took lots of walks.

At Christina's urging, her mother invited him to dinner more and more often. One night, at the table, he called her "Tina," the nickname William Bellios always used for his daughter. Everyone noticed, but no one said anything. From then on, Pat never called her "Christina" again.

Even though they were becoming much closer, Christina never met his parents. Pat didn't want her to.

"They come here for just three reasons, Tina," he said. "To cut my hair, to pick up my laundry, and to bawl me out."

"You mean your mother does your laundry?" Christina asked curiously.

"Yeah," he said. "I suppose I could get them washed and ironed at a laundry. But she pins the right shirt and pants together afterward so I know which goes with which."

It struck Christina as very odd, but she knew how preoccupied Pat often got with his studying. She was glad, though, that they'd been alone when he'd talked about it. If Karen had heard *that,* she thought, I'd never live it down.

Pat's class would be the first to graduate from the University of Arizona Medical College, and during the final semester a member of the senior faculty gave a big party to commemorate the occasion. Christina was so proud when Pat asked her to go with him! She and Karen spent hours choosing just the right outfit and doing her hair so it was at its waviest and shiniest. Just before going downstairs, she put on a trace of makeup. Pat's expression when he came to the door told her that he was pleased. As they drove off to the professor's house in the car Pat's parents had just given him, Christina knew that they made an eye-catching couple.

And indeed, when they walked into the party, people stared. Pat seemed nervous and uncomfortable as he escorted her from group to group, introducing her to his classmates and teachers. But she knew that he was something of an outsider. He had told her how rarely he spoke to anyone at the medical school. He had told her, too, how some people looked down on him because he didn't spend a lot of money on clothes or on entertaining. That wasn't his fault, Christina thought. He didn't have any money to spend.

For the party, Pat had dressed as well as he could. He had worn his Nehru jacket, a style that had not been fashionable for several years. Christina thought she noticed several people staring at it, or winking at their friends and nodding in Pat's direction. But everyone was very nice to her. That was what Pat needed, she thought, someone to bridge the distance between him and other people. She knew she could do it if he gave her the chance.

Two days after the party, Pat told Christina he wouldn't be graduating with his class. He was going to fail pediatrics and surgery, two of the required courses.

"Pat, there's still time in the semester," Christina said, trying to be practical. "Maybe you could do extra labs, or another paper. Why don't you ask them? They might say yes."

"Tina, you don't understand," he said angrily. "It wouldn't do any good. It's got nothing to do with my work. Those two guys don't want me to graduate. One of them told me as much—he said someone like me shouldn't be a doctor. How do you like that—'someone like me!' "

"But have you asked them what you could do specifically—"

In a rage, he cut her off: "No! You think I would go crawling to them? No way. If they're out to get me, fine. But I'm not going to play their game. This isn't my fault; it's theirs. But I wouldn't give them the satisfaction."

Christina stopped trying to make suggestions. His anger was so intense, she couldn't even try to console him.

When he rang the bell next day, Christina braced herself. But the fury was over; now he was elated. Charity Hospital in New Orleans, his first choice for internship, had accepted him.

"Of course I'll have to take the pediatrics and surgery courses again this summer. But if I pass them I can start at Charity in September.

"Pat! You mean the med school will let you just repeat the courses you failed? You see, they aren't really 'against you' at all, are they?"

He didn't want to discuss it. "Never mind them, Tina. I'm just thinking about New Orleans. It's such a great city. There's so many things I want to do there."

Suddenly he looked at her. "Why don't you come with me, Tina?" he asked. "We could get married."

She didn't love him; she knew that. And although they had met four years ago, she didn't feel she knew him well at all. Yet that was part of his attraction: a certain mystery she couldn't easily penetrate. She felt an excitement, a sense of future possibilities that had been missing in her other relationships. Out of that, she thought, love would come.

"All right," she said. "I'll marry you."

Christina had finally met Pat's parents, on their last visit to East Broadway. She didn't get much of an impression; Pat had made the introductions and she had talked to them only briefly. But she was looking forward to knowing them better, now that she and Pat were getting married.

When Pat called to tell them about the engagement, Christina stood beside him, assuming she would take the phone at some point to say how happy she was to be joining their family. But it turned out that Pat's mother did not want to speak to her at all.

When Pat broke the news Christina could hear his mother's angry "No!" followed by several minutes of angry, excited yelling. It seemed to go on forever. Pat stood rigid, listening. He did not try to argue and after a while he hung up.

There was no need for Pat to relay his parents' reaction to Christina, nor any way he could soften it. Shocked, she tried to remember what she might have said to alienate them, but there was nothing. Pat, however, seemed to recover quickly— with or without their blessing he was determined to go ahead. "Let's set the date, Tina," he said, and they did: May 31, 1971, which was the Sunday after Pat's medical school graduation. The dean of the medical college had agreed that Pat could attend the ceremonies and wear a cap and gown.

Christina's parents could not understand the Henrys' opposition to the marriage. When they questioned him about it, Pat was evasive. "They just don't think I should get married right now," was all he would say. "Please don't worry about it. The way things are going, I doubt they'll even come to the ceremony." He seemed amused, almost defiant, that his parents were taking it so hard.

A few days before his graduation, Pat invited William and Athena to the graduation ceremony. They accepted, partly to please Pat and partly because it was a chance to meet the Henrys and try to smooth things out.

On the morning of the twenty-ninth, the day of the convocation, the phone rang in Athena's kitchen. Her caller barely waited for her to say "Hello" before introducing himself.

"This is Jason Henry, Pat's father. Listen, I'll get right to the point: My wife and I would appreciate it if you and your husband would stay away from the ceremonies tonight. I'm sure you understand. When they get married it'll be your day. But today is ours."

Athena didn't know what to say. The Henrys' hostility upset her, but she didn't see any way out of the situation. "Mr. Henry, I'm sorry you feel that way," she answered finally. "But it was Pat's wish that we attend, and I feel that he should make the decision whether we go or not."

Later that morning Pat himself called, obviously furious

about his parents' interference. "Look, I invited you—you're coming," he announced. "That's all there is to it. Okay?"

Feeling awkward and uncomfortable, William and Athena agreed. This trouble between the families wasn't good, they thought, and it was so unnecessary. With only two days to go before the wedding, a peace had to be reached.

"Pat, do something for me," Athena said. "Please invite your parents to be our guests for dinner tonight before the graduation ceremony. William says to ask them to meet us at the Old Pueblo Club at six o'clock."

If they just get to know us, she thought, hanging up, everything will be all right.

Tucson was already a bustling Indian town—a *pueblo*—when the Jesuits sent by the Spanish discovered it in the seventeenth century. It was to that period that the name "Old Pueblo Club" referred, but by now, 1971, the city had a population of 300,000 and was growing rapidly. The Old Pueblo Club was on the twenty-first (and top) floor of one of Tucson's largest buildings, and with floor-to-ceiling glass windows on three sides, it had a view of the city, the valley, and the surrounding mountains unequaled by any other restaurant or office in Tucson.

To Christina's relief, the Henrys seemed impressed with the club. As everyone sipped their drinks, the sun began to set and the view became even more spectacular: the mountains on the horizon silhouetted against the copper-colored sky. But everyone was uncomfortable, nonetheless. The Henrys were not openly rude, but they were reserved and condescending. Christina watched, her stomach in knots, as Pat quickly knocked back two straight Scotches.

Then it was time to order dinner. The manager of the Old Pueblo, a personal friend of William's, came to take their order, an attention that was not lost on the Henrys. Everyone ordered the Pueblo's Friday night specialties: oysters on the half shell to begin, then dinners of shrimp, crab, and lobster. It was a rich meal, especially for Regina Henry, who had loudly declared herself to be on a diet. But when the manager returned later on with seconds of everyone's entrees, she quickly ate hers, then Christina's and Karen's, when they declared themselves too full to attempt theirs.

By the time the dessert cart was rolled to the table, Regina's appetite still had not waned. She selected several different concoctions from the cart and managed to get down a good bit of each. Her greediness was so extraordinary that Karen nudged her mother's foot under the table and widened her eyes in discreet astonishment.

Seeing the glance they exchanged, Christina quickly looked down at the tablecloth, mortified by Mrs. Henry's behavior. When Regina neatly placed her napkin beside her plate and excused herself to go to the ladies' room, Christina took the opportunity to escape from the table by going with her.

Regina did not speak to her as they made their way to the bathroom. Once inside, Christina went to the mirror to run a comb through her hair, while Regina went into one of the vacant stalls, leaving the door open behind her.

As Christina watched in the mirror, Regina bent down over the toilet, stuck a finger down her throat, and vomited. Without even glancing at Christina, she repeated the process. Then she came out of the stall, splashed her mouth with water at the sink, and dried her hands carefully with a paper towel. With Christina looking on, speechless with disbelief, she pushed open the swinging door and returned to the table.

The two families left the Old Pueblo and drove to the convocation separately. In the privacy of her family's car, Christina told her parents and sister what had happened. At the ceremony, the Bellioses no longer even pretended to be friendly; the two families ignored each other completely.

William Bellios put down his newspaper. He could see his daughter was thinking hard; she was disturbed in a way that a bride should not be on her wedding day.

"Tina, you must do what you think is right," he said. "Whatever you think is okay. But only you can decide. It is up to you."

Pat wasn't his parents, Christina thought. And it wasn't as if he didn't recognize how impossible they were. He hardly ever saw them, they made him so angry.

She had doubts, she knew. But so did every bride. No one could be entirely sure; Papa had just said so. Feeling more certain now, Christina smiled at her father. She felt she had made the decision her mother would have made, and her mother's mother. She put away her notes, went to her room, and began to dress for the ceremony.

The wedding was performed by Father Paul Koutoukas at

Saint Demetrious Greek Orthodox Church. Karen was Christina's maid of honor. The best man was a family friend of the Bellioses, as Pat had said he didn't know anyone who could stand up for him.

The Henrys did come to the church for the ceremony. They refused the seats in front reserved for the groom's family and took seats in the back pew. It was just as well, Karen thought, since Regina Henry was dressed entirely in white, as if she, not Christina, were the bride.

After the ceremony, Jason and Regina refused to stand beside the Bellioses in the receiving line. They also refused to pose for pictures. Christina could see the horrified expressions on her friends' and family's faces, but there was nothing she could do but pretend she didn't notice them.

There was more—but neither Karen nor Mrs. Kempf were going to tell her what they had witnessed early that morning. Just after 8:00 A.M. Regina had suddenly burst out of Pat's room and into the back yard screaming, "You're not marrying that Greek bitch! I won't allow it!" Pat and his father had come running out a second later and managed to get her back inside before the scene got any worse. Karen, who had been walking from her apartment up to the main house, heard everything. So had Mrs. Kempf, who was putting on coffee in her kitchen. But no purpose would have been served in telling Christina.

Regina spoke to her new daughter-in-law for the first time at the reception.

"You won't last for three months," she announced loudly. "You mark my words. Three months. That's what I give you."

The first days of their honeymoon were difficult for both Pat and Christina. There was a great deal they didn't know about each other, but they knew even less about sex—Christina by choice; Pat because he had never had a girl friend in his life. "There was no time," he explained. "I never did anything but work and study." Christina didn't mind. She was sure everything would get better. As time went by they would come to love each other, just as her parents had.

The newlyweds had stayed at a motel in Tucson for their wedding night. The next morning they'd eaten brunch with Christina's family, packed the car, and left Tucson. Their honeymoon was also to be a practical trip. They were on their way to Michigan, where Pat was enrolled in a surgery course at the university in Ann Arbor. It was one of the two courses he had to pass that summer in order to graduate.

Their belongings and wedding gifts almost filled the 1969 Mercury, leaving room only for themselves and Trykie, an eight-week-old kitten Christina's students had given her. She curled up in Christina's lap when they pulled out of the Bellios driveway and slept most of the way to Michigan.

Pat drove all the way. Christina offered to spell him every few hours, but he insisted on doing all the driving himself. "I know how to save gas," he told her. "I can get the maximum mileage out of this car." Christina soon learned that he had other ways of saving money as well. At night he carefully compared motel rates before selecting the cheapest. In restaurants he always picked the least expensive meal, then gathered up the packages of salt, pepper, and sugar from the table. When they left a motel, he took whatever was portable: soap, shampoo, tissues, toilet paper, and ashtrays. If Christina objected, he would tell her, "Listen, we paid for this stuff."

It was during this long cross-country trip that Pat finally explained why his parents had been against the marriage. "You came along at the wrong time," he told her. "I was just about to graduate, and they were getting ready to enjoy what I had achieved. They considered me an investment in their future, their retirement. You stole all that by marrying me. I don't know if they dislike you personally, but I suspect they do. I mean, they don't like Greeks to begin with."

Christina sat dumbstruck, staring blankly out at the highway, too upset to reply. She thought back over every time she had been with his parents, trying to think of a single incident where she might have done something wrong. As far as she remembered, she had gone out of her way to be nice to them, to treat them with all the respect a daughter-in-law owed to her husband's parents.

"It's nothing personal," Pat went on. My parents don't like Jews either, or Italians." Then he laughed; he was remembering, he said, how upset his mother had been at the wedding. "I think I enjoyed that the most," he said. "She's always tried to manipulate my life, but this time it didn't work."

Christina didn't respond. She was too upset. She was also thinking about what Pat's mother had said at the reception—that Christina wouldn't last three months. She had not said the marriage wouldn't last, but that she, Christina, wouldn't last. She wondered what Regina Henry had meant by that.

From her first sight of Ann Arbor, Christina loved it. The lush shrubbery and green lawns of the campus were new to her, so different from the stark desert around Tucson. The day they arrived they drove for hours until they found a small apartment that was inexpensive enough for their budget.

The apartment was cramped and filthy, but it didn't matter to Christina. She knew she could make it spotless, and besides, the summer session only lasted six weeks.

She spent the next two days cleaning, scrubbing every surface until she had washed away all the accumulated filth. She was proud of having made the seedy apartment livable, but Pat never commented on her hard work. He seemed oblivious to his surroundings. But she understood. He had more important things on his mind than their dinky little apartment. He studied continually, getting up early and going to bed late. Often he worked straight through meals, covering the table with a mound of books. Christina did what she could to help. She hauled library books back and forth, rather than have Pat lose valuable study time. In the evenings she tried to find things to occupy herself that wouldn't make noise or otherwise distract him. And she took over Priscilla's job of doing his laundry and coordinating the various shirts, pants, and ties for him. It wasn't laziness on his part, she saw. He simply had no sense of style or color, of what could be worn and what couldn't. Once she realized that, selecting his clothes became a special task that she enjoyed performing.

To help keep track of their money, she set up a bookkeeping system for the everyday household finances. Pat was pleased when she showed it to him.

"That's great, Tina," he said. "Just one thing—any time you want to spend more than ten dollars, I wish you'd ask me first."

Christina laughed. "Are you serious?" she said. "That could turn out to be a little difficult."

"I know," Pat said. "But it's got to be that way. I've got to know where the money is being spent."

Christina didn't really mind the tight budgeting. His mother had lent Pat a thousand dollars to finish school and make the move to New Orleans—a loan secured, at her request, by her son's personal note. Christina assumed that Pat simply felt as she did: that any amount of scrimping was worth it if it saved them from asking Regina for more.

The first weeks in Ann Arbor flew by. Christina was happy. Pat's inattentiveness was understandable; she knew the pressure he was under. On weekends he would take short breaks and they would have lunch and see Ann Arbor together. She and Pat would take walks, hold hands, and sometimes stop to kiss. He seemed to relax and enjoy himself. Later in the evening he would go back to his books, studying frantically as if he were afraid he'd fallen behind.

It was a while before Christina noticed how moody he had become. He would be fine at breakfast, but when he came home later he would act distant and uncaring. Sometimes he ignored her completely. At other times he would become angry for no reason at all. Pressure, Christina thought, and consoled herself with the thought that the six weeks would soon be over.

It was during the fourth week of the summer session when the first outburst occurred. Christina was ironing in the living room when Pat walked by and called the kitten.

"Trykie, come here. Come here to me. Trykie, do you hear me? Come here." But the kitten ignored him. He called to it again, louder; then he started really yelling.

"Come here, cat. Now. Come here." Frightened by the anger in his voice, the kitten scampered into the bedroom and under a bed.

"Damn it, come back here. Come back here, you son of a bitch." By now the cords of his neck were standing out as he screamed.

Racing into the bedroom, he lifted the bed and lunged after the tiny kitten. But Trykie was cowering up against the wall, and Pat was unable to reach that far. Furious, he slammed the bed frame against the wall, pinning the kitten for a second. That was long enough for Pat to grab it, cutting his forearm on a jagged edge of the bed frame as he did. He didn't pause; didn't even notice the cut.

Christina was terrified. She had never witnessed such anger.

Stunned, unable to react, she stood trembling, as Pat came out of the bedroom with the kitten. He held it by the neck, smacking it with his free hand. She tried to speak, to tell him to stop, but she couldn't find the words. "Please," she whispered as Pat flung the kitten away, throwing it down hard against the floor.

Then he turned and rushed at her. He was trembling, his eyes squinting with rage.

"Nothing runs from me, nothing!" he screamed, his face inches from hers. "I hate it when anything runs. It makes me violent." Then suddenly as if he were flicking off a switch he controlled himself. His voice became calm, flat. "Don't you ever run from me," he went on quietly. "Don't you run. It makes me violent. I'd see you dead first." Christina stood speechless, unbelieving, yet afraid to say anything that might provoke him further. He stared at her a second longer, then suddenly realized his arm was bleeding. Without a word he turned and quickly walked to the bathroom.

It was the kitten's pitiful cries that snapped Christina out of her shock. Her first impulse was to find the cat and give it comfort, but no matter what he had done, her first duty was to Pat and the wicked cut on his forearm. She went to him cautiously, and in a whisper offered to help.

He began talking to her as if nothing had happened. In a professional, clinical voice he explained to her why the wound needed stitches and why he couldn't take the time to get them now.

Once the bleeding was stopped and the bandage wrapped, she went to find Trykie. For the next half hour she cuddled and stroked it, trying to stop its trembling and wailing. Eventually the kitten calmed down, but from that day forward it walked with a twisted, unnatural hop in its hind legs.

Christina never discussed the incident with Pat. It had been so frightening and upsetting that she couldn't talk to him about it. Not thinking about it was harder. That night, and for many nights after, long after Pat was asleep she would lie in bed and remember. She saw Pat's angry, distorted face and heard the kitten screaming. Then she would hear, over and over, the words he had so calmly said to her. He had not shouted them in a fit of anger. He had spoken in a soft, deliberate voice, as if he wanted her to make no mistake about what he was saying.

*   *   *

Pat passed the surgery course at Ann Arbor. Now there was just one more course to take, pediatrics, this one at the University of New Mexico Medical College. Again they packed up all their belongings and headed cross country, this time to Albuquerque. Again Pat drove and Christina sat with Trykie on her lap. The only variation from their previous trip was Pat's list.

Pat had typed it all out. It was a list of things to be done each day, including detailed instructions to remind himself to do everything from driving the car to looking under the motel bed in the morning to be sure they wouldn't forget anything. Faithfully he would check himself against the list. Sometimes he would have Christina take it out as they drove and enter new reminders on it.

In Albuquerque Pat found them a small, run-down trailer in one of the poorer sections of town. The landlords were gracious and friendly, but they were just as poor as Pat and Christina and hadn't been able to do much with the trailer before they rented it. It was old and dirty and, Christina found, impervious to soap and elbow grease. Although she attacked it with the same energy and enthusiasm as she had their first apartment, the place looked the same when it was finished as it had when she'd begun. Christina had to console herself that they would be there for only five weeks and that, however it might look, it was clean.

What bothered her more was Pat's increased moodiness. She would try to figure out what had triggered a particular mood swing, but usually she could find no explanation. There was no way of telling what had thrown him into a mood, or what would bring him out of one.

Once, several weeks into the summer session, he left for the day without saying good-bye, grabbing his lunch bag and mumbling to himself as he barged out. He was gone only ten minutes when he suddenly burst back into the trailer, shouting at her: "You fucked up again, Tina. You forgot to remind me to shave." He marched into the bathroom, shaved, then left again without saying a word.

When Pat finally finished the pediatrics course they were free for the rest of the summer. From Albuquerque they drove directly to Tucson to visit Christina's family. The pressure was off Pat and he was happy and relaxed. Christina breathed a sigh of relief. It was a good time for them both.

Although they had been away for less than three months, the family was as excited as if they had been gone for years. Every day Athena Bellios prepared special meals. In the evening they sat around the table, talking, joking, and having fun. Christina was delighted to see Pat return to his old self. He was warm and affectionate to her again, and apparently happy. She had told her mother over the telephone about Trykie, but not about Pat's threat. No one mentioned Trykie's limp, or the ragged three-inch scar on Pat's forearm. The incident was best forgotten. Christina did not mention her husband's moodiness, even when she was alone with her mother. That was something between her and her husband.

She was confident that she and Pat would work out their problems. Once he started practicing medicine and earned money of his own, he would be fine. Perhaps he wasn't as affectionate as other men, but that was not his way. She was sure he loved her, and sure she would one day grow to love him.

On the drive to New Orleans, Christina decided to try even harder to make life better for Pat. She would make an all-out effort to be positive and reinforcing at all times.

Her plan of action decided, she spent the rest of the trip putting it into effect. She spoke excitedly about living in New Orleans, and encouraged Pat to talk again and again about the places he wanted to visit. She also expressed admiration for his new status as a doctor, as someone starting out to fulfill a new career, all to good effect. By the time they got to Louisiana, Pat was brimming with enthusiasm.

The Las Brisas Apartments on Chef Menteur Highway were everything their last two homes had not been—new, clean, and landscaped with palm trees and flower beds. The tenants were young people—executives, doctors, and lawyers—all starting out in their careers. The neighborhood was one of the better sections of the city. Although she was tired from the long drive, and from sitting in the car for several hours in the humid heat while Pat checked into Charity Hospital, Christina was immediately excited. Here was a place where she could make a comfortable home.

The manager, upon learning more about them, asked if

they'd be interested in getting a special rate by having Christina work part time as an assistant manager.

"No, she's not interested," Pat answered before she could reply.

"I don't want you busy with something else when I come home," he told her later. "I don't want you too tired to do what you have to do as my wife. And I don't want people bothering us when I'm home. Your job is to be ready when I come home in the evening."

Christina nodded and said nothing. It hadn't been a job she particularly wanted, but she had expected Pat to jump at the chance of saving on the rent. Later on, when she suggested she help out by getting a job substitute teaching, he was equally emphatic. He didn't want his wife doing anything but taking care of him.

Pat worked hard at the hospital. As a new intern he drew a shift requiring him to stay at the hospital for three days straight, catching a few hours' sleep whenever he could. Then he had a day off. But if he felt pressured, Christina couldn't detect it. Meanwhile, she was continuing her "total effort" campaign. She did her hair and chose her clothes to please him. When he arrived home she was ready with dinner, the apartment was clean and straightened up. If he chose to discuss his shift with her, she listened attentively. Her interest was genuine. Aside from the wives she met in the laundry room, he was her only social life.

Pat refused to socialize with anyone who worked at Charity Hospital. He saw those people all day; he didn't want them knowing anything about his private life. Eventually Christina met another couple in the apartment building and invited them for dinner. Tony and Eloise were friendly and entertaining, and Christina was happy to see that Pat seemed to like them. The two couples saw each other for dinner every few days, and Christina was thrilled to have Eloise to talk to during the day. After a while she came to wonder whether Pat genuinely liked Tony or whether he just liked being the recipient of the other man's generosity. Eloise and Tony were somewhat older than the Henrys, and better established financially. They frequently offered things to the Henrys—a three-speed bicycle that Eloise had bought but never rode, a fishing rod and reel when Tony got a new one for his birthday, and so on—things which Pat never failed to accept even if, as in the case of the fishing rod, it was something he probably would never use. But this was just a mild suspicion of Christina's, nothing more, and she tried not to let it spoil her new friendship.

When Pat had a day off, he and Christina had fun doing things together. They often went walking in downtown New Orleans, limiting themselves to window shopping since they didn't have the money to do anything else. For Pat's birthday Christina spent ten dollars for a little mixed breed dachshund they named Weenie. Pat didn't complain about the money; he loved getting gifts.

It was historical New Orleans that Pat loved most. With Christina in tow, he trudged all over the French Quarter and into the surrounding countryside, taking pictures of everything. Christina found the Quarter as charming and interesting as he did. She loved the porches and balconies, the elaborate wrought-iron fences and gates. They would often spend Pat's whole day off going through the streets and shops, through Andrew Jackson Park, eventually stopping at some spot where they could watch ships passing on the Mississippi.

Several days before Christmas of 1971, Christina's sister Karen came to visit and a peace was struck. Pat made a real effort to get along with her, and devoted his free time to showing her the treasures he'd discovered, pointing out all the sights that a first-time visitor would want to see.

One day Pat discovered something he'd missed before. They had just visited the French Market on Decatur Street and were walking north on Conti Street. Just past the intersection where Dauphine Street meets Conti, Pat spotted the Musee Conti, Museum of Wax. With childlike excitement he insisted they go inside immediately.

As they walked through the entrance, all three of them blinked. The entire museum was in darkness, the only lighting provided by the life-size, brightly lit exhibits. It was like being in a theater with a series of different-size stages. They quickly understood the setup. Visitors walked through a dark, winding hall and came upon each lighted display. In each were lifelike wax figures, dressed in period costume, acting out historical scenes dating from the founding of New Orleans in 1699.

As Pat, Christina, and Karen walked through the darkened halls they were all struck by the realism of the scenes. Pat was particularly intrigued. But when he reached the thirteenth exhibit he stopped and stared in complete fascination. Christina and Karen had to go back for him. He stood before it, motionless, for over five minutes. When Christina called to him he didn't respond; he just stood and continued staring.

The exhibit was entitled "The Haunted House of Madame Lalaurie." It showed a dark, unfinished attic, with black slaves chained against the wall and to the floor. Their white mistress stood near them, dressed in a pink silk gown, holding a huge whip in her hand. She was assisted by her personal servant, a neatly dressed black male.

The exhibit originated in stories of a real antebellum New Orleans lady, Madame Delphine Lalaurie, and her mulatto servant, Bastian. The wife of a wealthy doctor, and the toast of New Orleans society, Madame Lalaurie threw extravagant parties on the main floor of her house while at the same time she kept slaves in the attic upon whom she repeatedly committed atrocities too incredible for human belief. The exhibit is so realistic that the agony and fear of the slaves can be seen clearly on their faces. Pat went back to stare at the exhibit three times. Finally, when the manager told him it was past closing time, he relented and finally left. Christina and Karen kidded him about his fascination with the exhibit, but he ignored them.

Christmas with Karen was fun. Together the two sisters prepared a small feast for dinner, and Christina borrowed an old record player from Eloise so they could have some Christmas music. The truce between Pat and Karen lasted until she was safely on the plane back to Tucson. Christina was delighted. The visit had been a success.

After Christmas, however, Pat's moodiness started again. He would often come home angry and remain that way for hours, or else he would come home and ignore Christina. One evening he told her that the people he admired most were the Indians and Orientals, because they were able to conceal what they were thinking or feeling. They had the self-control not to give anything away in their faces.

Another day he came home and handed her a note he had written her. Christina unfolded it, but couldn't read what he'd written. It wasn't just his handwriting; the letters seemed to come from a different alphabet.

Pat laughed at her puzzlement. "Give up, Tina?" he crowed, "Look, it's easy. Just hold it up to the mirror."

The note had been written backward. That was peculiar enough. But Christina still couldn't read it. She could read the words, but taken together they didn't make sense.

"That's part of it too," Pat explained eagerly. "It's like a code. You don't use the real word. You use another word that will remind you of it."

Christina could only wonder who all this elaborate subterfuge was designed for. But she didn't ask Pat. Later that evening he went back to ignoring her. He sat calmly, impassively, for hours, his face expressionless. Like all of his moods, this one eventually lifted. There was nothing Christina could do but wait.

The apartment was immaculate. Christina had cleaned and recleaned twice, out of boredom as much as fastidiousness. The dinner and dessert were ready; she had only to heat up the main course. She had changed outfits twice before selecting a colorful hostess skirt and a white scoop-neck blouse. Her hair was freshly cut and washed. She looked her very best.

After three days without anyone to talk to, except for Eloise for an hour one afternoon, she had begun to feel the walls of the apartment closing in on her. The endless hours of boredom were beginning to take their toll. Christina badly needed someone to talk to.

Pat would be tired when he got home. He'd been working in the Emergency Room at Charity for the past three days. But maybe he would stay up for a while and talk to her. Even if he was in one of his moods she was sure she could get him out of it.

"You should have seen it this weekend," Pat said, coming through the door. "They were really going at it."

Christina greeted him with a kiss, but he just kept on talking, preoccupied with telling her all the grisly stories that had transpired at the Emergency Room.

"The Saturday night knife and gun club was really wild. We had a guy in there that someone—" He stopped talking for a second, as if thinking about something, then went on in a slower, more deliberate voice. "If someone did something to me like that, I'd get even. I'd get even no matter how long it took me. I'd get them and take them someplace where no one would ever be able to hear them. I'd tie 'em down, spread eagle, and then I'd start. First I'd stick pins in their eyes, then I'd push my thumbs back into their sockets and crush their eyeballs. Smash 'em. And they'd feel the pain. A lot of it.'' He seemed very pleased with himself.

Christina had followed him into the bedroom and was listening, dumbfounded. He placed his medical bag on the dresser, then began to remove his watch, but his mind was obviously still on his fantasy. Numbed by what her husband had just said, and by his obvious pleasure in it, she sat down on the end of the bed and stared out the window. She didn't want to look at Pat's face.

''They'd probably pass out eventually. The pain would be too great. But I'd bring 'em back. I could keep them conscious. I know how. Once I'd brought 'em back, I'd put pins under their nails and into their genitals. They'd scream forever but no one would be able to hear them, because we'd be out in the swamp or something. Then I'd take a knife and cut off parts of them.''

Christina was becoming ill. She couldn't believe what she was hearing. But Pat wasn't finished.

''If you put a knife in the lower abdomen—stick it straight in—you can pull it up in a single movement and cut someone wide open. We see it all the time at the knife and gun club. That's one of the most painful ways to die, lots of pain. They'd feel themselves opened up; their intestines would come out, but they couldn't do a thing, nothing but scream and nobody to help them.''

Pat had never talked about anything like this before. Yet Christina sensed that while this may have been the first time he had let it out, it was not the first time he had thought about it. This plan was something he'd worked out carefully over a period of time. As if in a trance, she sat motionless as he finished.

''You know how I'd end it? You know? I'd take explosives— not big ones; they'd have to be small, or I wouldn't be able to stay close enough to watch. I'd take the explosives and shove them up the rectum if it was a man. If it was a woman, I'd put it in her vagina and in her ass. Then I'd light the fuses and watch their faces. They'd know what I was doing. I'd stand close and watch while they went off. Then, after a while, I'd let them die. If I wanted, I could keep them alive for days with shocks or injections. I'm a doctor. I know how to keep them alive. But finally, I'd just let 'em die.''

Christina thought she would vomit. She had just heard from her husband's mouth thoughts so wicked and so cruel that no one in his right mind would have imagined them. She made a conscious effort not to visualize what he had just described. But the words were too vivid. For the first time since she'd met him, for the first time in over three years, she realized there was something in Pat that was horribly, horribly wrong.

But Pat did not give her time to think more about it. Having gotten this all out, he seemed to become the old agreeable Pat again. He sat down to Christina's special dinner as if nothing at all had transpired, and for several weeks thereafter he remained the Pat she had known. They went about New Orleans together and made plans for the future. After a couple of months Christina had almost succeeded in forgetting that terrible evening. Every young doctor, she knew, was shocked and upset by the gruesomeness he or she witnessed in the Emergency Room. Some quit medicine because of it. And some, she told herself, might have reacted as Pat did, by going temporarily a little crazy.

When Pat suggested a vacation trip to Florida, Christina was delighted. Her isolation from friends or professional acquaintances had begun to weigh heavily on her. Her life was in a vacuum with Pat. The trip would be such a welcome change.

Pat was excited too. He devoted all his free time to their vacation plans, and spent entire evenings making up lists of what to take. He had borrowed camping equipment—a tent, air mattress, and lantern—from Tony and Eloise, ''because,'' he told Christina, ''it's cheaper than staying in hotels. We can camp out all the way to Florida, and when we get to the water, I'll teach you how to snorkel.''

By the time they reached Florida the weather had turned even warmer. Every night they camped near a lake and swam before dark. For the first time in months, Christina was having a wonderful time. One afternoon they stopped early at a YMCA campsite, and Pat spent an hour taking pictures of her floating in an inner tube, all outfitted in her snorkel and flippers.

The next day they stopped early again and found another

place to swim. Pat had located the spot, a beautiful lake surrounded by tall moss-draped trees and thick vegetation. The lake was cold, but the day had been hot and humid and Christina loved the coolness of the water after the long drive.

They swam out together until they could no longer touch bottom, then treaded water. Christina stretched out and floated on her back with her eyes closed, relaxed and peaceful. When she opened her eyes again Pat was looking past her, off to one side, and smiling. He was enjoying the view, she thought. "Tina, wait here for me," he said then, "I'm going to get my camera and take some pictures."

Christina lay back and closed her eyes again as Pat swam to shore, hurried up to the car, then rushed back to the lake with his camera. She opened her eyes when he called to her from the lakeside.

"Over there, Tina, swim over there." He used his hands to direct her in the direction he wanted, shouting because she was so far from shore.

"Now over there, over there," he yelled again, directing her in the opposite direction.

She followed his hand signals, wondering if he could really shoot good pictures from so far away. Again and again he directed her, moving her back and forth on the large lake, until suddenly he stopped and ordered, "Tina, do exactly what I tell you. Swim this way as fast as you can, and don't turn around; don't look back."

Obediently she started toward him, thinking: why shouldn't she look around? . . . Why did she have to swim as fast as she could? His words spun in her mind. Something was wrong, she realized. He was warning her about something. Panicky now, she stretched her arms further and kicked furiously. The shore seemed miles away. She raced for it, straining, clawing and kicking, her heart pounding as much from fear as from physical effort. The fear caught in her throat and she gasped for air, still not daring to look back to see if anything really was gaining on her.

Gulping for air now, she drove harder and harder for shore. Seconds later one foot touched the silty bottom, then the other. Exhausted, she kept going, half swimming and half walking till she reached the point where the water was only a few feet deep. There she stumbled and fell forward, gasping for air as she crouched on her hands and knees.

Out of the corner of her eye she caught sight of something low in the water. It moved closer. She was so weak she couldn't stand. She couldn't get away. The water erupted beside her. Something wide and tapering, several feet long, twisted out of the water, then slapped it, spraying water high into the air. It was less than six feet away. Christina screamed, lunged for the shore, and crawled frantically up the beach, sobbing out of control.

Pat rushed over to her, but not to help. His legs straddled her body as he focused on her with the lens, shooting picture after picture of her in hysterics. Then he stood back and started to laugh. Christina turned her head away and covered her ears, but her hands couldn't stop the sound of his laughter.

"Did you see it?" he asked at last, when she had gained control of herself. "That was an alligator. Did you see it?" He couldn't stop grinning.

"Why?" she gasped, between sobs. She sat up, too exhausted, too frightened to do more. "Why did you do that?" she asked, still weeping.

He looked at her blankly, and for a moment a half smile caught at his mouth. Then, without a word, he shrugged and walked off, leaving her alone on the beach. Leaving her without an explanation or apology.

The rest of the evening he ignored her. Still numb with shock and terror, Christina said nothing, sat there silently at dinner, unable to eat, while Pat wolfed down his meal. How could he have done this? she wondered. He was her husband. How could this be? While she lay awake most of the night, Pat slept soundly. In the morning he chatted over breakfast about what they would do that day, as if nothing at all had happened the day before. "I can't wait," he said cheerily, "to visit Disney World."

Christina forced a smile onto her face. "That will be nice," she said, pushing back her thoughts of yesterday. Things would get better, she was sure; they had to. After all, Pat was her husband; she was his wife. It wasn't supposed to be like this, like it had been, yesterday. It was supposed to be like it was now, today.

For the rest of the trip Pat behaved normally. Sometimes he seemed moody or angry, but he would recover himself quickly. Christina tried not to think about what had happened, but it was hard. When they got back to New Orleans, Pat had a new nickname for her. Whenever they were alone and no one could hear, he called her "Toad." She tried not to think about that either.

Charity Hospital operated a small clinic in Pineville, Louisiana, and each intern was required to spend a month of his internship working there. Pat's turn came in July, immediately after their vacation.

Christina had been excited about the move but when they got to Pineville, her enthusiasm wilted. She had thought New Orleans was terrible in the summer, but she soon learned that Pineville was ten times worse. The heat in central Louisiana was debilitating; it sapped your strength, drained all your energy. Nightfall brought a little relief from the temperature, but not from the humidity, an invisible blanket that was almost smothering. Christina could only be thankful that, unlike several of the doctors' wives, she was not pregnant.

The apartments allotted to the rotating doctors were no worse than others Christina had lived in so far. It was the insects she couldn't stand. Nothing she tried would get rid of them; the roaches seemed to thrive on insect spray. But what really scared her were the fire-orange and black flying insects that looked like huge grasshoppers. Just the sight of the ugly creatures was enough to give her chills. Nevertheless, the apartment was where she spent most of her lonely days, as Pat continued his policy of not socializing with his colleagues.

In New Orleans she had broken him down just once. There had been a hospital Christmas party and all the doctors had chipped in twenty-five dollars apiece.

"I don't call it 'chipping in,' " Pat had told her angrily, "when they automatically deduct the money from your check. I told them I didn't want any part of it, but they went ahead and took the money anyway."

Eventually Christina had persuaded him that they ought to go. But Pat had been on duty for the first hour of the party, and when he and Christina arrived most of the food had already been eaten. Pat complained loudly that he had been cheated, and the evening was ruined for both of them. No, there was no way to persuade him to socialize with the other two doctors in Pineville.

She was elated, then, when Pat announced one evening that he would take her out to dinner on Sunday. She knew it would be to the clinic cafeteria where the meals were free for doctors on Sundays, but it didn't matter. She pretended they were going somewhere exciting. Dressing up in a linen skirt and flowered blouse, she behaved as if they were going out to a formal evening social, not just to a cafeteria.

Pat played along. He hurried ahead to open the car door, seated her with great politeness at the cafeteria table. He talked and joked with her throughout the meal, and Christina forgot for a while the boredom, the blanket of humidity, the cruelties that had come between them. It was one of the nicest evenings of their marriage. When dinner was over, Pat even rushed to open the cafeteria door for her.

He went out ahead of her to the car, and as she approached she thought she saw him reach for something in the back seat. But she didn't really pay attention. The heat in the car was unbearable, but Pat told her to roll the windows up; he would run the air conditioner.

The car began to cool immediately, and for a mile or so they drove in silence. Looking over at Pat, Christina saw that he was smiling. She smiled back. A few minutes later she noticed that he was still smiling. She was about to ask him why, when from the corner of her eye she caught a movement. On the back of her seat was one of the large reddish-orange and black grasshoppers. Pulling back, she yelled, "Pat, look! It's one of those things. Get it!"

"I was wondering when you were going to notice it," he said, smiling.

Before she could say anything more, another one flew over the seat, hit the windshield and bounced back on her lap. Several more flew over. In seconds there were at least a dozen flying frantically inside the car. Christina screamed as one caught in her hair, and others landed on her bare arms and neck.

She screamed at Pat to stop the car but he just kept smiling. She realized then that he was trying to drive and watch her at the same time, not wanting to miss anything. She cringed and pulled back against the door, desperately trying to slap them off. They were landing on him, too, but he didn't mind.

Christina had just pulled out the one in her hair when another one got tangled. She was becoming hysterical. She tried to open the window, but Pat reached across and grabbed her arm. The shell-like bodies of the insects kept hitting the glass with a sickening, cracking sound as they, too, tried to escape. Screaming and pleading with Pat only made him laugh harder. For a second she thought of jumping out of the car, but Pat had speeded up. No matter how many she pulled out of her hair, her imagination told her she was covered with them.

When Pat pulled into the parking lot at their apartment, Christina jumped out and brushed at her clothes frantically, knocking away those insects still clinging to her. She ran her hands through her hair, over and over, making sure they were gone. She was shaking and trembling, her blouse pulled out, hair going every which way. Tears streamed down her cheeks while Pat stood staring and smiling at her.

"How could you do that?" she yelled over and over. "How could you do that to me? You know how I hate them. Why'd you do that?" He answered with a smile and a shrug of his shoulders, just as he had weeks earlier in Florida.

Alone so much of the time, Christina had endless hours to sit and think. It was impossible to push away her thoughts about Pat any longer. She knew, unquestionably, that there was something dreadfully wrong with her husband. Yet his "sickness," as she had come to think of it, wasn't something constant; it came and went without warning. Sometimes it wouldn't reappear for months; sometimes it would return in a day. She didn't know what, if anything, she could do. She felt helpless, and totally at his mercy.

He had begun to talk about torture again. He would be reading the newspaper, or watching a program on television, when something would set him off and he would start talking about revenge. He described each of his scenarios as vividly as he had the first, but each time there were new variations. His imaginary victim was always someone who had crossed him.

"If someone did something to me that I didn't like, I'd get him for it," he told Christina fiercely one night. "No matter how long it took. Even if he got sent to prison I'd get him. I'd wait twenty years for his sentence to be up, and then I'd be outside with a shotgun."

What frightened her most about these stories was that Pat's face would be bright with pleasure as he talked. He would be as intense and excited as he'd been that day at the wax museum, standing before the Madame Lalaurie exhibit.

But what he enjoyed most was her reaction. He'd almost wrecked the car trying to see her panic and fear when the insects were crawling all over her. He had been so thrilled, so very thrilled.

The more she thought about everything, the more upset she became. She realized that only she was aware of this side of Pat. No one else was ever present when he said or did frightening things. She had not told anyone about her experiences nor could she. A Greek wife would never speak against her husband.

All she could do was pray. On a shelf in the apartment she had placed an icon of Christ, a Bible, and a spray of palm from the previous Easter. Kneeling there, she prayed that Pat would be all right again. And she prayed desperately for herself, that she would have the strength to endure the atmosphere of intimidation in which, increasingly, she lived.

She had always dealt with Pat's moods and fantasies by not resisting them, by making sure that she said or did nothing to upset him. But each time she did so, she felt she was giving up a part of herself. Pat's ranting descriptions of torture and murder were beginning to affect her. Slowly, her personality was changing. She was afraid of him now and she was becoming withdrawn and timid. And the more fear she felt, the more powerful Pat seemed to become.

Pat finished his internship and, rather than be drafted into the army, volunteered for the United States Public Health Service. He was assigned to a government clinic in Mobile, Alabama, and he and Christina drove there in October 1972.

As she had before their move to New Orleans, Christina rededicated herself to her marriage and resolved to make a bigger effort to be loving and supportive. Pat was excited about his new assignment and she joined willingly in his good spirits. Looking back, Christina saw those first three months in Mobile as some of the best in her marriage.

Pat's job at the Public Health Service Clinic seemed perfect. The clinic itself was small: including secretaries, nurses, and administrators, there were fewer than twenty people. More important, as a group they were friendly and easygoing, taking their cue from the chief doctor, Don Unverferth. Unverferth was everything anyone could ask for in a supervisor.

Not only was he thoroughly competent, he was well liked and respected by the entire staff. Christina found him as charming and gracious as everyone else did; Pat seemed happy working under him.

Without tension and pressure at work, Pat came home each evening in a good mood, and Christina made sure that nothing happened to upset him. The fits of anger and moodiness ceased; there were no more dissertations on torture and murder. Pat seemed more at ease with himself than she had ever seen him.

Their apartment at Yester Oaks Village was small—a bedroom and bath upstairs, kitchen and tiny living room down below—but it was clean and modern. Best of all, there were people Christina's own age all around her. She met some of her women neighbors, and they talked and visited frequently. But it was with the woman who lived next door that she formed the strongest friendship.

Janis Tyler, several years younger than Christina, was as pretty and energetic as a cheerleader. Blond and attractive, giving and warm, she was just what Christina needed in a friend. The two women liked each other, they spent hours talking. Janis's optimism and enthusiasm were contagious. Both young wives shared the same dream—to have a baby.

Right after Christmas, Christina's mother visited them and Pat seemed genuinely excited to have her there. He had read up on the history of Mobile and on the first day of Athena's visit he took her and Christina for an hours-long tour of the city. He said he wanted Athena to see all the important sights of Mobile, but every place they visited, it was he who jumped out and photographed everything, from every possible angle—the beautiful old houses in the city, the antebellum mansions and plantations in the country, the waterfront houses built on concrete stilts to withstand gulf storms and high water. And although he talked incessantly about each place, he seemed to be speaking more to himself than to them. Of all the places he took them to, it was the swamp that most captivated him.

Leaving the highway, he drove right into the swamp on a spongy dirt road that was no more than two narrow, parallel tracks where grass didn't grow. Christina warned him that it wasn't safe, but he ignored her and kept going.

The swamp wasn't much of a tourist attraction—some tall grass and trees draped in green moss. But Pat seemed to see something more in it. He snapped several shots and then, "to get a better angle," got out of the car and climbed up on its roof. Christina could only look at her mother apologetically as they sat in the middle of a swamp, on a deserted dirt road, listening to the metallic pop the roof made as Pat moved around on it taking pictures. When at last he was ready to leave, the car had sunk six inches into the mud. It took them half an hour to extricate themselves.

Later, when they were back home, Christina told her mother the news: she thought she was pregnant.

"She's not," Pat cut in abruptly. "She just thinks she is."

But Christina knew she was right. Even though she was only, at most, a few weeks along, she could feel the changes in her body. She wanted a baby more than anything—someone she could love, someone to love her. Trykie, her crippled cat, was her only source of affection. Even at his best Pat was not interested in affection. They still had sex, but not since the first few months of their marriage had he put an arm around her or hugged her. She couldn't remember the last time he told her he loved her. He shunned her attempts at showing affection; he wasn't interested. But a baby would be different. A baby would change her life.

She had always loved children. As a little girl she had dreamed of the day she would have a baby, and, years later, teaching young children had been much more than just a job to her. Just the thought of a baby lifted her spirits.

But Pat's attitude was puzzling. It wasn't as if she hadn't discussed having a baby with him. He had seemed willing, though not exactly enthusiastic. He had even suggested that the best time to be pregnant was now, while all his medical expenses were covered by the government. Yet here he seemed to be against it, but she didn't want to risk angering him by reminding him that he had agreed to it.

The night before Athena returned to Tucson the Henrys gave a party. When she approached Pat with the idea, Christina had quickly mentioned that her mother had offered to pay for everything. To her surprise, he had immediately agreed.

She and her mother had cleaned the house and then cooked for several days, preparing every Greek delicacy imaginable. The party was a complete success; everyone came, had a good time, and went home late. Christina went to bed tired but glowing, proud of herself and proud of Pat. Every guest that evening had seen Pat as the congenial host. He had fixed drinks and talked hospitably with everyone.

At one point, though, he had been alone in the kitchen with Athena. Dropping his smile he had said, "You know, Mom, I hate this. I really can't stand it." Then, a guest had come in for a refill, and Pat had greeted him cheerfully. For the rest of the evening, Athena marveled at his performance.

When Christina visited the gynecologist several weeks later, he only confirmed what she already knew: she was two months pregnant. Seeing on her information card that her husband was a physician, the doctor asked her if her husband had come with her. When she told him that he was in the waiting room, the doctor sent his nurse to ask Pat to join them in his office.

"Congratulations, Dr. Henry," he said, extending his hand for Pat to shake. Christina's heart sank when she saw Pat's smile. She had learned long ago to read his face, although he was certain no one could. This smile wasn't a real smile; Pat was hiding his feelings. She had hoped Pat would grow accustomed to the idea of her having a baby, but she realized now that there was no hope of that. His expression told her all too clearly how angry he really was.

Pat bought a new camera. It shouldn't have surprised her—he was enthralled with photography, and had taken hundreds of slides in Tucson, New Orleans, Pineville, and Florida. They were all neatly arranged in wooden storage compartments he'd made out of cigar boxes. He loved to look at them. Christina had given him a Carousel projector for Christmas and he'd spend hours at a time going through his collection. They still had no screen, so he projected them on a wall of the living room.

But this new camera was expensive. Pat had bought it at the local air force base, but even at the PX's reduced price it had cost him $250. She couldn't believe that the man who lectured her about turning off lamps not just to save electricity but to save wear on the bulbs, who often drove to motels to get free ice from the hall machines, who siphoned gas out of his government car into his own car, was the same man who had just spent all this money on a camera when he already had one. But she made no objection. She couldn't remember ever seeing Pat so excited about anything.

It was a few nights later when she first saw it. He was sitting in the darkened living room, staring at the slide on the wall. In his lap was his camera, and he was stroking it. It was dark; Christina looked again, squinting to make sure. That was exactly what he was doing. Like someone petting a cat, he rubbed his hand over the camera while staring intently at the wall. After that evening she made a point of watching whenever he spent an evening with his slides, which was now three or four times a week, sometimes every night—he held the camera gently and stroked it as if it were a living creature. Eventually Christina stopped watching. She would sit in the other room, waiting for him to decide it was time to eat dinner.

The new camera spurred his interest in taking pictures. At first it didn't seem to matter what he photographed. He'd follow Christina, taking shots of whatever she happened to be doing—washing dishes, cooking, talking on the phone. It made no difference. Suddenly he would appear with his camera and take pictures. It didn't take long, however, for her to realize that there was a common denominator: the more inappropriate the time and circumstance, the more unflattering the picture would probably be, the more likely he was to snap one. If her hair was in curlers, if she was wearing a housecoat, if her nose was red and running, he would turn up with the camera.

About this time Christina began having morning sickness—or in her case, morning, afternoon, and evening sickness. It was worst in the evening, when she was trying to prepare dinner. She would get so sick she'd become too weak to keep climbing the stairs to the bathroom. One evening, after vomiting several times during the afternoon, she placed a large stainless steel bowl on the floor beside the couch where she was lying. When she felt sick she'd grab the bowl. When Pat came home and saw this, he swooped down on the scene. It was his idea of a perfect picture.

She begged him not to, but he ignored her. As she lay on the couch, too weak and too sick to move, her face pale and drained, her hair loose and messy, Pat gleefully took photographs. Later when they had been developed and returned to him, he proudly labeled them "Tina Making Chunks."

The camera became the most important thing in his life; it was with him constantly, not just in the apartment but wherever they went. She began to resent it, then after a while to hate it. He intentionally used it to torment her. Just when she thought he'd taken every possible photograph of her, he came to her one evening with a new idea. He wanted to use color filters, then hold a glass paperweight over the lens while he shot the picture. Ignoring her protests, he insisted that she smile, stick her tongue out, and make a face. Several times he changed filters to get different colors. Then trembling with excitement, he asked her to scream; he wanted a picture of her screaming. She refused. Without bothering to argue, he stepped forward and kicked her in the leg as hard as he could and took his picture at the instant her face crumpled in pain. It was the first time he had hurt her physically. Christina ran into the bedroom, closed the door, and cried, as much out of fright as pain. Later when she composed herself, she reached the same conclusion she always did. Tolerate it, avoid upsetting him, forget that it ever happened. She didn't know what else a wife could do. The thoughts of leaving did not even enter her mind.

When her parents called a week later to invite them to Tucson for Easter, Christina said yes without waiting to ask Pat. Her parents had offered to pay the air fare; she knew she could convince him to go. And she needed the trip. Now, in her fourth month, her nausea was finally passing. The chance to get out and go someplace for a while was just what she needed. Seeing her parents would do wonders for her.

Pat had ignored her since he'd taken his last series of pictures. It was as if she wasn't important any more. He talked to her only when he had to. She knew it had to do with the pregnancy, but she didn't know how to deal with his resentment. She was too close to the situation to see it clearly, she thought, to understand what was happening between them. A visit home would help her focus.

And Pat was all for the trip. As long as it was free, she didn't even have to coax him.

The visit to Tucson only made things worse. Christina's parents were overjoyed to have them, but try as she might, Christina could not enjoy herself. Pat was acting affectionate, kissing her, holding her hand, and talking a silly baby talk, but she knew it was only for her parents' benefit. When they were alone it ceased immediately. She tried hard to behave as if she were happy but it was hard.

Athena Bellios was not taken in. She saw clearly that Christina had become much more quiet and reserved, while Pat was more aloof and demanding. He seemed to consider himself more important, more the center of things.

The baby was the key. Knowing how much her daughter loved children, Athena had expected her to be much more excited about the pregnancy. When the two women were alone Christina did seem happy about it, but she never discussed the baby when Pat was present. Sometimes she would even change the subject. Athena Bellios understood without having to be told: the marriage wasn't a happy one.

On the third day of their visit, Christina's nausea returned. She sat down to dinner with the family but couldn't eat a thing. Thinking it would help to lie down, she told everyone she was going to bed early. Pat surprised her by saying that he, too, was tired and would also go to bed.

Her parents had given them the main house, while they stayed in one of the apartments in back. The bedroom they were using had twin beds, pushed together to share a common headboard. It was still light outside when they lay down. After a few minutes of trying different positions, Christina found one that relieved the nausea enough to allow her mind to wander. Finally, feeling secure in her parents' home, she fell asleep.

It started like a dream. There was a noise, the sound of an animal growling. Then it stopped. Seconds went by, perhaps a minute, then it started again. It happened several times. Not until she opened her eyes and listened did she know she was awake. The room was dark; she'd been asleep for hours.

It began again, a low, growling noise coming from somewhere in the room. Christina sat up in bed and whispered, "Pat, do you hear that?"

He didn't answer.

"Pat, what is it? Pat?" She reached over and tried to find him.

"Pat, don't you hear that? Pat? Where are you?" Her eyes adjusted as she asked the question. She could see him on the far side of his bed lying on his right side, facing her. His eyes were open, looking at her. When she said his name again, he curled his lips back from his teeth and let out a low, gutteral growl.

"Pat, stop that. Stop it."

He kept growling. Then she saw his hair. It was standing on end. He continued to lie there, looking at her, growling deep in his throat, his lips curled like a vicious dog's.

Frightened of him now, she started out of bed, crawling for the edge of the mattress. It was too late. With hands held like claws over his head, and screaming loudly, he tackled her before she could escape.

The impact knocked her to the floor. "Pat!" she screamed, "let me go! Please." But with his hair standing up and his face contorted, he continued to rake his fingers down her body, clawing her, growling and snarling like a mad dog.

Athena Bellios was on her way to the main house to get something she'd forgotten, when she heard her daughter's terrified screaming and pleading, and the loud animal noises. Running the short distance to the house, she pulled open the sliding door and ran down the hallway. When she reached the bedroom she was shocked at what she saw: Christina on the floor, Pat crouched over her, growling like an animal and clawing her.

It took Athena only a step to reach Christina and grab her arm. Only then did Pat see her. Immediately he dropped his hands, stood up, and began laughing.

With an arm around her daughter for support, Athena led her to the living room. They collapsed on the large couch and Athena held her, trying to stop the hysterical sobbing. Christina's nightgown was ripped in several places; her body had red marks where Pat's nails had raked her. Aside from that, she had not been physically injured.

In the bedroom Pat could be heard—still laughing. Finally, when Christina could manage to talk through her sobs, she asked desperately, "Did you see him? Did you see him?" Athena held her tighter and told her that yes, she had seen him. She had certainly, and she too had been terrified.

Christina did not stop crying for almost an hour. She let out emotions she'd held in for months. After a while, Athena knew that her daughter was crying for something more than what had just happened.

When Christina's father came into the living room looking

for Athena, he found his daughter still upset and his wife comforting her.

"What has happened?" he asked sleepily.

Athena shook her head. She knew better than to tell the truth. Her husband would never tolerate what had happened. With a gun in the house, she knew he would do something drastic. Instead she said, "Pat has been playing a game and it's upset Christina, probably because she's pregnant."

Coming to her side, William asked in his heavily accented English, "Why you cry, Tina? What is the matter?"

"I don't want to go, Papa. . . . I don't want to go."

"Where? Go where?"

"To the Grand Canyon. I don't want to go." She was thinking already of the next day. Pat had asked to borrow her mother's car to drive to the Grand Canyon so he could take pictures. She was afraid now of being alone with her husband.

"But Tina, you must. He is your husband; you must go where he goes. He is your husband."

Still sobbing in her mother's arms, Christina could tell him nothing. And neither could her mother.

As it happened, the Grand Canyon excursion was uneventful. Pat wanted Christina to climb over a railing and pose for him out on a ledge, but did not press her when she refused.

When they returned to Mobile Pat left her completely. He acted as if she were of no importance to him whatever. His slide show was his social life; it was presented nightly, sometimes for as long as three or four hours. The slides taken through the glass paperweight lens became his favorites. They created horrible, tortured distortions of Christina's face. In some, the glass so altered her eyes and teeth that they were practically unrecognizable as human features. Pat liked to project these slides on the wall, then stare at each one for several minutes. Appalled at their hideousness, Christina asked him to get rid of them, to throw them away.

He looked at her incredulously, as if to say, "You must be joking." Then he said loftily, "These slides are for company, Tina. When we have people over, these are to show them. From now on they're the company slides." He spoke to her all the time now as if she were a child, in a condescending singsong. He knew she hated it.

The entire collection of paperweight slides were neatly labeled "Tina distorted." She knew he would never destroy them; next to his camera, they had become his most prized possession.

A few months later Don Unverferth, Pat's supervisor, left the clinic and Pat became the new director. The change in him occurred instantly. As he detailed to Christina his plans for changes and improvements, it became clear that he had been waiting months for this opportunity, yet she had had no idea the promotion was something he'd wanted. But what surprised her most was the contempt he revealed for Don Unverferth. As she listened, she realized that Pat had resented everything about him—his competence, his personality, even his looks. She had thought she could read Pat; now she wasn't sure any more.

Dr. Henry began his new regime the very first day. That evening he delighted in telling Christina how he had chewed out people who had it coming, how he'd changed procedure and assignments, and how he'd reassigned vacation dates that he didn't approve of. His petty tyranny soon carried over to the apartment. He found fault with Christina constantly and he was often angry and vindictive. But there was a new edge to his old moodiness. He now considered himself a very important person, much more important than ever before, and of course this meant that Christina was much less important than ever before.

Christina tried to take cover from this new barrage of unpleasantness. She avoided Pat whenever she could, bent his way when she couldn't. She would do anything to sidestep a confrontation. Only the thought of the baby to come kept her spirits up.

"Tina, you're so docile, so wifely," Pat would tell her teasingly. But he was pleased with the way she was behaving, she could see that, pleased that she was so completely cowed and intimidated. He had won. But of course that was only right. A person as important as he was deserved to win.

Athena Bellios had had enough. She knew Christina would never speak against her husband, nor would she permit her mother to ask certain questions. But Athena could read the signs. When she talked on the phone with Christina, she noticed what was not said as much as what was. Christina talked excitedly about the baby, but she never mentioned a word about how Pat felt. When she talked about anything besides the baby, her voice was flat and uninflected. Some topics she would not discuss at all.

Athena made up her mind to visit again, as soon as possible. The baby would be coming soon. Whatever the problems between them, she was sure that Pat would not cause difficulties for Christina if she was present.

She arrived in Mobile late in August, several weeks before Christina's due date. This time there was no need to read between the lines. For the first time Pat behaved in front of her as he always did with Christina. He didn't bother to change his evening routine, or to tone down his unpleasantness. The difference in his demeanor was startling. Everything had to revolve around him and what he wanted. He didn't put on any display of affection. When he came home in one of his moods, he didn't care in the least that Christina's mother was there to see it. The first night Athena saw him sitting in his chair, looking at his slides for hours on end and stroking his camera, she went to talk to Christina.

Christina broke down in sobs, admitting to her mother that this had been going on for months. But even then, out of loyalty, fear, and shame, she held things back. She didn't mention the distorted photographs, or how Pat had kicked her to make her scream, or the slides labeled "Tina Making Chunks."

At night, Athena would lie awake on the couch in the living room, worrying. Her powerlessness upset her as much as anything. Her beloved daughter was trapped in a marriage to a man who made her life totally miserable. There was no love, no sharing, nothing between them, yet they were married and about to have a child.

No solutions occurred to Athena. She and her husband had given Pat and Christina thousands of dollars worth of wedding gifts; they'd sent them money each month that Pat was in school and doing his internship; they'd given them furniture and anything else they could think of to help. But now she could give nothing but love and emotional support. She couldn't see any way out for Christina. It never occurred to her that Christina should leave him. A marriage *was* for better or worse.

One evening a week before the baby was due, Pat came home in higher spirits than usual. He even sat with Christina and her mother in the living room and chatted pleasantly.

Athena, who was cooking dinner, left for a minute to baste the chicken. The moment she was gone, Pat pulled Christina to her feet.

"Time to practice my judo," he said, and before she could react, he had grabbed her, turned slightly, and thrown her over his hip. Athena walked in just as her daughter hit the floor.

"My God!" she cried as she ran to Christina.

Pat pretended to laugh. Then he said coldly to Athena, "Don't worry, Tina is as strong as I am. She won't get hurt."

"She won't get hurt because you won't do that again." Athena crouched over her daughter, keeping herself between Christina and her husband. "What do you think you're doing?" she went on angrily. "You could have hurt Christina and the baby. What kind of father are you?"

Ignoring her fury, Pat turned his back on the two women and left the room. Afterward, he acted as if the whole episode had been a joke, and there was nothing Athena could do about it.

When Christina felt her labor pains begin, she was ready. She had waited a long and difficult time for this moment. Her mother and Janis Tyler had spent the last week working hard to keep her spirits high, and now she was happy and excited, not at all apprehensive.

Pat was ready too. As the women raced around the apartment getting everything together for the hospital, he made certain not to forget his camera. He took his first picture at the hospital just as the anesthesiologist was about to give her an injection. But Christina didn't notice him, even when he followed her into the delivery room. This was her moment, and she was focused totally on her child.

Patrick Steven Henry was born on September 7, 1973, weighing nine pounds, twelve ounces. Christina's parents sent orchids. Her sister Karen, who had become engaged, sent a beautiful assortment of flowers from herself and her fiancé. Janis sent a bouquet, as did several of the women from the clinic. Pat didn't send anything. He had photographed the entire delivery, not as a record to be shared later with his wife, but as more entertainment for his private world.

Christina called the baby "Paddy." She loved holding

him, nursing him, changing him, and just standing by the crib watching him as he slept.

But caring for him was exhausting. Athena did as much as she possibly could, but it was Christina who had to wake up and nurse the baby at 4:00 A.M. and again at 8:00. She had been home from the hospital for several days, but she was still feeling weak and drained.

One Sunday morning Athena insisted that Christina go back to bed after the 8:00 A.M. feeding and rest for a few hours. Christina had gratefully obeyed, and now she lay alone in the bed, drowsily watching Paddy sleep in his crib near the bedroom door.

She thought back to his last feeding. To her amusement, he had kept falling asleep as she nursed him.

"Paddy," she'd said softly. His eyes had opened half way and he'd begun nursing again, only to fall asleep again in a minute or two. Holding him in her arms, she had realized at that moment that his very existence depended on her. She could hold him, love him, be good to him without fear or rejection or disapproval. Now, as she drifted off to sleep, she knew she had never been so happy in her life.

His first cry woke her, but not fully. As she rolled over sleepily toward the crib, his cry changed, became a scream, something she'd never heard before. She was fully awake in seconds, jumping out of bed and rushing to the crib.

It was the baby's arm. He was wearing a knitted crib jacket with short sleeves, and she saw instantly that his right arm, bare below the elbow, had turned blue.

This couldn't be happening. She grabbed the baby, then screamed for her mother. Downstairs in the kitchen Athena heard and ran for the staris.

The tiny arm was entirely blue, from just below the shoulder to the tips of the fingers. Christina was rubbing and massaging it, trying to restore circulation. Athena's first thought was of her younger brother who had been born a "blue baby." Several seconds later, Pat casually entered the room. He strolled over to the crib, stood beside Christina, and looked at his son for a second, then announced calmly, "Probably a congenital heart defect. But they won't be able to do anything, not for a while. When he's four years old or so they'll cauterize it."

Her baby's life was in danger! Christina's face, tears streaming down her cheeks, reflected her agony. Athena, too, began to cry at Pat's diagnosis, but then quickly caught herself. She couldn't upset Christina more than she already was.

Leaving his frantic wife still working to restore the baby's circulation, Pat strode out of the room without once offering any help. After long, anxious minutes, Christina and her mother saw the arm return to normal. For the next several hours Christina held her baby clasped against her as if her body could somehow transfer its strength.

The pediatrician's office was crowded, even at 8:30 in the morning. Christina had no appointment, but when the nurse heard what had happened she made sure Paddy was seen immediately. Twice the doctor asked her, with a puzzled look on his face, to explain what she'd seen. Twice he checked the baby thoroughly. When he put his stethoscope to Paddy's tiny chest and listened, Christina searched his face for the slightest trace of a frown, but there was none. He found nothing. Patrick Steven Henry was quite healthy, he assured her. But a single arm turning blue was something he'd never seen or heard of before. It occurred to him that perhaps she had been mistaken, or was exaggerating, but her precise description and calm manner of speaking were not consistent with new mother hysteria. As there was really nothing he could do, the doctor advised her to watch the baby closely for any recurrences and not to hesitate to bring him in if there was the slightest question. He said there was no possibility of congenital heart defect.

For the next several weeks, whenever she heard the baby cry she would rush to the crib immediately, afraid of what she might find. Each time she would quickly scan his body for anything similar to what she'd seen that Sunday. She worried even when he wasn't crying. Sometimes when he was asleep, and his breathing was hard to detect, she would nudge him slightly with her finger, and each time he moved or stirred she felt a grateful relief. Several weeks passed without incident before she began to relax her vigilance.

Athena could not remain in Mobile indefinitely; the apartment was too small for all of them, and her husband needed her back in Tucson. His health was not good. Yet she had to find some way to protect Christina and her child. Eleven days after Paddy was born, she boarded a flight to Tucson. Karen's flight landed in Mobile just hours after her mother's left.

Karen arrived just in time to help them move. Even before the baby came, Christina and Pat had realized that they needed another bedroom. But Pat had insisted on finding an old house to rent, which was cheaper than renting another apartment.

Christina hated to leave her friends in the apartment building, but of course the decision was up to Pat. She knew he would not think of consulting her. Besides, her best friend at Yester Oaks Village was Janis Tyler, and now something had come between them.

One night over dinner, Christina had told Pat how surprised Janis's mother had been that Pat hadn't sent his wife flowers in the hospital.

As soon as she spoke she knew she'd made a mistake. Pat stopped eating, threw down his fork, and exploded into a tirade, cursing Janis and her mother for interfering in his affairs. In the end he declared that Janis, her husband Rick, and Janis's mother were all forbidden ever to set foot in his apartment again.

Christina had no choice but to be honest with Janis. She told her what had happened and apologized for being so indiscreet. The trouble was, however out of proportion Pat's response had been, Christina would have to obey him.

"Listen, don't worry," Janis told her reassuringly, "we'll figure out ways to see each other. Besides," she laughed, "Ricky can't stand Pat. He'll be happy he doesn't have to see him any more."

Christina liked the house Pat had found. Located on Reed Street, in an older section of Mobile, the house was a single story, with a high gabled roof and huge shade trees that would keep the house cool in summer. Its rooms needed work but they were large and spacious. Aside from the master bedroom, there was a bedroom for the baby, and another that Pat could use as a den. Pat particularly liked the unfinished attic. At one end someone had laid enough floorboards to form a deck covering less than a third of the total attic. A small cot and an old desk were the only furniture on the deck. There were no walls separating the floored area from the rest of the dark space. A single light bulb hung from the roof by a wire. Pat thought it was a perfect place to give insurance physicals, his latest moneymaking project.

As soon as the previous tenants left, Karen moved in with

a woman she'd hired and scrubbed and cleaned the entire house. It was still less than a month since the baby had been born, and Christina was very grateful to her for doing all the heavy work. Pat would never have let her hire someone to help. But after Karen helped her sister pack everything in the apartment for the move, she had to leave. She was to be married the following month, and was flying to New York to meet her fiancé's parents.

Christina knew the house could be charming. It was old-fashioned and in bad condition, but all it needed was a few repairs and some new paint and wallpaper. Her modest plans were all easily affordable on Pat's salary, but he steadfastly refused to spend money on someone else's house. New furniture was also out of the question. He wouldn't consider it. Only after much discussion and a little pleading was she able to convince him that the baby's room had to have a rocking chair. Reluctantly, he agreed to spend forty dollars on one she'd found advertised in the newspaper. Later on, she would sit in that rocking chair when she made the most important decisions of her life.

In the end, her parents sent them some old pieces of furniture and gave Christina the money to buy a crib and a chest of drawers for the baby. Then they also bought her a washer and dryer.

On the whole, however, the house remained just as it was: run down, in need of paint and repairs. Being poorly insulated, the house was always uncomfortably chilly in the winter but Pat had given strict instructions that he was the only one to touch the thermostat. To be sure his orders were followed, he carefully checked the meter against each bill. Even though she dressed warmly, Christina was always cold, but Pat refused to use the furnace unless it snowed. She took special care to see that Paddy was always dressed warmly and covered each night with blankets.

She couldn't tell how Pat felt about the baby. Sometimes he played with Paddy, held him on his lap and talked baby talk like any other father. Other times he would ignore him completely. As the days passed, the second pattern began to predominate. Often Pat would come home, fix a drink, go into the den, and show himself his slides for hours. Later he would go to bed without seeing the baby or even asking about him.

His feelings about Christina were clear enough. He was more impatient with her than ever. No matter how hard she tried, nothing pleased him. Under other circumstances she would have laughed at the absurdity of some of his criticisms. Grabbing her arm one day as she was doing the laundry, he directed her to look at the lint filter on the washing machine. "Do you see that? Look at it, Tina. See these? See these blue threads? That's my pants. That's our clothes being wasted. You're wearing them out by washing them so often."

Christina didn't bother responding. She was too tired for an argument. No matter how hard she'd tried, she had not been able to fully recover her strength. When she told Pat she thought she should see a doctor, he dismissed her statement out of hand.

"There's nothing wrong with you. I'm a doctor; ask me. There's no need to spend money on another doctor."

One day Janis Tyler came to visit her while Pat was at the clinic. It was obvious to her that Christina wasn't well, and she immediately offered to give her the money to see a doctor. Christina thanked her profusely, but she refused to accept the money. Janis thought she knew why: Christina was afraid of her husband.

At dawn one cold October morning, when everything outside was covered by a light frost, Christina was awakened by the baby's cry. She'd heard that scream only once before. Instantly she sat up and started out of bed, but Pat stopped her. "Leave him alone. He's all right. There's nothing wrong with him."

"Yes, there is. Pat, listen to him. Something is wrong."

"Leave him alone. . . . He's all right."

Ignoring him, she jumped from the bed and ran down the short hall to the baby's room. Paddy was screaming louder, more frantically. When she got to his crib and looked down, she couldn't see him at all. Instead she saw his blanket wrapped in the shape of a cocoon. The screaming was coming from inside it.

Grabbing the small bundle, she tried to unwrap it but couldn't find the edges. They seemed to be folded and tucked. Finding a corner she pulled it free and worked frantically to get the rest of it untangled. The blanket was wound around him so tightly he could barely breathe and she was desperate that he would suffocate before she could get him free.

When the blanket was finally unfurled, the baby's bluish-red face was her first sight. She grabbed him and held him while he screamed louder and louder until he ran out of breath. She walked back and forth across the room, holding him and talking to him in a soft, reassuring voice. Minutes passed before color returned to his face and his panicked screams turned into his normal cries. It was only then that Pat came into the room and asked what had happened.

Still frightened by what had happened, she described how she had found the baby suffocating in his blanket. He listened quietly, then said, "Calm down, Tina. He probably just turned over and got tangled up in the blanket." Then, just as he had done before when she had found the baby in distress, he left the room without even bothering to look over his child.

Christina sat down in the rocking chair beside the crib and reconstructed what she'd seen. The baby had never turned over before; he was still too young. Even if the baby had turned over for the first time, how could he have wrapped the blanket around himself twice and so tightly?

But it *had* to have been an accident. Whatever her suspicions, one single thought kept her from reaching the obvious conclusion: no person, not even Pat, could do such a thing to an innocent, helpless child. She held onto that single thought like a talisman, desperate to have it be so.

But her suspicions, once formed, stayed with her and haunted her during the weeks and months to come. She knew what she had seen; she just could not accept or believe it.

Karen came to visit again in November. She was shocked at how much Christina had changed in a single month. Her face was pale and gaunt, with purple shadows under her eyes. She looked like someone who had been sick for a long time and had not yet fully recovered.

When the two of them were alone, Christina explained that she wasn't sleeping much at night. Karen had heard from her mother about the time the baby's arm had turned blue; now Christina told her about the blanket incident.

"I just can't afford to sleep," she told her sister. "Suppose I missed a sound, or a cry, or something that meant Paddy was in danger again and needed me?"

Although she was unaware of the true nature of Christina's

suspicions, Karen was alarmed by her sister's desperation.
She hoped that, in the course of her visit, she could help
Christina relax.

The two sisters certainly had plenty of time together. Pat
was as openly unsociable with Karen as he had been with
Athena. He would come home, speak to them briefly as he
fixed a drink, then climb the stairs to the attic, where he
would stay for several hours. Karen was puzzled; she couldn't
imagine anyone wanting to spend hours up there. Christina
explained that he often gave insurance physicals in the attic,
to make extra money, but she had to admit that most of the
time he was up there by himself.

Knowing that Christina wasn't well enough to keep house
as she would want to, Karen tackled a few of the major jobs.
She was cleaning out the refrigerator when she discovered a
piece of sandwich meat that had turned green.

"God, Christina," she said, "what is this, a penicillin
factory?"

"Oh, I know—but Pat won't let me throw it away,"
Christina answered.

Holding the meat between forefinger and thumb, Karen
pretended to hold her nose with the other hand as she dumped
it into the trash.

It took Pat less than an hour after he arrived home to
discover this wastefulness. He sorted through the trash until
he found the meat, then demanded to know how Christina
could have allowed this.

With Karen there to bolster her courage, Christina began to
giggle. Both their smiles faded, however, when Pat carefully
cleaned off the meat with his fingernail and ate it.

The following evening, Christina sat in the kitchen as her
sister fixed dinner and they reminisced about their childhood.
Then Karen told Christina about how on her last trip to New
York she and her fiancé, Andres, had found a wonderful
apartment. She would be moving in almost immediately, as
soon as she could get her things packed in Tucson. Then she
and Andres would work on the apartment—scraping floors,
painting, wallpapering—and it would be perfect by the time
they were married.

They continued gossiping as Pat sat down with them for
dinner. But Karen could see he was bored by wedding plans.
Politely turning the conversation in his direction, she asked

all about his promotion at the clinic, and whether he had any idea what he would like to do next. Pat answered all her questions curtly. Exasperated, Karen gave up and fell silent. Then Pat began steering the conversation in the direction he wanted to go. He started with something he had read about, a crime in the newspapers, and then, to Karen's surprise and disgust, began the litany, by now familiar to Christina, of what he would do to someone who offended him.

Christina sat mortified and humiliated. He had never mentioned these horrible things to anyone but her. Now Karen would know what dreadful thoughts went through her husband's mind.

"Please, Pat, you're being disgusting," she said, but he went on and on.

"Pat, stop—you're upsetting Karen," Christina once again interrupted. Again Pat ignored her.

Karen was appalled but she thought she could see what was happening. Her sister's pleas only spurred Pat on to more grotesque descriptions. It was Christina's horror that he thrived on.

To test her theory, Karen sat expressionless and looked directly at her brother-in-law while he talked. After several minutes his enthusiasm lessened. In another few minutes, he seemed uncomfortable and then quickly dropped the subject.

Late that night, after everyone had gone to bed, Karen was awakened by the sound of a dog barking.

Weenie, she thought, Christina and Pat's dog, who was in the back yard. She was trying to go back to sleep when she heard doors slamming and Pat swearing. Now fully awake, she lay still in bed, listening. There was a pounding sound, and then Weenie yelping and crying. The back door slammed a second time, and then she heard Pat yelling to Christina, "If you ever wake me in the middle of the night again, I'll take a sledgehammer and smash in the head of his crib. That'll give him something to really cry about." Then there was silence, and no other noise for a long time. Eventually Karen fell back to sleep.

But Christina did not. She had awakened Pat to ask him to check on the dog; if he went on barking, she had said, he would wake the baby. That was what had triggered his outburst. Afraid that the baby might cry again, she crept into his room and picked him up. Cradling him in her arms she sat down in the rocker and lulled him back to sleep. The rocker did not creak; it moved back and forth silently on the carpet.

Christina's mind worked as she rocked. She told herself that Pat had spoken in anger—he wouldn't really do what he had said to the baby. But her mind returned to the blanket. Unless Paddy had somehow entangled himself, which seemed more and more unlikely, that blanket had been wrapped around him deliberately, calculatedly.

From there her mind returned to the first incident, the time the baby's arm turned blue. For the first time she tried to visualize everything that had happened that morning. First she had heard the cry. Then she had heard it again, louder. Then she had rolled over, turned toward the crib—and it was at that point that she remembered. Pat had been going out their bedroom door just as she turned over. *He had been in the room!*

She sat back in the chair, cold with shock. It had never occurred to her that he had hurt the baby then. *But he could have.* If he had squeezed the baby's arm hard enough he could have cut off the circulation and made it turn blue. It was possible. He could have been responsible for both incidents.

But she was just guessing. There was nothing she could prove. As the sun began to light the baby's room that morning, she realized that no one would ever believe her. Yet she had to do something; she couldn't just sit and wait for something else to happen. She began to plan what she would do if Pat someday went into a rage. She could grab Paddy and run to a neighbor's. Better yet, she could run to the car and drive with the baby to Janis's apartment. But none of these plans were any good, she realized—not if Pat really went after the baby. There was only one thing she could do, and that was to never leave the baby alone with Pat again. She would never give him the opportunity.

In the morning she apologized to her sister, but Karen passed off the disturbance as something she had been almost too sleepy to notice. When she returned to Tucson that November, she told her mother everything she had seen and heard. Neither of them told Christina's father. In the last few months William had discovered he had a serious heart condition. His blood circulation was so poor that he could not walk even short distances without pain. As long as he could do nothing for Christina his wife and daughter would not alarm him. The two women would have to cope as best they could: Athena would return to Mobile in a month; she could use the Christmas holidays as an excuse. In the meantime, she and Karen would keep in close touch with Christina by phone to be certain she was all right.

When Athena arrived in Mobile just after Christmas Day, bearing her usual gifts of enthusiasm and cheerfulness, she thought Christina looked a little better than Karen had described. But there was no question that she should have been healthier and stronger.

Pat was not at all as Karen had described him; he was friendly and pleasant. But again, Athena was not taken in. Remembering his behavior on her last visit, she took no comfort from his apparent good spirits. She knew now that he was capable of putting on whatever performance he wanted others to see, and she thought she knew why he was putting on this performance for her: he suspected that Karen had reported back to her, and that she had come to Mobile to monitor Christina's well-being.

At Christmas Pat had outdone himself. Even Athena was impressed by his gifts to Christina. It was not that she liked the fake fur coat and hat he'd bought—they were neither tasteful nor stylish. What mattered was that he had gone out, on his own, and selected something special. It was a gesture of caring, and once again Athena found herself hoping that everything would work out.

Christina didn't tell her mother about the Christmas party at the clinic just a few days before. Pat had told her to be ready to go at 3:30 in the afternoon. He would arrange for someone from the clinic to pick up her and Paddy and take them to the party.

She had just gotten into the shower at 2:30 when the doorbell rang. Wrapped in a robe, she answered the door to find two women from the clinic.

"I'm sorry, I wasn't expecting you till 3:30," she said. The women looked surprised.

"But Dr. Henry was very specific," one of them answered. He said you'd be expecting us at 2:30—now."

Feeling embarrassed and somewhat foolish, Christina told them to go ahead, that she would meet them there later. By the time she and the baby were dressed it was past 3:00. When she called Pat to say they were ready, he told her not to bother, the party would be over soon. So she and Paddy stayed home that afternoon, just as, it was now clear to her, he had intended, but only after he'd embarrassed her first.

The last day of her mother's visit Christina sat in the rocking chair with the baby in her arms and opened her mind to thoughts she'd never permitted before. She had always tried to bury the mistrust and fear, but now that she had Paddy to protect, she had to force herself to see Pat as he was.

The viciousness was always with him. It seemed to come and go, but in fact when he seemed normal he was simply pretending in order to gain some advantage. During the day he could practice medicine and be an executive, but in the evening, alone with her, he made no attempt to mask what he really was. It amused him to terrorize her. He thought nothing of risking her safety, and that of the baby, in order to dominate them. Once—how long ago it seemed now—she had thought that Pat loved her. Now it was frightening to guess at what he really felt.

As she admitted the truth to herself, she felt a great relief. Her next thought was the one against which she had long barricaded herself: leaving him. For an instant she visualized herself at 1409 East Broadway, safe in her parents' house with Paddy, safely away from Pat. But it was just a mental escape, a fantasy refuge. The price of going home was too high. It would destroy her father. It would go against everything he and his brothers stood for, had worked so hard for. The shame would be too much.

When her mother walked into the baby's room, Christina looked up, tears coursing down her cheeks, and said, "What would it do to Papa? It would kill him. . . . I know it would. He wouldn't be able to stand it."

Without being told, Athena understood what her daughter was thinking. And that afternoon Christina talked openly about her marriage to her mother for the first time. The loyalty she owed Pat had ended. She had endured being abused and endangered by her husband, because it was her duty to do so, as well as in the hope that things would eventually get better. She could not and would not endure it for their child.

Once she had begun to reveal all the horrors in her marriage, Christina did not hold back. She went over each incident in detail. Athena did not interrupt. She was relieved that Christina was at last letting out what she had been holding in for so long. There was no need for her to ask questions or give her opinion. She knew where the conversation was eventually going. In the end there would be but a single question, and it had only two answers. Since both of them were undesirable, if not unacceptable, only Christina could make the decision. She offered her daughter the only words she could: "Whatever you decide, your father and I will be with you." As she spoke, she could only guess what effect a divorce would have on William. She knew he would stand by his daughter, but what it would do to him she didn't know.

Christina did not decide what she would do that day, and because she didn't, she had in effect made a decision. For the time being, she would stay.

As soon as her mother left, Pat ended his performance. First to go were the Christmas presents. The fur coat and hat were returned, although, to his annoyance, the store refused to take back the hat because it had been worn. Pat was livid at the thought of the money he'd wasted.

In January Christina observed that his moods were deepening. On the surface his general routine stayed the same. At night he would come home, pour himself a strong drink, and then do one of two things: disappear into the den to look at slides, or stay in the kitchen and force Christina to listen to a detailed monologue about his murder fantasy. He had hit upon a new detail—how the knife he plunged into the victim's abdomen would have to be sharpened on both sides, so it could cut as it was raised.

The change she saw was in his increasing remoteness. When he stayed in the den, he seemed to lose touch with everything around him. If she tried to talk to him, he seemed not to hear her. He had ignored her many times before, but this was different—it was not deliberate. If he did answer, he would respond slowly, forming his words with obvious difficulty. There were times when he came down from the attic as oblivious of her presence as if he were sleepwalking. Then one evening she discovered the reason.

He came home as usual, said a few angry words as he fixed his drink, then walked into the den. Needing to know what he wanted for dinner, she followed. From the door of the den she saw him preparing to swallow a gray and orange capsule.

The next morning she found the container. The gray and orange capsules were sixty-five milligram doses of Darvon. The combination of drugs and alcohol were the cause of his deepening moods.

Christina realized that this might be an opportunity to solve their problems. As a doctor Pat had to know that what he was doing was dangerous. If she could persuade him to get psychiatric help with that problem, maybe other things would change as well. And maybe, in time, he would get down to whatever it was inside that had created his anger, his hatred.

Christina knew this was the best chance she was likely to get. But when Pat came home the next night she didn't have the courage to approach him. The same thing happened the next night. The third day she spent hours getting up her nerve. When Pat came home she waited a few minutes, then followed him into the den.

He was seated in his chair, staring straight ahead at nothing. She stood at the door for a second, then spoke his name softly. He looked up at her, but did not answer.

"Pat, there's something we have to talk about. Something isn't right. Don't you know something is wrong? You need help, Pat. You need to get some kind of help."

"It's too expensive."

"You've got to do it anyway. You need help; you know that."

"I can't do it through the clinic. The women there have access to my file. They'd find out."

"That's okay; you don't need to go through the clinic. You can go someplace else. Please, Pat, you've got to try."

Before she'd even finished she saw him tuning out, lapsing into one of his states. He looked away at nothing and sat staring again. When she called his name, he either ignored her or didn't hear her. She stood there another few moments, then went back to the kitchen.

She couldn't talk to him. She should've known she couldn't reach him. Even worse, she saw now she might have made a mistake. If he remembered their conversation tomorrow he would resent it. She was his inferior and hardly the person to advise him to do anything. The more she thought about it the harder she prayed that he wouldn't remember. But in the days that followed it was clear that he did.

Within a day or two Pat changed his routine. He neither drank nor took any kind of drugs. He talked to her every night, and his speech was fluid and intelligent. But under the guise of having a conversation he would deliver a nightly lecture. These talks were rambling, and spread over several weeks, but taken in sum, their message was clear: women had no rights whatsoever in the South.

Explaining that he had been reading extensively on the subject, he informed her that most of the southern states, including their home, Alabama, had not changed their laws since Civil War days. Today's women had no more rights than they had a hundred years ago. In fact, they really had none at all, as the law recognized only the rights of men.

Before she could say a word, he began giving her examples of cases that demonstrated his point. In one instance a woman left her husband—ran off without his permission. The husband called the authorities and had her brought back. In court the decision of what to do with her was her husband's. The authorities simply asked him what he wanted. In another case he'd read about, a woman had run away from her husband, taking their child. The authorities returned them both to the husband, but the husband refused to take his wife back; he no longer wanted her. He was given the child and the wife was divorced. In both cases, he said insistently, the law allowed the husband to do whatever he wished.

It was as if he'd read her mind. Christina sat listening, not knowing if what he was telling her was the truth. He was probably lying, she knew, yet she dared not disregard what he was saying. Pat was telling her what was going on in his mind. Somehow he knew she was thinking of leaving, and he was warning her.

As the days went by, Christina found herself dreading these little "talks" more than she had his moods. Another night he casually pointed out that if she ever turned against him, no one would believe her stories. "I'm a *doctor*, Tina. Who would ever take your word against mine?"

Although Christina knew what he was trying to do, it didn't make any difference. He had set out to undermine her confidence and he was succeeding. No one in Mobile knew the real Patrick Gerald Henry. People saw him as an intelligent, handsome young man in a responsible position. Only her mother and Karen knew what horrors he was capable of. If she told the authorities even half of what he had done to her, they would think she, not Pat, was the crazy one. Christina found herself wishing he would fall back into his moods. At least then he had left her alone.

Then one night there was no lecture. Pat talked about what had happened at the clinic that day, and asked her what she had been doing. More than a week went by that way, and although Christina knew better than to be fooled, she couldn't help relaxing a little.

One night as they sat down to dinner, she thought of something Paddy had done that day. "Do you remember that stuffed seal Karen sent Paddy?" she began. "Well, today I had him on the table dressing him—"

"Christina." In a flat, unemotional voice he interrupted her. "You know, Christina, Paddy is yours now but someday he'll be mine."

Christina looked back at him, incredulous, waiting for him to explain what he meant, but he did not go on. His face was a perfect blank. Neither smiling nor frowning, he watched her fear spread as his words sank in.

He had accomplished what he wanted. He had touched her in her most vulnerable spot: the baby. Christina knew exactly what he was up to, but it didn't matter. He was sending her a message, and the message had had its effect. . . .

It was in the afternoons that Pat's little lectures really took hold of Christina. With a new baby and a large house to take care of, she found it easy to keep busy. But in the afternoon, when the baby was napping and she knew Pat would be coming home soon, she could not help thinking about her situation.

Her thoughts were always the same. Whatever escape route her mind pursued, it always reached a dead end with the fear that Pat would somehow take her son away. She thought of going to her church for help, but for the first time in her life she was afraid to talk to a priest. She would have to tell him about the blanket incident, the long discussions of torture, the time Pat had thrown her to the floor a week before the baby was due. Could he possibly believe her? And what if he decided that she needed help herself? It would be only natural for him to go to her husband, that nice young man who held such a responsible position. And then Pat would have a witness on his side to help him take Paddy.

Christina didn't know how many more lectures she could take. Then one night Pat came home while she was preparing dinner and walked straight to the stairway leading to the attic. Relieved, Christina did not even try to speak to him. Perhaps he would stay up there all evening.

He did not. After no more than a few minutes he came back down the stairs and stopped behind her in the kitchen.

Speaking slowly, in a low voice, as if telling a ghost story to children, he asked, "How would you like it if I took you up to the attic where the spooks and spiders are? How would you like it if I tied you up in the dark places up there and let them crawl all over you?"

Christina turned to look at him, thinking he was joking. The words "spooks and spiders" sounded childish, as if they were not meant seriously, but his face showed no sign of a smile. Still not certain, she answered, "You couldn't do something like that and get away with it."

"I can do whatever I want to you."

She was about to answer back when he caught her by the wrist and twisted her arm; at the same time, with the other hand, he grabbed a carving knife off the counter and held it to her breast.

"Who's going to stop me," he challenged.

"My parents, I have a family. You can't do anything to me. I have a family." As she said it, she wrenched her arm from his grip and pulled away. At that moment, for some reason, she wasn't afraid. Staring defiantly into his eyes she repeated, "I have a family. You can't do anything to me."

Staring back at her, the knife still in his hand, he answered softly, "Yes, they're halfway across the country . . . by the time they got here it would be too late."

Without letting her reply he threw the knife on the counter and walked out of the kitchen. As soon as he was gone the fear found her and she began to cry. She'd stared him down this time but what would happen tomorrow?

The next day, after Pat had gone to the clinic, her friend Janis Tyler came to visit. At the sight of her, Christina's eyes filled with tears. Wanting someone else, someone in Mobile, to know what was really happening, she led Janis to the kitchen and started to talk. For the first time, she spoke freely, telling Janis what had just happened the night before and much, much more. She was confirming what Janis had always suspected about the Henry marriage, but as she listened Janis saw that the situation was worse than she had ever imagined.

"I've been thinking about this so much, Janis," Christina said, her voice trembling with the intensity of her feelings. "I used to think Pat loved me, and of course he didn't. But he did want me to belong to him. He didn't want me to work, or have friends, or do anything but take care of him. He didn't even want you to come near the house. I knew he was unsociable, and impossible, but I just never put it together this way. Oh God, I wish I had—because that's what's the matter about the baby.

"He thinks I betrayed him by having the baby. If he couldn't stand me having you for a friend, can you imagine how he feels about Paddy? I've never been able to believe he did those things—what I said about the blanket, and Paddy's arm turning blue—but it's got to be true. Because that's when it started with the camera. It wasn't till I got pregnant that he started being really weird about all that. I think he used the camera to replace me."

Both women knew where Christina's outburst was leading. Janis waited a moment, then asked the question Athena had left unspoken: "Are you going to leave him?"

Christina still had no answer. But seeing Janis that day had made her feel stronger. She and Paddy were no longer by themselves. There was someone in Mobile who had listened to her and believed her.

It was no more than a week later that the baby developed diarrhea. Christina was not alarmed. She was probably putting too much Karo syrup in his water bottle. And then Pat decided to intervene.

He came into the nursery early one morning. Standing behind her, near the door, he announced that he had something for the baby's diarrhea. The instant he said it she was alerted. Glancing over her shoulder, she saw that he was holding out a small plastic bottle for her to take.

"Just take the capsule that's in here, pull it apart, and dissolve it in his milk. That should take care of it," he instructed.

She knew he was expecting her to give it to the baby right then, while he watched. Without hesitating, she answered, "Put it on the dresser and I'll give it to him later. I have to change him before I feed him."

The next moments took forever. She finished what she was doing as slowly as possible, taking every extra second. At last Pat left the nursery, and minutes later she heard the back door close and the car start. She hugged Paddy to her in relief.

As she fed the baby that morning, her eyes were focused on the small white bottle sitting on the dresser. Although barely two inches tall, it seemed the only thing in the room. When the baby was fed, she returned him to his crib. Then she read the label on the bottle and went to the telephone.

The pharmacist was aghast. In no uncertain terms he told her she was not to give the baby that medication. In that quantity it could be fatal to a child of his age. It was a narcotic, he informed her, implying she was crazy to have suggested it in the first place. She thanked him and hung up before he could ask any further questions.

Standing with her hand still on the phone, Christina forced herself to accept what she had just learned. Pat had tried to poison their own child. For once everything was perfectly clear. There was no other possible explanation.

Consciously, she calmed herself. She had to get away. He'd tried to harm Paddy at least twice, probably three times; he'd try again. She could not hesitate any longer. The only question remained was how. She picked up the phone again and called home. As soon as she heard her mother's voice she began to cry.

"Christina, what is it? Please tell me. You've got to calm down enough to tell me!"

She was upsetting her mother. But it couldn't be helped. She had struggled mightily to keep herself from calling her parents the day after Pat had threatened her with the knife; she had known how badly they would take it. But now she told Athena everything that had transpired during the last several weeks: the pills, the lectures, the "spooks and spiders," the knife, and then the last—Paddy.

When Athena spoke, it was in a voice Christina had never heard before. "Christina, you've got to come home. You can't stay there. You've got to get out."

"Yes, Mama, I know. But I'm not ready. I've got to have a plan."

"Just come home now," her mother ordered. "Wait till he's gone during the day, take the baby and *come*."

But Christina didn't think she could do that. Pat had told her that women in the South had no rights. She didn't know if that was true or not, whether he had been lying to her. But she couldn't take the chance. If she were stopped at any point and brought back to Pat . . . or if he caught up with her before she could make it to Tucson . . . No, she had to have a foolproof plan. If only he would go away for several days or a week on a trip . . . Or if there were some natural reason for her to go to Tucson with Paddy with Pat's knowledge and approval—then she could make good her escape. She had to have a plan.

But there was yet another consideration, one that Christina broached with a heavy heart.

"What will Papa say?"

"Your father does not feel good these days." Athena answered carefully. "I do not want him to know these things, when he cannot do anything to help. But I will tell him that Pat threatened you during an argument. And that he made a mistake and gave you medicine for the baby that could have hurt him. After you are home, when you are safe, then he can know the truth. And he will say the same thing I do: You belong with us."

"Thank you, Mama," Christina whispered. She knew Athena was deliberately making it seem easy, but for once she didn't care. She was just glad she could go home.

That afternoon Christina flushed the narcotic capsule down the toilet and threw away the container. She worried for a long time about just what story to tell Pat about the medication when he got home but, as it turned out, her concern was for nothing. To her astonishment he never mentioned the capsule to her again.

Just when he'd pushed her to the point of desperation, just when he'd forced her to discount her family's honor and the tenets of her religion, Pat gave Christina the opening she needed.

It was only a few days after he'd tried to give the baby the capsule. He had come home more animated than usual, but he let several hours go by before telling Christina the reason.

"The dermatology convention is going to be in New York City this year," he said, as they were getting ready for bed. "I wanted to go, and now I've gotten the Public Health Service to agree to pay for it. I'll be gone five days the first week in April."

Even before he'd finished speaking, Christina realized what was being given to her. Her prayers were answered. She had a way out.

But April was two months away. That was a long time to keep Pat from picking up her thoughts. It was also a long time in which to think about what he had said the first month they were married: "Don't you ever run from me. It makes me violent. I'd see you dead first." She hadn't really believed him then, but now that she knew what he was truly capable of doing—and would do—she realized that leaving him would be the most dangerous thing she had ever done in her life.

It was William Bellios who deflected any suspicions Pat might have had about Christina's leaving him. And he did so ironically enough, because he could not agree to Christina's deceiving her husband.

Athena had given him only a sketchy idea of what was happening in his daughter's marriage. William suspected she was withholding some of the story, but he never imagined anything as shocking as the truth. Given what he did know, divorce did not seem inevitable to him. He agreed that Tina should come home for a visit; it would be good for both her and Pat to have time alone to think things over. But if she stole away while Pat was out of town on business, left without her husband's knowledge and consent, a divorce would surely follow.

There had to be another way. If a divorce was to come, then it would come, and they would face it. But he wanted Christina to have the option of returning to Mobile if that was what she eventually decided was best. He had not seen his daughter in over a year. If he could sit down and talk to her he'd know what to advise her.

The plan William put together took advantage of his own failing health. His heart had been bad for years, and now the poor circulation that resulted was seriously weakening his legs. Walking was very painful, but the cardiovascular surgeon he consulted had deemed him too frail to survive an operation on his arteries. His chances of surviving arterial surgery were at best fifty percent. It would be safer, the surgeon said, to amputate the legs when it became necessary.

William had accepted that advice. But now he was changing his mind. He wanted the operation on his arteries. And if he underwent such a dangerous operation, surely Pat would have to let Christina come home to be with him.

But first he had to persuade the surgeon. Accompanied by his personal physician of twenty-five years, William paid a visit to the surgeon.

"Doctor, I understand what you say," William told him. "But this is what I say: better I die than have no legs."

The surgeon looked at William's doctor. "Doesn't he understand that the odds of his surviving are no more than half?"

The other doctor smiled. He knew William well. "He understands. But there's something I should tell you about Mr. Bellios: this old man is one tough Greek. He'll make it."

"All right," the surgeon finally agreed. "Let's set a date. How about a week from today?"

"No," said William quietly, "April." He knew Pat would be more likely to let Christina leave if he were out of town at the time.

The surgeon studied him across the desk. This patient had wanted the operation—had campaigned for it, in fact—and now, as soon as everyone agreed to proceed, he wanted to delay for two months. "Mr. Bellios, a postponement could mean that you would lose your legs after all. It could even be fatal."

William was adamant. No surgery until after the first week in April.

Exasperated, the surgeon stood up. "Mr. Bellios, please come with me. We'll see if the surgery can wait." Leading the way out through his waiting room, he took William to the sidewalk. Then, looking the old man in the eye, he said, "Let's see how far you can walk."

For a long time William had been able to manage no more than a few short, stiff-legged steps. Now he took those steps, then kept on taking more steps. He was in great pain almost immediately, but he was determined not to show it. After a few more minutes of walking, the pain was unbearable, but his face betrayed nothing. Twice he walked completely around the medical building, then he could not force himself another step. He had walked farther that day than he had been able to in months. The surgery was delayed until April.

Christina endured the next two months in a special kind of hell. Pat had agreed, grudgingly, to her visiting Tucson. He could think of no reason to object, especially since the Bellioses were paying her air fare. But it was as if he could not let her out of his sight until he was satisfied that her subjugation was complete.

Her confidence and dignity were his targets. With special viciousness he criticized her housekeeping, her appearance, even her ability to care for Paddy. "You're too stupid to bring up a child, Tina," he told her. "How do you expect him to learn anything from a drone like you?" At the same time he taunted her with her own increasing nervousness. "You're the one who needs the shrink, Tina. Someone at the clinic was just saying that you seemed a little—unstable."

To demonstrate his point, he pointed to the skin infection she'd developed on her hands. The sores refused to heal, no matter what she did, but as usual Pat insisted that she did not need medical attention. When the condition continued he treated it himself, by lancing the sores. They got worse; several of her nails came loose and fell out, but he still insisted on continuing that treatment.

Her hands were proof of her mental condition, he informed her. "When they see your hands, they'll know you're a neurotic, Tina. Look at them. It's true, you know."

As the weeks went by and both of their departures came closer, Pat's approach became more insidious. Having noticed that Christina never left him alone with Paddy, he began to take a special interest in his son each evening.

One night, holding Paddy in his lap, he began to talk about the softness of the baby's skin. He was leading up to something, but Christina knew from experience that he would draw it out. He went on to talk about the softness of Paddy's skin, in particular, and then, when he felt he had her full attention, he began to talk about how common it was for adults to commit sexual acts with small children.

Christina tried to play Karen's game of not giving him a reaction, but she knew her husband too well not to be genuinely frightened. Calmly Pat went on to discuss the specific physical acts that men could perform with small children. At that moment, Christina came very close to panic. All she wanted to do was to grab the baby and run for help, but she resisted. Instead, she went to her husband, took the baby as calmly as she could, and said it was time for bed. Pat did not demur; he simply looked up and smiled, as if to approve her passivity. That was the first of several nights he spent playing with his son. And each night Christina was drenched in fear. Fear that she struggled to hold back not only for her sake, but for the baby's.

The day the airline tickets arrived, Christina trembled as she opened the envelope. The tickets would be a source of strength until she left Mobile, a tangible proof that it would soon be over.

She slid the tickets out of the envelope. There had to be some mistake. There were two tickets to New York, none to Tucson. Although she had been told never to bother Pat at the clinic, she called him immediately.

"No mistake," he said. "The operation isn't till a week or so after you were supposed to get home. Instead of wasting time out there you can spend a few days in New York with me, then fly out there with Karen and still be in plenty of time."

"But there's no ticket to Tucson here," she said weakly.

"I know. We can pick it up in New York."

Christina hung up determined not to let him throw her. But the uncertainty took its toll. She even slept less than she had before and became even jumpier. Each day drained more of her strength but not her determination. She never challenged Pat or stood up to him. Her only consolation was that Pat was probably interpreting her behavior as the submission he was looking for.

That was all that mattered—that he trust her enough to let her leave New York alone.

As the day of departure drew closer, Christina was given a reprieve from Pat's attentions. Just as he always did before a trip, he became totally caught up in plans and preparations. Every day he was to spend in New York had to be scheduled carefully to include as many tourist sights as possible. He also spent hours compiling extensive inventories of what he would need for the trip. Three-quarters of the items on the inventory were photographic equipment and supplies. His big purchase was a special attachment that made it possible to take pictures of one subject while pointing the camera in another direction.

"What's so terrific about that?" Christina asked.

"You're just not very bright, are you, Tina? That way you can take someone's picture without his ever knowing."

With Pat's attention directed elsewhere, Christina had a chance to make her plans. If nothing else, Pat had taught her to be cunning. She had never had to deceive anyone before in her life, but now she was glad she knew how. Just as Pat had shown her, she made a mental list of eventualities and went about preparing for them.

It was a given fact that Pat would go into a rage when he discovered that she was not coming back. He would take his revenge on anything she'd left behind, and the thing she loved best was Trykie. The cat had been her closest companion during the entire course of her marriage, the only thing that had loved her till Paddy was born. Weenie, she knew, was safe; he was one of Patrick's possessions.

Having heard Pat talk for hours about dismemberment and degutting, she knew exactly what he would do. But his enjoyment would come from making sure she knew. When she thought of receiving the pieces of Trykie's body in a box, she knew what she had to do.

Several weeks before they were to leave, she mentioned to Pat that she didn't like having a cat in the house with the baby. It wasn't sanitary. A few days later she commented idly that she wasn't really paying enough attention to Trykie anymore; she was too busy with Paddy. A week later she told him she was still trying to decide what to do about Trykie, especially since they couldn't leave him alone while they were gone. If Pat was paying any attention to her musings it wasn't evident.

A week before they left she packed the sterling silver and some of the other expensive wedding gifts and gave them to a woman she'd met at Church. Christina had told her that she and her husband would both be out of town and they were afraid of burglars. That evening she told Pat about her plan before he could discover that the items were missing. He agreed that it was a good idea and never thought to ask the woman's name.

Carefully selecting the best of the baby's clothing and

bedding, as well as her own, she packed it all in cartons and shipped them to Karen in New York. Preoccupied with his preparations, Pat didn't notice that they were missing. Nor did he pay any attention two days before they were to leave when she told him that she had found a new home for Trykie.

Christina now worried incessantly that Pat would suddenly put all the pieces together. It would be all right if he simply forbade her to go to Tucson. She would simply wait till he left for New York and then disobey him. But what if he left her behind but took Paddy with him? Whenever she thought of that possibility, all Pat's spoken and unspoken threats flooded into her mind.

The night before they were to leave, Pat subjected her to one final humiliation. She was working hard to get everything ready to go, and with no help from him she had fallen behind. It was well after 11:00 P.M. when she ran through a drizzling rain to pick up the last load of laundry from the shed out back where the washing machine had been installed.

It had rained harder during the day and the path was very muddy. She had just started back, picking her way carefully around the bad patches, when she saw Pat coming to meet her. Weenie, the dachshund, was trotting along beside him.

Thinking he had come to help, she held out the heavy laundry basket, filled to overflowing with clean clothes, for him to take. But he didn't take it. In one quick movement he stooped down and scooped a rubber bone of Weenie's out of the mud. Then he threw it into the basket she extended, splashing mud and dirty water over everything.

She would have to run another load. She would be up long past midnight. Pat stood expressionless, waiting to see what her response would be.

"Pat," was all she said, putting into the single word all of her sadness and despair.

He looked at her for a moment, then, apparently satisfied, turned and walked back to the house. The next day they flew together to New York.

The morning he was to deliver her to Karen's apartment was the morning she had lived for, a time she had thought would never come. She prayed that nothing would happen, not now, at the last minute.

For these few days in New York, everything had gone

well. Pat attended a few meetings at the medical convention, but spent most of his time engrossed in picture taking. One night he had returned to the hotel at 3:00 A.M.; he had been in Central Park, he'd explained, taking night shots. "Lots of interesting people in Central Park," he said. "Especially after midnight."

Pat had been so busy with his camera he had even allowed Christina to go to Fifth Avenue alone to pick up her ticket to Tucson. When she held that ticket in her hands, she believed for the first time that she really would be free.

Pat carried her luggage and the baby's up to Karen's apartment, but didn't stay to chat. He had a full day of sightseeing scheduled and he was anxious to get going. Christina forced herself to say she would miss him, but Pat didn't bother with such formalities. He said good-bye to her and his son without a trace of affection, real or pretended, and walked down the hall to the elevator. His camera hung from his shoulder in a leather carrying case, all the companionship he needed.

Waiting impatiently at the elevator, he had no inkling that the woman he thought he dominated was about to escape him. But as the two metal doors finally parted to admit him, Christina was already behind the locked door of Karen's apartment, weeping uncontrollably. After all those years of nightmare, she was finally free of him.

As she came to the end of her story, Mrs. Henry's hands were shaking and so was her voice. She was almost hysterical, but she looked me steadily in the eye, as if pleading with me to believe her.

It wasn't easy. Her story was so lurid and dramatic. Various parts of it, like the alligator incident, were especially hard to accept. Yet, I was inclined to believe her. As a professional law enforcement official, I had interviewed hundreds of witnesses over the years, and I had developed an instinct for recognizing who was telling the truth and who was exaggerating, imagining, or lying. I had no single set of criteria; every person was evaluated individually. I had been observing Christina Henry closely and was impressed by several factors: her rapid, almost frantic speech; her way of directly meeting my eyes; and her incredible memory for detail. Yet some of the best pathological liars are specialists in all three of those categories.

The fourth, and the decisive, factor was Mrs Henry's fear. It was written all over her, and it was genuine. I could feel it, it was so palpably *there*. And, after watching her for a couple of hours now, I had realized something else: it was her fear that robbed Christina Henry of her attractiveness.

But still, with all my experience, I knew I could be fooled. I needed something more than just Mrs. Henry's story. I needed corroboration—something to tie her story to the physical evidence. The moment she had described the double-edged knife her husband had intended to use to degut someone, I realized she had given me some corroboration. But I needed more evidence than that; I needed something that would eliminate any possibility of coincidence.

For a few minutes I fished around, asking various questions that I had noted on a yellow legal pad. Then I moved on to the question I most wanted an answer to.

"Mrs. Henry, there's one last thing I have to ask you. It has to do with what your husband said about torturing people in the swamp. He said he would do various things to them, and then he would kill them with explosives."

She nodded.

"Okay. What kind of explosives did he plan to use? Did he ever talk about that? The kind of explosives they'd be?"

"They had to be small ones. He said he'd use firecrackers, so he could stand close enough to watch."

"Goddamn!"

Mrs. Henry jumped, startled, but Agent Wallace, sitting across the room, knew what I was feeling.

What she had just told us was proof, absolute, that she was telling the truth. Christina Henry had never been shown, or been told of, the contents of Dr. Henry's briefcase or the inventory of evidence found on his person on December 6. There was no way she could have known that, on the day he was arrested, Dr. Henry had been carrying the following: forty-one safety pins, 380 feet of twine, a hunting knife—surgically sharpened on both sides of the blade—and twenty-three firecrackers. He had brought with him to Tucson, to the home of Christine Bellios Henry, everything he needed to carry out the revenge he'd been fantasizing for years.

And, unless I could stop him, sooner or later he'd be back to try it again.

PART TWO

The Investigation

CONVINCING me had been Christina Henry's job. My job was to convince the jury I hoped we would someday face. The history of the Henrys' marriage, awful as it was, provided only scraps of evidence—and they were, at best, circumstantial. From a legal standpoint, we had not yet begun to build the case.

For my next session with Mrs. Henry, I asked her to bring her parents. I needed to question the three of them simultaneously, before they could figure out what I was interested in and discuss their testimony in advance. I wanted their spontaneous answers and reactions.

To this meeting I also invited Carol Eley, a law student who was working as our legal researcher while preparing for the bar exam. I wanted Carol's impressions of Christina Henry and her parents, and I also thought that Mrs. Henry would feel more at ease if one of her interviewers was a woman. She was an exceptionally modest and retiring person who obviously found it difficult to talk about private matters.

They came to my office on December 16. Mr. Bellios spoke with a heavy Greek accent. He was very thin and obviously not in good health. Mrs. Bellios was short and plump and looked like everyone's grandmother—very warm and pleasant, with a smile I found myself returning automatically. She spoke English with a barely discernible accent.

I suggested we begin by going over the events of December 6. "What's the first thing you did?" I asked Christina Henry. "What's the first thing you remember?"

"I got Stevie dressed and started over to the apartments to have coffee with my father." Her parents, she explained, now lived in the rear apartments, while she and Stevie lived in the main house. Mr. Bellios was semiretired but still went downtown to a job every day at 7:15. Most mornings Christina and Stevie managed to visit for a few minutes before he left. On December 6, she remembered, by the time she and Stevie went out the back door it was already 7:15. Glancing around, she saw that her father's car was gone. They had missed him that day. Christina also saw, across the street, a man who appeared to be looking at her. She stared at him, and he stared back. He seemed to be writing something as he was looking at her. She described him as bulky or stocky, wearing a dark coat and some kind of cap pulled down over his ears. His hair was black and shoulder-length.

Could she tell me anything else about the man?" For example, did he have a briefcase?"

"Yes, I think so," she said. "I'm almost sure he did." She paused, as if she were seeing him again as she had that morning. "Yes," she said, "he did have a briefcase."

She remembered thinking that the man looked like a professor. That wouldn't have been unusual, because many professors walked by the house on their way to the university, which was only a few blocks away. But when the man bent down to pick up the briefcase, his mannerisms reminded her of Patrick. But this man was heavier, much heavier, and the hair wasn't right. Besides, it made no sense. Her ex-husband was back in Maryland. She decided it couldn't be him.

Holding Stevie's hand she walked on toward the apartment. But she didn't stop looking at the person across the street, nor did he stop looking at her. She entered the apartment feeling somewehat shaken, but soon dismissed her suspicion as silly. It could not possibly have been Patrick.

She was back up at the main house when the telephone rang. It was about 9:30, she knew, because she had been expecting the mother of one of her pupils to call, and she'd been looking at the clock. When the phone finally rang, she had automatically checked the time again.

"Mrs. Henry," I interrupted, "if you can, I'd like you to try to quote me this conversation as exactly as you can—what the caller said to you and what you said to him, as precisely as you can recall it."

She had picked up the phone and said, "Hello," then realized that her mother had picked up the extension phone in the apartments. She said, "Mother, I've got it," and her mother hung up. As soon as she did the caller said, "I'd like some information about the Broadway Boulevard Kindergarten and Preschool." Upon hearing just that first sentence she knew that the caller was her ex-husband, even though he was trying to disguise his voice. Just having to talk to him made her afraid, even though at the time she assumed he was calling from Maryland. She immediately tried to think of an excuse to get off the phone. She was too fearful to confront him and too polite to just hang up.

I stopped her and again asked for the exact words. She recalled saying, "I'm sorry, I'm just about to leave. Can you call back?" The caller said, "I have a four-year-old. I'm near you; I'd like to see what you have to offer."

She became even more upset and desperate to get off the phone. "I'm sorry," she said, "if you'll leave your name and number, I'll call you back." The caller said his name was Tim LaShanta, at which point she broke in, saying, "I'm sorry, I have to go." The caller said, "Then you can't give me any information about the Broadway Boulevard Kindergarten and Preschool?" "No, I'm sorry," she said, and put down the phone.

Terrified, she grabbed Stevie and ran out the back door toward the apartment screaming, "Mother! Mother!"

"You won't believe this," she told her mother. "You won't believe who was on the phone! I just talked to Pat!"

After the phone conversation, the three of them—Christina carrying Stevie in her arms—left the apartment; checked the street to make sure it was safe, and immediately went in to the main house. Even now, just telling me the story, Mrs. Henry was becoming agitated.

"But the sixth of December was a Tuesday," I said. "Why wouldn't the caller have waited till the school was open and then dropped in for his tour?"

"I never opened it that Tuesday," Mrs. Henry replied. She had just recently started the school, and had only three children who attended on Tuesdays. Two of the three were sick and the third child's mother had been scheduled to call that morning to say whether the child would be coming. It was that call she had been expecting when the phone rang at 9:30.

Changing subjects, I told her that Dr. Henry had made some notes on his trip to Tucson that we had in our possession. That agreed, Christina pointed out excitedly, with what she had already told us: that Dr. Henry didn't plan anything, not even a vacation, without making notes of everything he would do and everything he would take.

Christina Henry had also told us that Dr. Henry liked to write in code, and I silently wondered now if she could help us decipher what was written on the Ramada Inn stationery and the Hertz application. After hours of study, Agent Wallace and I had decided that the words on the back of the stationery were as follows:

> clean up
> ticket
> unb
> Box
> Suit etc
> pants
> paper
> plunger
> (meat)

9:05	331	Tu
10:15	Tu	car

> cab——U.
> prepare self; carry extras
> case   lights
>   feed dogs
>   activity
>   ck 1403 Key
>   inside
>   neighborhood
>   routes
>   phone
>   changing place
> In 1409
>   select window
>   tape
>   plunger
>   thru-open
>   find T
>   M T
>   out front; or rm window

```
1:00   Route
1:15   Change
1:20   Wrap Suit
              Box
       call cab
       mail

2:15   Airport—chg flt
2:40   Out Tu D
5:30   D
```

The words penciled on the Hertz application were easier to read. They were as follows:

```
Bill up at 5:00
Bill leaves in Ford 7:15
Tina out and around shortly
Guard enters yard 8:00
Crowell sweeps   8:20
School bell      8:30

Guard leaves     8:45

Broadway Boulevard Kindergarten
and Pre School          6240503
                        6238175

Tan buick wagon with luggage
          RTT 690

    V W   TGF   912

White Ford Wagon with luggage rack
          SYC 270
```

We didn't show these notes to Christina Henry or her parents. Instead, I began by asking if they remembered anything happening during the night before the morning of the sixth.

"No, not that I remember," Christina said immediately.

"How about the dogs?" I suggested, thinking of Dr. Henry's note "Feed dogs."

"Actually, there's only one dog," she corrected me. "We have a little dachshund named Champo, but our other dog died months ago."

"Do you think Dr. Henry knows that?" I asked, still without telling her about the note.

"I don't think so," she answered. "I don't see how he could." This explained why the note said "feed dogs" instead of "dog."

"Okay," I said, "let me revise the question. Did anything happen with the dog during the night?"

She thought for a second. "Nothing really happened," she said. "He barked twice, but that was all. Once early in the night and another time later."

I asked for more details and she explained that she had gone to bed early, only to be awakened by the dog's barking at about eleven o'clock. She was fairly certain of the time, as she recalled figuring out how long Stevie had been asleep and hoping that the barking wouldn't wake him. The dog quieted down soon. The second time she heard barking was between 3:00 A.M. and 4:00.

Then she sat forward in her chair; it was obvious she was becoming excited again. It was as though she was now understanding, for the first time, what I was getting at.

"Champo has two barks," she said. "One is his normal bark, when another dog or cat wanders into the alley or someone walks down the alley during the day. But the second bark is different. If a person comes into the alley at night, Champo sounds different. That's the way he was barking the second time."

Speaking and trying to remember at the same time, she recalled, "I got up and looked out the window to see what was the matter. Papa had gotten up too. I saw him at the door of his apartment with his flashlight. But it was too dark to see anything else; I couldn't tell who Champo was barking at. But it was his other bark."

Mr. Bellios, who had been listening quietly, suddenly spoke for the first time. I noticed that when he told a story, he spoke in the present tense, as if reliving what had occurred.

"Dog bark and I get up. It was 3:30, I know. I look. He keep barking, and he don't be quiet. I go to door. I tell him 'Champo, be quiet,' but dog does not obey. Dog run to fence. Same spot in fence. Keep running to fence and bark, and then come back, and then run back to fence again. He don't stop. He keep barking. I say, 'Champo, stop that noise, come here,' but he does not obey. I flash my light, but I don't see nothing. Then after a while, I close door, and go back to bed. I leave light on outside, don't turn off. Dog still makes noise but not so much now."

Mr. Bellios was certain the time was 3:30 because he had looked at the clock on the wall beside his bed.

I was thinking of Dr. Henry's notes. By 3:30 A.M. he was supposed to be on an airplane, on his way back to Dallas. Yet I suspected that it was, indeed, Dr. Henry that the dog had been barking at. We had known for some time that the doctor hadn't followed his original plan. Perhaps today we would find out why.

I decided to initiate another line of questioning.

"Mrs. Henry, please tell me again what happened that morning when you first left the house to go to the apartments. What was the dog doing at 7:15 when you went out?"

As she sat thinking, it was obvious she was remembering things that had seemed insignificant before. "He didn't move!" she then exclaimed excitedly. "He didn't get up and jump the way he normally does; he just lay there. He lay on the old couch that's on the porch and just looked at me without moving."

Normally Champo jumped up and down and got excited when she came out—so much so that often she had to push him away. But that morning he didn't even get up and follow her and Stevie off the porch.

Christina Henry's eyes were bright with anticipation. No matter how impassive I tried to be, she was quickly putting together what must have happened: Dr. Henry had been there during the night and had done something to the dog.

"Did you notice later in the day if the dog had been sick?" I asked them. Again Mr. Bellios replied first.

"He got sick. I saw. By the faucet, when I go to fill the water, I see he get sick in yard. I see it. Later I tell Tina what I see."

I asked Mr. Bellios to tell me what he had done that morning before leaving for work. He was able to recall his actions without difficulty, since he had followed the same routine for over twenty years.

"Every morning I get up at 5:00, always get up at 5:00.

Clean up, shave, then go get paper. Take flashlight to front yard, get paper, then come back and feed dog. That morning something is wrong. Dog doesn't eat. I say, 'Champo, come here eat.' He don't get up. Usually he excited to eat, but not this morning. He don't eat anything.''

Putting the times and activities in sequence, this was what Christina and her father had just told us: At 3:00 in the morning the dog was barking and running to the fence. At 6:00 the same morning he'd lain in the yard motionless, not wanting to eat. At 7:15, he'd moved to the couch on the porch, but still didn't move or eat.

All of this was consistent with Dr. Henry's notes. The murder plan mentioned ''meat'' and ''feed dogs,'' and the surveillance notes fit what we now knew:

> Bill up at 5:00
> Bill leaves in Ford 7:15
> Tina out and around shortly

The next series of questions explained the rest of the notes: ''Guard enters yard 8:00; Crowell sweeps 8:20; School bell 8:30; Guard leaves 8:45.'' Across the street from Mrs. Henry's house was an elementary school. Every day the school crossing guard came to the Henry house and parked his bicycle in the yard of the nursery school. He usually arrived between 7:50 and 8:00 A.M. and stayed about an hour. The bell at the elementary school rang at 8:30.

When I asked about ''Crowell sweeps,'' Mrs. Bellios answered for the first time. Mr. Crowell was an elderly neighbor who swept his front porch at the same time every morning; he'd followed that routine for as long as they could remember.

The license plate numbers and the vehicle descriptions written on the Hertz application described the vehicles owned by the Bellios family that were parked behind the house and apartments on the night of the fifth.

I had told Mrs. Henry and her parents that we had Dr. Henry's notes, and from the questions I was asking it was obvious that I had specific information. But none of them asked me to tell them what I knew or what the notes contained, and I did not volunteer to do so. These three people would be interviewed again and again and I wanted to keep them uncontaminated, for as long as possible, by any information other than their own recollections.

I told Mrs. Henry that we would talk again soon. As I escorted her and her parents to the door, Christina Henry suddenly turned to me, with more emotion and fear in her face than she'd let show during the interview.

"Mr. Stevens," she said agitatedly, "he'll come again. I know he will. He won't be satisfied. He's proud of the way he is, and the way he thinks things out. He doesn't stop. He keeps a grudge forever. He won't stop. He'll come back. He'll come for me again."

I tried to reassure her, to tell her we'd stay on the case, but she seemed not to hear me. "Mr. Stevens, he's brilliant," she said. "He wouldn't do something like this unless he knew there was a way out. He's told me that if you're going to lie and cheat, you'd better do it right. You'd better be prepared to back yourself up." She paused for a second, then continued. "He plans in advance. He's smart enough to have done this so that you can't catch him. I'm sorry, Mr. Stevens, I know I keep saying this, but you have to believe me." She was trying not to cry, but tears kept escaping down her cheeks, and I could see she was shaking. "I'm sorry," she kept saying, "I'm so sorry, but you've just got to believe me."

Finally I said as soothingly as I could, "Christina, tomorrow's the weekend. Let's meet again on Monday. Is it all right if I call you Christina?"

She nodded dumbly, still shaking.

"Thank you, Christina," I said. "Please don't worry. I *do* believe you."

And I did.

Based on what we'd learned in the two interviews, I saw that we had to move immediately. Agent Wallace had established that Dr. Henry had keys to the nursery school, and now I thought I knew why. The schoolhouse had been his back-up plan. On the night of the fifth, the dog had barked loud enough to wake up Mr. Bellios, who had come outside with a flashlight. When he went back in, he left the outside light on. This had prevented Dr. Henry from crossing the yard and entering the main house through a window. At 5:00 A.M. Mr. Bellios was up and around again, so no move could be made then. Dr. Henry's original plan had been frustrated, but he had been prepared for that possibility. As Christina Henry had told us, he thought everything through and planned well in advance.

He watched the house until 7:15, when she emerged with Stevie and saw him in his disguise. Then, perhaps while she was inside her mother's apartment, he had slipped into the nursery school and waited. At 9:30, he had called the main house and, disguising his voice, had said, "I'm near you. . . . I have a four-year-old. I'd like to see what you have to offer." The only possible purpose for that call was to lure Mrs. Henry into the school. If she had not recognized his voice, she most likely would have gone next door, expecting to meet a prospective client for her still-struggling business. And had she entered the schoolhouse, alone, she would have found Patrick Henry already inside, waiting to kill her.

That was my hypothesis. But if I wanted to prove it to a jury, I had to have physical evidence that he had been there. To convict him of attempted murder I had to prove that Christina Henry was not still alive because her ex-husband had had a last-minute change of heart, but because both his first plan and his back-up plan had failed. I immediately set one of my investigators, Ken Janes, to the nursery school to process it from top to bottom for any physical evidence, and also to take a Sheriff's Office identification unit, and photograph and take fingerprints of everything. If I could prove that Dr. Henry had been inside the schoolhouse, it would help me persuade the jury that he had kept trying.

The night after our meeting the lights burned late at the Bellios house. They sat in a small room, just off the kitchen, and talked of matters long since put aside. They did not revive their memories willingly. Forgetting Patrick Henry had been all too difficult, especially for William.

On Christina's first night home, the day she flew in from New York with Karen, the father and daughter had talked for hours. Speaking mostly in Greek, Christina had told him everything: Pat's fantasies of torture, how he had held the knife to her chest and boasted that her family could not keep her safe, the night he'd threatened to smash in the head of the baby's crib, and the day he'd given her the medicine that could have killed Paddy, and much, much more. When she was finished her father bowed his head. The man was a monster. His daughter had cause.

The next day William had gone downtown. He entered the lawyer's office and shook hands with the man who stood up behind the desk.

"I am here to see about a divorce for my daughter," he announced.

William had done what was right and necessary, but afterward he had not been able to prevent the shame. He had been a member of his parish, Saint Demetrious, for twenty-eight years, since before the church itself had been built. The Greek church and its congregation were a vital part of his life. In America they were his village. And in a short time all of them would know that William Bellios's eldest daughter had returned to seek a divorce.

He did not blame Christina; she had cause. But no one else would know that. The ghastly events that had transpired in her marriage would never be spoken of outside the family. When the divorce was final it would be recognized by American law, but not by his church or by other Greeks—by the village.

At that moment William had hoped he would not survive the surgery he was to undergo. But he had. And after several weeks of convalescence, he had even been well enough to lead a normal life again. But the members of his church had rarely seen him. For two years after Christina's return, William did not go to his church liturgy. He did not call his friends or eat with them. If they passed him on the street he turned his head so he would not meet their eyes. He could not speak to them.

Seeing his pain had been hard for Christina. But there could be no turning back now. Pat's behavior, in the months and years following their separation, only reinforced her belief that the man who had been her husband was capable of anything. Looking back now, she and her parents realized there had been signs then that Pat was not only malicious but dangerous. They had simply not wanted to see it.

After making the decision to remain in Tucson and get a divorce, Christina had called Pat and broke the news. He tried everything to persuade her to come home. For months he wrote letter after letter, pleading with her to change her mind, promising to make up for what had happened between them. He admitted that he'd made "mistakes" and that he'd been wrong about things he'd done and said. Claiming to love her and to miss her, he promised to receive her with open arms if she would only give him another chance.

Christina did not believe a word he said or wrote. She knew him too well by now. He would agree to anything until she returned. Then she would never get away again. She did not doubt that he would eventually kill her child. Never once did she consider returning. When that finally became obvious to Pat, when he realized that all his letters and phone calls had failed, he tried one last but quite different tactic.

When she found yet another letter from him in the mailbox, three months after she'd left, she expected it to be like all the rest. Inside the letter, however, Pat had enclosed a newspaper article. She looked at the letter first, but didn't get past the first sentence: "Hi, Tina, I sent this clipping because I thought about Patrick and I thought you would like to see it."

She opened the folded clipping: The headline read: KID-NAPPED BABY BACK HOME AFTER BEING FOUND IN A SWAMP. Below was the picture of a baby, Paddy's age, and his mother. To Christina the message was clear—come home or lose your baby.

After receiving Pat's warning, she spent every day of the next year in constant apprehension, expecting something but not knowing what. Wherever she went, whatever she was doing, the uncertainty and the worry were always with her.

Pat visited Tucson in January of 1975, before the divorce became final in April. He was reserved and polite, and seemed resigned to the end of their marriage. He had even agreed to return the Volkswagen Christina's parents had given them as well as clothing and other personal items that she had left behind, on the condition that her parents pay for the gas and the U-Haul trailer rental. When he arrived at the house, Christina made certain that both her parents were present. Pat played with his son for a few minutes, then took a series of photographs, while Christina and her mother kept a close and tense watch.

After the child was put to bed, Christina looked over the belongings Pat had returned. She noticed immediately that the hinges of her cedar chest had been pried loose. Knowing what had been locked inside, she checked immediately. Her father's pistol was missing.

"Pat, what happened to the cedar chest?"

"I opened it. I asked you to send the key, and you didn't, so I opened it."

"What happened to the gun?"

"I sold it, It was mine; Bill gave it to me."

She knew he was lying. In his letter containing the newspaper article about the child in the swamp, he had requested the key to the cedar chest. He'd mentioned he wanted to take the gun out and have it registered, "in case we ever needed to use it." She'd known what he was telling her, and she hadn't sent the keys. Now he had the gun anyway.

When a year after the divorce Pat remarried and moved to Baltimore, Christina had willed herself to relax. They had been apart for several years now and Pat had a new life; surely he wasn't thinking of her and Paddy any more. But her respite from apprehension was short-lived. Soon letters began to arrive suggesting that Paddy come to Baltimore for a visit.

Christina refused. She knew Pat didn't care about his son; he only wanted to get him away from her. Even though he offered to have his mother bring the baby back to Tucson, she refused. Long ago she had decided not to allow Pat to be alone with the child. She would never change her mind. Never.

When Pat visited Tucson with his new wife, Christina allowed them to see Paddy, but only in her parents' house, where she and her mother could be certain that nothing would happen. Annoyed by her continued restrictions, Pat filed a petition in August of 1976 to amend his visitation rights.

Pat asked the judge in Tucson Superior Court to lower his child-support payments and increase his visitation rights. To support his case he prepared an exhaustive memorandum, citing 138 different books, articles, and journals on the subject of child care and development. Having adopted his new wife's two children from a previous marriage, he now had a family in which to raise his child. For this reason, he claimed, he was the proper person to have custody, since Christina was not married and not able to provide a family structure.

Not a thing that had happened during the marriage was brought up at the hearing. Knowing she had no actual proof, Christina said nothing to anyone. Her attorney felt certain, however, that under Arizona law she would be able to retain custody, especially since her ex-husband had not asked for it when the divorce had been granted the year before. Christina was not so confident; not until the judge ruled in her favor did she feel at ease.

The entire experience had been frightening. Pat had come too close to keeping the prediction he'd made: "He's yours now, Tina, but someday he'll be mine."

Yet Christina knew how Pat felt about his son. The only reason he'd wanted him back was to take revenge on her. As she and her parents reviewed everything that had happened, they realized that the custody suit had been a warning they should not have ignored. Pat still hated her. Three years was nothing to him; a new wife and family didn't matter. She had crossed him and, it was all too clear to them now, that he intended, as he'd warned her, to "see her dead" if it took him twenty years.

Detective Janes did not find much when he processed the nursery school. Almost all the prints found by the technicians had been made by tiny little fingers, and the rest were unreadable smudges. Neither he nor I was surprised, considering the time lag, the activity in the school, and the fact that Dr. Henry had been carrying both cotton and rubber gloves in his briefcase.

Janes was particularly disappointed, however, that certain possibilities hadn't proved out. Christina Henry had mentioned earlier to Agent Wallace that she recalled some things that "weren't right" when she went into the school the day after Dr. Henry's visit. When he arrived Janes had asked her about them.

There were three things: first, the blinds on the windows facing east, in the direction of 1409, were not even. Normally she kept them both exactly level, but on that morning one of them had been left raised a few inches; second, her desk drawer had been opened and one of the files she kept in it, a manila folder containing her personal records, was pulled up out of place; and third, the toilet seat, which was always kept up for the children, was down that morning when she went into the bathroom before the children arrived. She admitted that she or her mother, who helped her at the school, or even one of the children or their parents could have been responsible for one or all of the things she'd noticed, but Janes was hopeful. He fingerprinted the blinds and toilet seat, and saw to it that a special chemical, ninhydrin, was used to raise prints on the manila folder. But none of these efforts to document Dr. Henry's presence in the school proved successful.

Janes did have one bit of good news though: the thin wood frame—the molding—that held the screen fast in the screen door had been carefully pried loose. Once the molding was loose, the screen could be pushed out and the screen door unlatched, as James himself successfully attempted to do.

To the casual observer, the door did not look as if it had been tampered with. The screen had been replaced in its proper position, then the molding, and then the nails had been pushed back in. The pry marks could be seen only by someone closely examining the door, and they appeared to be fresh. There were, however, no pry marks on the front door, which made sense. Dr. Henry didn't have to pry the main door open, since he had the key for it. He only needed to unlatch the screen door so he could get to the lock on the front door.

But there was a problem. Neither Christina nor her parents could say when the pry marks had been made. They had never noticed them before. The marks could have been ten days old or thirty days old; there was no way to tell.

Even though Janes assured me that he had complete photographs of the screen door and the marks, I had him bring in the door for further analysis and as evidence. He also took into evidence the floor mop and the bag from the vacuum cleaner that had been used to clean the school since the time of the suspected break-in. He also took miscellaneous hairs found inside the school and paint chip samples from the screen door, even though we had the door itself. If there was anything to be found, Detective Janes was going to find it.

I spent the weekend after my meeting with the Bellios family pondering our conspicuous lack of evidence. Detective Janes had called in his preliminary report late Friday evening, so I had plenty of time to contemplate what we did and didn't have.

Christina and her father would provide testimonial evidence. Their recollections of the night of December 5 would help me suggest that Dr. Henry had been outside their house that night at 3:30, had done something to the dog, and later had entered the school. But their testimony, taken by itself, wouldn't stand up under cross-examination. They hadn't seen anyone at 3:30 and, if pressed, they would have to admit that the dog could have been barking at almost anything. They would also have to admit that the dog could have gotten sick from any number of reasons besides poison.

What we needed was physical evidence to support their testimony, but so far there were only the pry marks on the screen door. We had no way of dating them, nor any way of proving that Dr. Henry was responsible for them. We also had the doctor's murder plan, in his own handwriting. That would be helpful, but our own witnesses would testify that he hadn't followed his schedule very closely. The murder plan wouldn't be worth much in court if the defendant obviously wasn't following it. In fact, a good defense attorney might suggest that his departures from the plan indicated something else: that he'd changed his mind about murdering Mrs. Henry before he even got to Tucson, and that he'd had another purpose in going to the house.

I went over everything again, trying to see where we'd missed a chance for additional evidence. For a few minutes I even considered having Champo put to sleep; an autopsy might reveal drugs or poisons still in his system or his tissues. Then I gave it up. Aside from the fact that Champo had probably saved his mistress's life, so much time had passed that the chances of finding something were less than remote.

When I went to bed Sunday night, my mind kept going back to the interviews, replaying everything Christina Henry and her parents had said. And in the middle of the night an idea finally came to me. If it worked, we might have something.

Monday morning, thirteen days after Dr. Henry had been in Tucson, I called Detective Janes into my office. We needed two things, I told him. The first was a blood sample from Champo, to be checked immediately for possible poisons or drugs. Second, I went on, with the straightest face I could manage, he had to go back to the Bellios house, find out exactly where the dog had vomited that morning, scrape it up, grass and all, and bring it back in a plastic bag. To make sure he got everything, he was to dig down and get about an inch of dirt under the vomit. "We're going to need it," I told him.

Although Janes did not say a word, his face told me just

what he thought of his assignment. He was brand new in our office, and a little nervous about working his first case with the chief prosecutor. If this was what the head office was like, his expression said, he was sorry he'd made it this far. Later on, when we knew each other better, we would have a good laugh over the incident. But that was still months in the future. For the moment, Janes stolidly did as he was asked, and came back with both the blood sample and a grass and dirt-filled plastic bag, which was placed safely in evidence.

We sent everything Janes had found on East Broadway—the bag of grass and dirt, the mop and vacuum bag, the paint samples from the screen door, and all the other physical evidence from the schoolhouse plus the items in the briefcase and everything taken from Dr. Henry at the time of his arrest—to the Alcohol, Tobacco, and Firearms laboratory in Washington, D.C. We requested that any hairs found in the floor mop or vacuum bag be compared to the wig that Dr. Henry had been wearing, and that any fibers found be compared to the fibers in his clothing—a long shot, but worth the try. The material contained in the dog vomit was to be analyzed for drugs or poisons. We also requested identification of the two clear liquids found in the small bottles in the briefcase, and a comparison of the paint chip samples from the screen door with a tiny dark spot on the ratchet screwdriver found in the briefcase.

In the meantime, Carol Eley was combing the law library for legal precedents that would help us make our case that "once the intent is clearly shown, the slightest acts in furtherance of it are sufficient to commit the crime." The hard part, for us, would be clearly showing Dr. Henry's intent. Even if his plan said "Murder Tina," as we all suspected, we knew he wasn't following the plan. A further legal problem was that, even if it was agreed that the plan showed intent, that intent had been formed in another state and was therefore outside our jurisdiction. We had to bring to court acts done in furtherance of the intent while he was in Arizona, and so far we had come up empty. Showing that he had walked down the street in strange attire taking surveillance notes would not be enough. We had to show that he had tried to kill his ex-wife but for some reason had not succeeded.

One afternoon Carol came into my office with a grin on her face. She'd found an old California case, dating from the

1940s, that was almost exactly what we needed. A man had told several people that he was going to kill his wife. He then went to her house with a loaded gun. One of the people he told had called the police and they were waiting inside when he got there.

The court had ruled that: once the intent to commit murder is clearly shown (in this case it was shown by what he had told people), then the taking of a loaded gun to the place where the crime is to be committed may be sufficient for the jury to find the defendant guilty of attempted murder.

Christina Henry had seen the doctor carrying his briefcase that morning, and we now knew what had been inside it—a loaded pistol and a knife. Carol and I both felt that the California case was enough of a precedent to allow us to charge Dr. Henry, and it might even help us convict him.

In the next few days, Carol unearthed several other cases built on the fact that the defendant had taken a weapon, or tool, to a scene where he intended to commit a crime. Regardless of which state had tried the case, the same principle was upheld: that taking the items needed to commit the crime to the scene of the intended crime may be sufficient for a conviction. In most of the cases, however, the defendant had been prevented from carrying out his intention. Sometimes the police had arrived and caught the defendant before he could do anything. While this did not fit our facts, the cases would still be helpful to us.

While Eley was conducting her research, Agent Wallace brought us some very interesting information discovered by George Boiko through American Airlines security in Dallas.

On the twenty-third of November 1977, someone using the name Terry Cordell had made a telephone reservation from Baltimore, Maryland, for a Dallas-to-Tucson flight. The flight was American Airlines flight 331, scheduled to depart Dallas at 9:05 P.M. on the night of December 5, and arrive in Tucson at 10:15 P.M. that same night. Then, on November 29, 1977, a week later, someone using the name Donald Vester had telephoned from Baltimore, Maryland, to reserve a seat on a flight from Tucson to Dallas. The flight was scheduled to leave Tucson at 2:40 on the morning of December 7, and arrive in Dallas at 5:30 that same morning. Even though he had actually left Tucson on the sixth, Dr. Henry's plan corresponded to these schedules.

The notation "9:05 331 Tu" appeared on the murder plan. At the bottom of the plan, the notation appeared, and below it was written "2:40 Out—Tu D" then "5:30 D." We interpreted this to mean that Dr. Henry had made the reservations as registered by American Airlines, but had planned all along to "chg flt"—to change his flight—from 2:40 A.M. on December 7 to 2:40 A.M. on December 6.

American's central computer also showed that Dr. Henry did not fly into Tucson on the flight he'd originally reserved from Baltimore. For some reason Terry Lee Cordell either missed or passed up flight 331 to Tucson and instead boarded flight 301 to El Paso. After a forty-five-minute delay in El Paso, he then proceeded to Tucson via Continental Airlines flight 75, arriving at 11:45, two and a half hours later than he had originally planned. No wonder he had found it impossible to keep to his written schedule.

Checking further, Agent Wallace discovered that this combination of American and Continental flights was the fastest way to get from Dallas to Tucson, once the American flight, 331, had departed.

Our next step was to interview the American and Continental flight crews to see if anyone remembered seeing Dr. Henry on his way to Tucson that night. We decided this could best be done with the help of the ATF, which has offices in every large city in the country.

Also to be interviewed was the crew from the Tucson-to-Dallas flight Dr. Henry had taken just before he was arrested, as well as Dr. Noah Fredericks, the man who had written a note to the captain about Dr. Henry. All of these people were found and interviewed in less than ten days.

Our case was improving. We could show that for some reason Dr. Henry missed his flight, but took the next available ones to fly to Tucson. He arrived at 11:45, just before midnight, and then at 3:30 in the morning the dog started barking at the Bellios house. By his own notes we could show he was there at 5:00 A.M. At 7:15 the same morning, Mrs. Henry identified him even though he was in disguise. Her description fit his appearance later on in Dallas, and his own notes confirmed he was there. At 9:30 the same morning, he called and tried to get her to come into the deserted school. We had only Mrs. Henry's identification to go on, but I was counting on the jury to know that a woman would recognize her husband's voice no matter how he tried to disguise it.

There was still a great deal, of course, that we didn't know. For example, how had Dr. Henry gotten into town from the airport? His plan mentioned two possibilities: "Tu car" and then "cab—U." We interpreted this to mean that he would either rent a car, have a car waiting, or take a taxi to the University of Arizona, just a few blocks from the Bellios house. Wallace and Janes would have to check out these possibilities with the car rental companies, using the names for which Dr. Henry was carrying I.D. They would also have to speak to every limousine and cab driver who had been on duty the night of the fifth or morning of the sixth.

There was a lot more work ahead, but Carol Eley and I were optimistic. Chuck Wallace was less so; he still didn't think we could make a case that would stick, though he was doing his damnedest to help us. Ken Janes didn't voice an opinion. But whenever we considered the evidence we were accumulating, the four of us did agree on one thing: Christina Henry was right when she had said her ex-husband would try again. Everything pointed to the fact that this was a man obsessed with the idea of revenge. And in the next few years Dr. Henry would earn quite a lot of money as a dermatologist. He could make another murder attempt himself, or he could simply hire someone else to kill Christina. A professional killing, especially if it were designed to look like an accident, would be almost impossible to solve. The only way to protect Christina was to put Dr. Henry behind bars. And we had to do it now. We wouldn't get another chance.

Two weeks later our case was torn apart in less than an hour.

Thelma, our receptionist, buzzed me to say that an attorney named Ron Sommers was on the line. I recognized the name from an interview with Mrs. Henry: Ron Sommers had represented Dr. Henry in Tucson during the divorce proceedings and custody hearings. If I was lucky, this call would provide me with some new information.

"I hear you're looking at my client, Dr. Henry, for some kind of criminal charges?" Sommers asked.

"I answered, "Yes, sir. We're looking at him, all right.""

"Why? All he did was come to see his kid. He just wanted to see his kid."

"Bullshit, Ron, you know why he came out here, and it wasn't to see his kid. You know what he had in that briefcase. What the hell was that all about?"

Sommers answered matter-of-factly, "I know what he had in there."

"Do you know, for example, about the gun, the knife, the gloves, and the glass cutters?" I was sure that he didn't.

"Oh, I know all about that stuff. I know what he had in there. But he never had the briefcase with him. He didn't have it at any time when he was in Tucson."

"What do you mean he never had it?" I waited to see how he would try to talk his way around it.

"If you check, you'll find he never had that case. He got it back from the airlines just before he got on board the plane to leave Tucson. In fact, there's a record of his losing it. If you go look, you'll see."

I couldn't believe what I was hearing. If he hadn't had the briefcase with him that morning, when Mrs. Henry saw him, our case was destroyed.

The lawyer seemed willing to give information, so I asked another question. "Hey, Ron, how did he get into town?" Neither Wallace nor Janes could find anyone who had rented him a car or driven him anywhere in a cab or limousine.

Hesitating very slightly, Sommers responded, "Well . . . he walked in."

"At one o'clock in the morning? You've got to be kidding."

Sommers went on to tell me the story his client had told him. Once Dr. Henry discovered the airlines had lost his briefcase, he decided just to come into town and see his child—to check on how he was living, and how he was being treated. The lawyer then hesitated again.

"He may have come to Tucson to do something originally," he said. "Hell, I don't know what he had in mind. I can tell you one thing, though: he didn't *do* anything. He just wanted to see his kid."

I told Sommers I would check out the lost luggage story and get back to him. If anything was going to happen regarding his client, I'd let him know.

I immediately dialed Wallace and asked him to go out to

the airport and check Sommers's story right away. Then I sat back to wait. My thoughts were not happy ones.

At best, Dr. Henry was lying. I knew Ron Sommers by reputation; he was an honest lawyer who would not knowingly lie to me. But his information came from his client, and I was sure Dr. Henry would say anything to cover for himself.

On the other hand, Dr. Henry was smart enough to know we'd check his story out. So what were the other possibilities? The most likely was also the worst: that Mrs. Henry had been mistaken; she hadn't seen a briefcase that morning. And if she had been mistaken about that, what else had she been wrong, or inaccurate, about?

However unavoidable that conclusion seemed, I just couldn't accept it. I'd seen the woman—talked to her, watched her. I was positive she wasn't wrong. If she said she'd seen a briefcase, she had.

Wallace called back in less than an hour. The lawyer's story checked out. There was a delayed luggage claim. It had been filed with Continental Airlines by Terry Lee Cordell twenty minutes after the flight from El Paso landed in Tucson. Wallace read me parts of the claim over the phone. It described a black briefcase lost somewhere during his flight from Dallas to El Paso to Tucson. Furthermore, an airline agent in Tucson had written on the bottom of the claim that the bag had been located in El Paso. I asked Wallace to make a copy of the claim and bring it to the office as soon as possible.

After I hung up I sat in my office, stunned. The weapons had to have been transported from Dallas to Tucson in the briefcase. It was the only luggage Dr. Henry had carried, and he had checked it rather than carrying it aboard. The knife and gun could have been concealed on his person, but he would have set off all the alarms when he tried to pass through security. No, the weapons had to have been in the briefcase. And if he hadn't had it with him in Tucson that morning, we would never prove that he had brought weapons or tools to the scene of the crime he intended to commit. Without the briefcase we had absolutely nothing.

When Wallace brought the copy of the luggage claim back to the office, we sat staring at it. The claim itself was a single piece of paper. On one side were blank spaces for information about the passenger and how the bag was lost. There

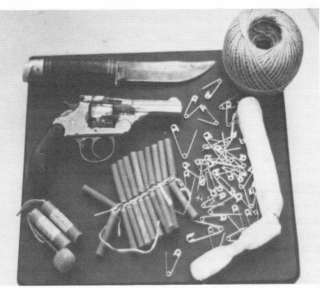

Dr. Henry's briefcase and its ominous contents: a hunting knife with both edges sharpened, a .32 caliber revolver, 23 firecrackers, 41 safety pins, 380 feet of twine, and a homemade blackjack.

clean up.

ink
Box
cont etc
paints
paper
plunger
(nails)

9:15 33' → Tu

10:15 Tu car?
cal → U.
prepare stuff; any extras:
Case lights
        feed dogs
        at time
        ck 1405 keg
                inside
        neighborhood
                routes
                phone
                changing place

In 1409
        select window
        tape
        plunger
        thru-open
        find T
        M T
        exit front ; or rear window

1:00 Route
1:15 Change
1:20 Wrap Suit
1:30 call cops Box
        mail
2:15 airport - chg plt.
2:40 Out Tu → D
5:30 D

The plan Dr. Henry scribbled on Ramada Inn stationery,
with the chilling notation: "find T, MT."

The wedding of Patrick Henry and Christina Bellios, St. Demetrious Greek Orthodox Church, Tucson, May 1971.

The Henrys and their son Paddy, their last Christmas together.

The scene of the attempt: Christina Henry's kindergarten, left, and the home of her parents.

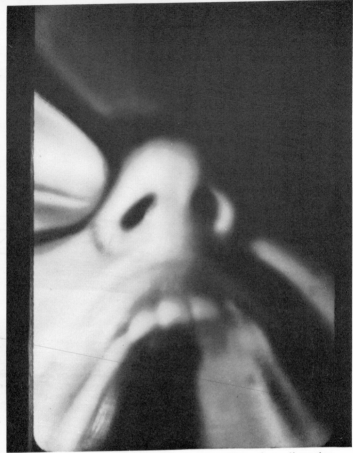

A photograph taken by Dr. Henry, through a distorting lens, of his wife in agony.

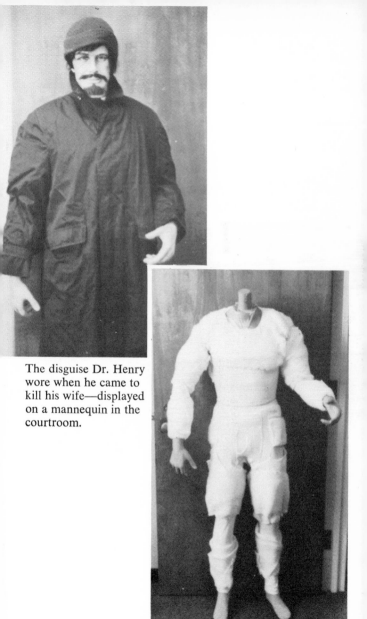

The disguise Dr. Henry wore when he came to kill his wife—displayed on a mannequin in the courtroom.

September, 1979:
Above, Dr. Henry
smirking at a news
photographer during
the trial.

Right, Henry being
led into the courtroom
for sentencing.

was also a space where the passenger could describe the bag. On the reverse side were illustrations of different types of suitcases and briefcases. The passenger was instructed to select the one most similar to his own luggage, and write down the number that corresponded to that illustration on the front of the form. At the bottom of the front page was space for the airline to state where and when the suitcase eventually was located.

That was what really killed us. There was nothing to stop. Dr. Henry from claiming, falsely, that his case had been lost. But the airline was backing him up. The form indicated that the briefcase in question had been located in El Paso by American Airlines. Both parts of the form—the lost luggage complaint section and the recovering information—had been signed by agents of Continental Airlines at Tucson International. The agent who had filled out the recovery information was called H. Smith. He was our last hope. Perhaps he had returned the case to Dr. Henry in time for him to take it to the Bellios house that morning.

Wallace called the airline from my office and received the final blow. According to a personnel supervisor, Horace Smith had not gone on duty the morning of the sixth until 8:00 A.M., which meant he could not have returned the briefcase before that time. Christina Henry had seen Dr. Henry outside with the briefcase at 7:15. She was positive about the time. But there was no way Dr. Henry could have had the briefcase that early. Wallace would locate Horace Smith to see what he remembered of the incident, but as Wallace left my office neither of us was expecting much.

I thought back to my first meeting with Christina Henry, when she had explained how clever and devious her husband was. She had meant her words as a warning, but I had taken them as a challenge. Before my duties as an administrator became so time-consuming, I'd inspected almost every homicide and major crime scene in Tucson. For eight years I'd picked the brains of countless detectives, learning their investigative techniques and tactics. And I'd attended countless autopsies. I had even taught the subject of investigation and trial preparation in our office, throughout the state, and in several other western states. My pretrial investigation and preparation is usually so thorough that often the actual trial was the easiest part of the justice process for me.

So when Christina Henry warned me of her ex-husband's cunning, I had been tempted to announce that the doctor had picked one of the worst places in the country to try to kill her. I would get him if it took me twenty years—not just to protect her but to satisfy my professional ego.

But now I was glad I hadn't said anything. In less than a month's time Dr. Henry had stopped my investigation cold.

As it turned out, the lost luggage claim was not the final blow. The real coup de grâce was delivered when we received the ATF laboratory's report on the physical evidence we had sent them.

Nothing. No hairs or fibers matched the wig or the clothing Dr. Henry wore. No hairs were found that were the color of his real hair. The bag of dirt and grass, which we had labeled with the official-sounding name of "vomitus," came back negative—no drugs or poisons. The lab did identify the different drugs taken from Dr. Henry at the time he was arrested. One of the pills Agent Rand had refused to let him swallow at the Dallas-Fort Worth Airport was a ten-milligram capsule of chlordiazepoxide hydrochloride, a tranquilizer commercially manufactured as Librium by Roche Products. Four other capsules were from Pfizer, Inc. Known as Vistaril, they contained twenty-five milligrams of hydroxyzine pamoate, which is an anti-itching agent. The remaining two capsules contained doxepin hydrochloride, an anti-depressant also manufactured by Pfizer, Inc. and marketed under the trade name Sinequan. The tranquilizers would explain the doctor's trance-like conduct aboard the aircraft and at the time he was arrested, when he stared off into space and appeared not to care what was happening around him. The anti-itching agent was probably to help him endure the wig and padded underwear.

The laboratory also analyzed the clear liquids found in the two bottles in the briefcase. One was acetone and water—nail polisher remover, and the other was a mixture of hydrocarbons—lighter fluid. The lighter fluid, we suspected, was intended as fuel for the hand warmer found in the briefcase. The nail polish remover puzzled all of us; we couldn't imagine its purpose.

Worst of all, the lab had produced evidence that tended to prove Dr. Henry's innocence. The vomitus contained no drugs or poisons, and the school showed no trace of evidence that linked Dr. Henry to a burglary. Ken Janes had already established that the screwdriver in Dr. Henry's briefcase could have made the pry marks on the screen door, but so could millions of other screwdrivers and tools. The stain on Dr. Henry's screwdriver had proved too small for the lab to match it to the paint chips taken from the screen. Under a microscope the stain looked like the right color, but no one could say for certain.

If we were ever able to charge Dr. Henry, the law required that all of these test results be turned over to the defense to help them in their case. A good attorney would take Mr. Bellios's testimony about the dog acting drugged or poisoned and demolish it with this lab report. He'd undoubtedly accuse the old man of paranoid fabrications or, at the least, an overactive imagination.

After Wallace delivered the laboratory findings to me, he delivered the rest. Mr. Horace Smith didn't remember a thing about the luggage claim. It was his signature on it, and he did go to work on the sixth, at 8:00 A.M., like he always did, but he didn't remember anything about the briefcase or the person he talked to.

I thanked Wallace and told him I'd call back when I had some idea where to go next. After hanging up, I closed my office door, asked Thelma to hold incoming calls, and sat there trying to think of what else we could do. Soon I was even more frustrated and depressed than before.

Yet later that same evening something did come to mind. The next morning I called Janes and asked him to find out what time Randall Butler was working the Continental counter. He was the agent who had received the luggage claim from Patrick Henry.

"Sure I remember him," Butler told us when we went to see him. "He caused a hell of a scene. Demanding that we find his luggage. He was angry as hell. I helped him fill in the delayed luggage claim."

"You mean this?" I asked, handing him the original document that Wallace had obtained.

"That's it. I remember that guy all right. He had on a wig and a fake moustache. Really weird. And he looked like he was wearing two pairs of clothes.

He came back to the counter three times. I remember that. He was so insistent that I remember checking the flight when it made its next scheduled stop, which was Phoenix, but the case just wasn't aboard. That made him madder than ever."

"Anything else? Can you think of anything else? How about the time? What time was it when you last saw him? Tell us anything you can remember. We're interested in anything."

"Mostly I remember him getting so mad and causing a scene. After the flight was checked in Phoenix, I remember we closed the counter. Continental doesn't have another flight until later in the morning, so we always close the counter. In fact, we closed later that night than usual because we had waited around to see if his briefcase was in Phoenix. He walked off toward the escalators and that's the last time I saw him."

"Can you give us any idea when that was? What time was it when you saw him walk away?"

"It was 2:00 or 2:30. Closer to 2:30. In fact, I'm sure it was later. It was real close to 2:30 A.M.

We talked a few minutes more and he introduced us to another ticket agent, Fred Edmond, who had been on duty that night, but he couldn't add anything more. Thanking them for their help, I gave them my card and asked them to call if they thought of anything else. Jane and I both stressed that nothing was unimportant. "Anything," I said, "anything at all."

Randall Butler's information had only strengthened Dr. Henry's defense. According to Butler, Patrick Henry had still been at the airport at 2:30 A.M. If he really did walk into town, as Ron Sommers had told us, he couldn't possibly have reached the Bellios house by 3:30, when Champo had started barking.

Just to be sure, I asked Janes to do some time and distance measurements. It was just as we'd thought. The shortest route from the airport to the Bellios house was 9.7 miles. Even a vigorous walker could not cover much more than a mile every fifteen minutes, so total walking time would have been at least two hours, probably more like two and a half. If Dr. Henry left the airport on foot at 2:30, he would have arrived at the Bellios house not at 3:30 but between 4:30 and 5:00—which was the hour at which his surveillance notes began.

If we went to court with this evidence the jury might well believe that Patrick Henry had walked into town with no more in mind than spying on the family to see how his son was being treated. In fact, the way things were going, the jury might even feel sorry for him.

On the sixth of January 1978, just a few minutes past 1:00 in the afternoon, Father Anthony Moschonas arrived at the Bellios home. He wore his vestments—the robe and the *petrahili*, the embroidered mantle—and he carried a small silver pail containing water he had blessed in church that morning. Athena Bellios and Christina welcomed him at the door.

It is a Greek tradition that on the seventh day of the new year, the feast of Saint John the Baptist, the priest should go to his people's homes and bless them. But today the Bellios family sought more from their priest. It had been a month since Patrick Henry had come for Christina, and they could not rid the house of his presence.

It was like an evil aura, they explained to Father Moschonas. Pat had brought his murderous intention to their house and it remained with them. There were two words in the Greek language that expressed what he had done: *kako patima*. Pat had taken a "bad step" against their home. Now the priest would exorcise his presence.

With Athena and Christina preceding him, Father Moschonas entered each room of the house and dipped the cross he carried into the silver pail of holy water. Then, with a quick motion of his wrist, he sprinkled the water into each corner of the room, cleansing the house of all trace of the evil Pat had brought there.

When the ritual was done, the priest offered a special prayer for Christina and her son. Then Athena composed another prayer. It was one she and Christina would repeat every day for the next two years.

"Dear Lord, please help those who seek to help us. Please give strength to Agent Wallace, Detective Janes, Mr. Stevens, and Miss Eley."

Father Moschonas made the sign of the cross. "May God hear and grant your prayers," he said.

Patrick Henry had pulverized our investigation, but oddly enough, the setbacks only made everyone more determined. If we had come to a standstill, so be it. While we were standing still we would review every signed statement, every piece of evidence, every last report, to make sure we hadn't overlooked a thing. More than anything else, it was the Bellios family, and the fear they were living with, that kept us going. Christina Henry had been through an unimaginable experience but, with the help of her family, had managed to survive. Regardless of our professional assessment of the case, we couldn't walk away from her now.

This phase of the investigation was painstaking and often tedious. Reports, statements, and documents prepared by law enforcement agencies in Dallas–Fort Worth and Tucson were collected and studied closely, until we were sure all available information had been gleaned from them. Statements from the attendants aboard all the flights Dr. Henry flew were reviewed several times for any possible information that had gone unnoticed. On the chance that one of the cabdrivers at Tucson International might have accepted an undeclared fare, Janes reinterviewed them with the threat that they might be questioned later under oath. The trip cards of each driver were obtained, as well as the dispatcher's records, to be certain that no fare was taken anywhere near the Bellios house that night or morning. Wallace interviewed the employees of every all-night business along every one of the most likely routes in from the airport. If someone was on vacation, or had gone to another job, Wallace located and interviewed him. Wallace also asked the ATF office in Baltimore to initiate a general background investigation of Dr. Patrick Henry.

Christina and her parents were reinterviewed several more times, in depth. Sometimes it seemed that we were just rehashing the same information over and over again. Yet bits of information surfaced in these reinterviews that I felt would be invaluable if we ever got to court.

One day we were discussing how Dr. Henry had photographed his wife in the water with the alligator, not warning her till the last minute of her danger. I learned, to my relief, that the Bellioses had not simply heard the story from their daughter—which legally was hearsay, and thus useless to us in court—but had actual knowledge: they had seen the slides the doctor had taken on one of the Henrys' visits to Tucson. Mr. Bellios only remembered seeing slides of Christina in the water and then other slides of alligators, but her mother clearly recalled one which showed an alligator swimming in

Christina's direction only a few feet from her. Even though they would be accused of lying to help their daughter, their testimony would help prove Christina's truthfulness and her husband's demented attitude toward her.

I questioned them again about the night those slides had been shown, trying to establish whether they remembered the week, month, and year they had seen them. But in the midst of discussing these details, Mrs. Henry and her mother both remembered something much more important: that other people had been present at the slide show.

The principal of the school where Christina Henry taught before her marriage had stopped in to see her while she was in town, and his wife had come with him. They had seen the alligator slide too. Almost as important, they had heard the exchange that followed between Dr. Henry and his mother-in-law.

Shocked at what she saw projected on the screen, Mrs. Bellios had turned to her daughter. "Christina, why on earth would you do a thing as foolish as that?" she asked.

Dr. Henry had answered for her. Laughing, he told Christina's parents that she hadn't even known the alligator was there.

I could only hope that the principal and his wife had been shocked enough to remember the scene and what Patrick Henry had said. I had known all along the alligator episode would be hard to sell to a jury. Two unbiased witnesses would go a long way toward doing the job for me. But I needed their unbiased testimony. The couple no longer lived in Tucson, but I made Mrs. Henry and her parents promise not to contact them under any circumstances, until I'd talked to them first.

Excited by this discovery, I began stressing to Christina Henry the importance of independent proof.

"Is there anyone else like the principal?" I asked her. "Anyone who has seen, for example, the distorted slides your husband took with the glass paperweight?" When I heard her answer, I had to believe our luck in this case was turning.

"I can't remember showing these slides to anyone. But, Mr. Stevens, I have them. The slides, I mean. When I left Pat I didn't want him to show them to anyone else. He used to call them the 'company slides,' and I knew he'd keep showing them, even after I was gone. So I took them."

I asked her to drive home and bring them back immediately. She did so, and laid them out on the desk in front of me.

Those slides were everything she'd said they were. The grotesque distortions of her face had been heightened by color filters, and the results were incredibly eerie. Some were green, some purple, and all were dreadful. Among them was a slide she'd mentioned in our first interview, the one in which her husband had kicked her to make her scream.

Also in this group were the slides taken during her pregnancy. On the cardboard edging was written: "Tina Making Chunks." The distorted slides made with the paperweight were labeled: "Tina Distorted."

I looked over the entire bizarre collection and imagined a jury's reaction. There in front of me was a record of Christina Henry's private hell. If we could only get to court those slides would prove she was telling the truth about her husband's perversity. If we could only get to court.

Among the evidence we reexamined were Dr. Henry's own notes and plans. Having been told he sometimes wrote in code, we didn't want to miss any clues, evidence, or information that might be hiding right in front of us. I ordered each of the documents and papers bearing his handwriting to be photographed and enlarged to five or six times their normal size. That done, they were placed in my office where we could concentrate on them, study them, and speculate on what they meant.

The front side of the Ramada Inn stationery was the most puzzling. After considerable study, our reading of the words that appeared was as follows:

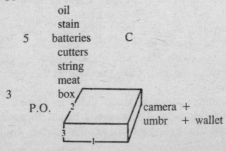

```
            Main            genetic
            A
2
            Mc Desirtt  on HLA
   record:   Main
            B  Katy on HG
   record:   Main
            C  Immunology
1
                    82
```

Detective Janes solved the most cryptic part. He came to my office one day and announced that he'd figured out the numbers "1," "2," and "3" appearing on the left-hand margin of the paper.

First he'd taken the green metal box found in the briefcase—the box that had contained the knife and the pistol—and had held it against the left-hand edge of the Ramada Inn stationery. Once he had done that he'd seen that the measurements of the box corresponded to the numbers written on the paper. The distance from the top of the stationery to the number 3 on the margin was the height of the box. The distance to the number 2 on the margin was the depth of the box, and the distance to the number 1 was the width of the box.

It all seemed elaborate and pointless, but the diagram near the other margin of the stationery proved Janes right. It was a picture of a box, with the numbers "3," "2," and "1" indicating its height, depth, and width. There was no disputing that Dr. Henry had done what Janes was suggesting—the question was, why had he done it? What was it for?

After a lot more mulling and speculating, I came up with a guess. To test it out I asked Janes to get the gun, the ammunition, and the knife and put them back in the metal box. Then he was to take the box to the post office and ask the clerk how much it would cost to mail it from Tucson to Baltimore.

The postage, Janes learned, came to $5.18—which was within pennies of the value of the stamps Dr. Henry had been carrying in the briefcase. I was sure, then, that he had planned to mail his weapons back to Baltimore after using them. And that might explain the numerical notations. He wouldn't want to deal with the postal clerk who might ask what was in the package. But to mail the box himself, he would have to be sure it would fit through the post office mailing slot.

That was where the size notations came in. Instead of taking the box itself to the post office to test the height and width of the slot, he could take the sheet of stationery instead. It was a plan that could have been devised only by a man who loved to be mysterious.

We all figured out the bottom half of the page, but Janes confirmed it. He obtained from the American Academy of Dermatology their program for the meeting in Dallas that Dr. Henry had attended. "Main A," "Main B," and "Main C" were lectures being given at the conference on the morning of the sixth. The speakers' names were listed in the program, showing us that what we had read as "Mc Desirtt" was "McDevitt" and "Katy" was "Katz." Dr. Henry had abbreviated the subjects of those doctors' lectures as "HLA" and "HG."

These were the lectures that Dr. Henry knew he would miss if he didn't arrive back from Tucson on schedule. Janes guessed that he had planned to record the lectures, possibly for use as an alibi, showing that he had in fact been in Dallas that morning. This speculation was supported by Henry's notation, further up the page, of "5 batteries C": C batteries would be the right size for a tape recorder.

Along with "batteries," Dr. Henry had listed up above "oil, stain, cutters, string, meat, box." The last four were self-evident, and all were in our possession except the meat, which I assumed he'd fed to Champo. "Stain" could have represented the bottle of Clinique makeup found in the briefcase. "Oil" was the only one that really stumped us.

But no matter how many pieces of the puzzle were deciphered, the lost briefcase was a stumbling block. As long as its disappearance and recovery were verified by Randall Butler and Horace Smith, we were unable to claim that Dr. Henry had transported a weapon to the Ballios house.

Yet Christina was certain about the briefcase. It was the case that had led her to assume that the man lurking on the street was a professor, and she specifically recalled the man leaning over to pick it up. It was possible she was mistaken, but I had trouble believing that. I had spent a great deal of time with Christina Henry, questioning her closely, rephrasing my questions and approaching subjects from different angles. In all that time she had never changed a story or tried to give information she really did not recall. The other possibility was that she was lying, but I dismissed that idea in seconds. Christina Henry and her parents radiated integrity. She wasn't capable of sustained deception.

But Patrick Henry was. Once again his wife's warning came back to me: "Mr. Stevens, he's brilliant. He wouldn't do something like this unless he knew there was a way out. He's smart enough to have done this so you can't catch him. He plans everything in advance."

Was it possible that the brilliant Dr. Henry had contrived to lose his briefcase in order to provide a defense? But how could he have left the briefcase behind in El Paso, where eventually it was found, and still have carried it into Tucson with him that morning?

I began to consider the use of hypnosis on Christina Henry—it was the only way I could think of to determine if she'd really remembered a briefcase, and to see if she had any new information she hadn't already given us. However, the legal risk was substantial.

Hypnosis has been used in law enforcement for years; my office has used it several times without problems. But as yet no high court in Arizona has ruled on whether additional testimonial evidence obtained by use of hypnosis is admissible evidence during a trial. If the Arizona Supreme Court, or one of its appellate courts, ruled that evidence obtained from Mrs. Henry under hypnosis was not admissible, we might lose other parts of her testimony as well. Dr. Henry's attorney would surely argue that we had improved her recollection by hypnosis, therefore she should not be allowed to testify at all, or should only be allowed to testify to that which she knew before going under hypnosis. In other words; by hypnotizing Mrs. Henry we might disqualify our primary witness from ever taking the stand.

In the end we didn't really have a choice. The delayed luggage claim was a barrier we couldn't surmont. Without new evidence we would never get to court.

The Israelis were the ones who perfected the use of hypnosis in law enforcement. Knowing that the mind acts much like a camera, they developed hypnosis as a way to let the brain play back what it has recorded. Suppose they were investigat-

ing the terrorist bombing of an airport. The Israelis realized
that as the bombs were being planted, there had been people
all around sitting and waiting for their planes. As they waited,
they had watched other people walk by. Under hypnosis these
witnesses were often able to go back in their minds and resee
everyone who had walked by and what they had been carrying.
Out of this might come a description of the person or persons
who had planted the explosives.

In much the same way I wanted Mrs. Henry to resee the
morning of December 6—the street, the man, and, if it was
there, the briefcase. To perform the hypnosis, I enlisted Dr.
Harold Russell, the Tucson Police Department psychologist, and
Dr. Walter Lindsey, a retired dental surgeon who was one of
the original seven founders of the American Society of Clinical Hypnosis. Dr. Lindsey used hypnosis in his dental practice for over twenty-five years. We met in a small room at
police headquarters.

"Christina, this is Dr. Lindsey," he began. "Do you hear
me? Fine. Now Christina, I'm going to ask you some questions about the event that took place on December 6. The
time is now 11:20 A.M., the twenty-fifth of January. From
now on, when I ask you questions, you can see the answer
to the questions." Dr. Lindsey's voice was smooth, without
inflection, yet it held our attention. I almost found myself
becoming mesmerized along with Mrs. Henry.

"Now, we have a screen up on the wall in front of you,
and on this screen you will be able to see a picture of what
will take place on the morning of December 6, and if you
open your eyes, you can see that picture on the wall. You can
open them, you can look right up there on the wall. You will
see something there. What's happening on the morning of
December 6? Would you tell me what you see?"

"A man."

"I didn't hear that."

"A man."

"You see a man. Where is this man?"

"Across the street."

"Across the street from what?

"My school."

"From your school. Okay, Christina . . . Tina, I'm going
to pin this microphone right on your blouse here, and it
doesn't weigh anything, so it won't bother you at all. Now

remember that you're watching a moving picture, like a movie or television on the wall, and you're sitting here with Dr. Russell, Randy, and myself, and you're perfectly relaxed, and what you see in the picture is not going to disturb you at all. Do you understand that?''

"Yes."

"Yes, okay. Now would you tell me again where this man is?"

"He's across the street." Christina's voice was just above a whisper. She spoke slowly, like someone talking in her sleep.

"Across the street from what?"

"From my school . . . the yard."

"All right. And how tall is this man?"

"He's tall."

"He's tall. Okay. Would you please tell me what kind of clothes he has on."

"A sort of black coat and a thing on his head. Dark. Just see dark on his head."

"Can you tell me what it is? Look real close."

"Close . . ."

"You can magnify it—that picture—and zero in real close, just like they do on TV when they get a close-up of a person's head. So you just close right in on that head so you can see better. What kind of thing does he have on his head?"

"Dark, dark hair, black."

"He had black hair. What about, does he have any—"
Mrs. Henry interrupted ". . . very dark hair."

"What kind of hat?"

"Hat—close—on his head down low, so . . . above his eyebrows."

"What is that thing on his head?"

Christina sat in a recliner chair, her eyes wide open, staring intently at a television screen that wasn't there. Now she extended her hand to adjust an imaginary dial. Only one light, a desk lamp, had been left burning in the small, windowless room we were using, and Mrs. Henry could see little besides the smooth, distinguished face of Dr. Lindsey, who sat just a few feet in front of her. Dr. Russell and I sat, quiet and inconspicuous, in the only other chairs in the room.

As we sat watching, Dr. Lindsey asked Mrs. Henry to go

through everything she saw, heard, and did the morning of the sixth. She described the man on the sidewalk, his clothing and briefcase, then the conversation with the person on the telephone.

Unfortunately she gave us no more information than we already had. We needed the hidden details her subconscious mind might possess. At this point, I asked Dr. Lindsey if I could question her, since I knew specifically what we needed.

"Christina, now you're going to go outside, and I want you to tell me now . . . remember . . . this time I want you to spend more time on that focus. Go outside, now tell me what you see."

"Just walking. I see the yard over at my school and that man."

"All right."

"Black coat, man in the black coat, watching and writing."

"All right, I want you now to get hold of the dial and focus in, and go to the man a little closer. Study his head, and study the face and the head. . . . What can you see there? Okay, you're looking at it. Good."

Christina sat forward in her chair, hand turning a knob that wasn't there, first staring, then squinting as she looked at a blank wall. She was seeing him closer and better than ever before.

"Yes." Her voice was a little more emotional, a little higher.

"All right, and you don't see anything on his face—or you do see something on his face?"

"Black, just see a lot of black, low and . . . face looks a little bit dark."

"Okay, study it carefully now, Tina. What do you see up there?"

"The man has on a moustache! Black moustache!" She spoke so excitedly that she startled me.

"All right."

"Not little one."

"Tell me about—"I started to ask for details, but she interrupted.

"Kind of bushy kind."

"Good. Work the knob now, see if you can get any closer. That's it, all right, can you see it up on the screen now? Tell me about it."

"Black, bushy moustache, big. Not the little, thin kind, the big kind."

We had learned from Randall Butler, the Continental Airlines agent, that Dr. Henry had a moustache, but, as with all the information derived from other sources, we hadn't told Mrs. Henry. She hadn't mentioned a moustache before, and there was no way she could know about it now, unless she was seeing it. I moved her forward, asking twenty or thirty other questions, but only really interested in our eventual destination: the briefcase.

"Okay, all right, now go back to your big picture, and I'm going to have you change your focus again. I want you to go down to the briefcase, get hold of the knob and focus in on the handle. Okay, that's it, the knob is coming right in. There. No, there, just below that handle. Is it all right? Good, focus, very good. Now tell me what it's made of. You're squinting, so you're looking hard."

"It's not standing up. . . . The handle isn't right." My heart was racing; I was trying not to show any excitement.

"It's not?" was my only comment.

"No . . . it's down. . . . It doesn't look—"

"Is something wrong with it?" I asked, trying harder than before not to show anything in my voice.

"It doesn't look really . . . it's not . . . it's not standing up right. It looks a little like it's not good, something was wrong with it." She was sitting forward again, squinting, trying to see better.

"All right, so something's not right, something's not right here. Okay, now try . . . just keep thinking. No, now look at it closer. Turn your focus closer; it's fuzzy. There, there. Very good, now tell me, what's wrong with it?"

"It's broken and it's not working right."

"Okay."

"It doesn't look right . . . handle."

"All right. Is it attached on both ends?"

"No, one end only."

"One end only is attached?"

"Other end looks a little bit like it's not in right, like it maybe doesn't go right."

"All right, that's excellent. While you're looking at it, tell me what the handle is made of."

"It's dark like the briefcase."

"Okay."

"I think . . . just see black."

We had never given Mrs. Henry the opportunity to examine the briefcase, and she had never mentioned the handle to us before. There was no way she could know that the handle was broken—unless she was seeing it that morning.

I was so relieved it was hard to continue the interview, but we went on. At one point, several minutes later, I asked her to look at the man's shoes and tell us what she could see of them. She turned the knob, squinted and stared for a few seconds, then said, "Looks not dark on the feet, like light. Like not, not dark like the coat, his shoes. . . ."

"Okay."

"Lighter."

"Okay."

"Maybe . . . maybe sneakers, not sure."

"All right."

"Not sure, can't tell."

In yet another attempt to verify the accuracy of the information she was giving us, I questioned Christina as to her activities just before she received the phone call at 9:30. She answered that she had been working on her checkbook and making a list of things to buy Stevie for Christmas. She was asked to describe her notations, and to tell us the things that appeared on her list. Later we would verify this information with the actual records.

Before the doctors brought Mrs. Henry back to full consciousness, I asked them to tell her that she wouldn't remember anything of the interview that had just been conducted. By taking away her recall, we ensured that she would have no more information to give, when she testified, than she had before going under hypnosis. The day before, the twenty-fourth of January, I had had her come to my office and we recorded an interview covering the same areas that I knew we would cover when she was hypnotized. The next day, the twenty-sixth, I would have her come back for a third interview to show that the hypnosis had not altered her unaided recall.

When she was interviewed the next day she did not recall that the man wore a moustache, that the handle on the briefcase was broken or that the man wore sneakers. This information was located only in her subconscious mind.

Once she was conscious again, Mrs. Henry desperately wanted to know what had happened, and whether she had been of any help. I had to tell her that, for certain legal reasons, I couldn't reveal anything about her interview. She did not press me further, though she was clearly disappointed.

I was very curious about whether the testimony we had just obtained would stand up in court—if we ever got there. The trial judge might let us use Mrs. Henry's testimony about the broken handle, and we might win the case. But later on the higher courts might rule that her testimony should not have been used, in which event the case would probably be reversed and the conviction thrown out.

But we couldn't worry about what might happen years down the line. Our present task was to prove, independently, what Mrs. Henry had told us under hypnosis: that Dr. Henry had carried his briefcase with the broken handle that morning.

In the meantime, other pieces of her recollection under hypnosis were verified. No record had been made in Dallas of what shoes Dr. Henry had been wearing when he was arrested, and his footwear had not been taken as evidence. On the off-chance that Jerry Lloyd might remember, Detective Janes called him in Texas.

"Sure, that's easy," Lloyd said. "I haven't seen those kinda shoes in years—the old black and white tennis shoes. I remember, 'cause I told my boss—he was with me when we went to court the day they turned him loose—'Things must be tough in the medical profession. Look at the shoes he's wearing.'"

Janes also went to Mrs. Henry's house and checked the notes and paperwork she had been doing before the 9:30 call came through. Her computations and Christmas list were just as she had described them. He brought those papers in and they, too, were placed into evidence.

I now had to face it: Patrick Henry had planned his moves much better than I had wanted to admit. Unable to know in advance if he would succeed in killing his ex-wife, he had taken steps to protect himself either way.

If his attempt succeeded, he knew he would be suspected immediately. But he would probably never be indicted. Patrick Henry hadn't traveled to Tucson from Dallas that night; Terry Cordell had. We knew now that they were one and the same, but we could so easily have missed getting that information. If it hadn't been for the sharp eye of Gene Zarr, Dr. Henry would never have been arrested in Dallas carrying identification in the name of Cordell. Without that break we could have spent years trying to link him to Tucson the night of the murder.

The delayed luggage claim was intended to protect him if his murder attempt failed. I was fully prepared to believe that Dr. Henry had researched Arizona law and knew exactly what we would have to prove in order to get a conviction: that he had brought a weapon to the scene of the crime he intended to commit. On the remote chance that Cordell might be discovered, and found to be Dr. Patrick Henry, he had arranged proof that Cordell didn't have the briefcase containing the weapons, which also constituted proof that Dr. Henry didn't have them. It seemed farfetched, yet that was exactly what had happened.

The scene Terry Cordell had created at the Continental counter the morning he'd arrived in Tucson had been designed to draw attention to himself. He'd wanted Randall Butler and the others to remember him. There was no other reason why he should have stayed at the airport for two and a half hours after his arrival, much less for him to have returned to the counter three times demanding they find his luggage. And his plan had worked: Randall Butler distinctly remembered that Mr. Cordell stayed at the airport until 2:30 A.M., and that he left without his briefcase.

Whenever I found myself doubting that Dr. Henry could really have planned it all, I reminded myself of the clincher. It was Ron Sommers, Dr. Henry's own attorney, who had let us know about the lost luggage in the first place.

It was not Dr. Henry's cleverness that most impressed me, however. It was his arrogance. He had known from the start that if Christina Henry was found murdered the police would inevitably come to him. She had almost certainly told her family something of what happened during their marriage, and her parents would repeat what they knew to the investigating officers. Fully recognizing the tremendous risk he was up against, he had gone ahead with his murder plan anyway. Having considered the odds, he felt capable of beating them. He was willing to gamble everything on the superiority of his intelligence, knowing that the penalty for failure was life in prison or death.

The day after Christina Henry underwent hypnosis I called Chuck Wallace and Ken Janes. I had sat up half the night plotting their next assignment.

"Pack your suitcases, gentlemen," I told them. "And dig out your warm coats, if you've got them. I hear it's real cold back East this winter."

On Sunday, January 29, both men flew from Tucson to Baltimore. Their assignment was to humble Dr. Henry's arrogance.

On Monday, the Baltimore streets were slick and icy and the gray sky threatened more snow at any moment. The air smelled of heating oil, a noxious oily smell. People on the sidewalks were walking fast, their shoulders pulled up and necks pulled down. At bus stops people stood with their backs to the wind, stamping their feet to keep the blood circulating.

Chuck Wallace was cold. He sat stiffly on the passenger side of the front seat, his hands in his coat pockets, his collar up. Ed Witterman, an ATF agent in Baltimore, was driving. Ken Janes sat in the back seat, alternately amused by and sympathizing with Wallace's misery. More than anything Wallace wanted to do the job and get himself back to the warm desert.

As they drove through the suburbs of Baltimore, toward the town of Catonsville, Janes tapped his fingers on the seat beside him. He was excited to be in Dr. Henry's world, seeing his new life. Dr. Henry was quite a mystery, but Janes did not expect to understand him. Henry had an unlimited professional future, a new wife and family. But he'd been willing to risk it all to kill a woman who'd left him. There was no way Janes would ever understand a man like that.

But what about his new wife, Nancy Henry? She had married a man other people described as a monster. She had let him adopt her children. What kind of woman was she? Janes was very curious, and he would know more about the new Mrs. Henry very soon.

Ed Witterman announced that they were now on South Ridge Road, and Janes looked out the window, trying to assess the neighborhood in which Dr. Henry had chosen to live. Although still blanketed in several inches of snow, the trees were large and probably shady in the summer. There were snow forts and sled ruts everywhere, suggesting to Janes that the neighbors were mostly young couples with growing children. The houses were brick, but not set very far back from the road. It was a nice neighborhood—not the most expensive, but more prosperous than most he'd seen that morning.

As Witterman pulled over to the curb, both Wallace and Janes felt the excitement. The whole routine they were about to perform was designed for one thing: to get one piece of information from Dr. Henry's wife.

Wallace, Janes, and I had worked it all out before the two of them had left. We knew from the passenger manifests that Terry Cordell had been a counted passenger on the flights from Dallas to El Paso and El Paso to Tucson. Most likely he had, in fact, arrived in Tucson via those flights. We also made sure, by checking schedules, that there were no other flights from Dallas to El Paso before 8:00 in the morning, so the case could not have arrived later in the night.

Given these facts, we could think of only three ways Henry could have done it. Our favorite was that he had taken two briefcases out of Dallas. Ken James suspected that he had deliberately left one behind in El Paso and checked the other onto the flight to Tucson. Upon arriving here he picked up the one he'd checked, hid it someplace at the airport, then claimed that his case was lost.

We went to the airport and looked for places where the briefcase could have been hidden. A locker was the obvious choice, except that airport lockers are now deliberately situated so that passengers must pass through a security checkpoint to use them. Dr. Henry couldn't have gone from baggage pickup to the locker area without the briefcase setting off the checkpoint alarm.

We discovered other possible hiding places in the open terminal area, like trash cans or vacant airline counters, but such places were too risky: the case could be found by someone other than Henry. Outside the terminal there were several other places, but they also involved the risk of discovery, unless he had a car waiting in the parking lot. Still, he might have assumed a calculated risk.

Our second theory was that there was only one briefcase. Henry checked it aboard the earlier American flight, the one that he didn't take, so the briefcase was already in Tucson when he arrived. The problem there was figuring out what briefcase had been located in El Paso.

Our third theory was that he had had an accomplice—but that complicated the case so much that we didn't want to think about it unless we had to.

The trouble with all these theories was that there was no way to prove them. Airline passengers are documented, but the movement of their luggage is not. The numbers on luggage claim checks do not represent particular flights. We could try to track Dr. Henry's movements from Baltimore to Dallas, Dallas to El Paso, then El Paso to Tucson—but I couldn't help thinking there had to be a short cut.

I wanted Wallace and Janes to get the information we needed from Nancy Henry. Their approach would be a little underhanded, but entirely legal. With everything Dr. Henry was putting us through, we all rather enjoyed the idea of taking the war to his home territory.

The three men walked up to the door and knocked. They knew who would answer. Patrick Henry was still a senior resident at the University of Maryland Hospital's Department of Dermatology, and they had chosen to call when the hospital said he would be on duty.

An attractive young woman opened the door.

"Good morning—Mrs. Henry?" said Ed Witterman. "Are you Mrs. Patrick Henry?"

"Yes, I'm Nancy Henry. Can I help you?"

"Mrs. Henry, I'm Agent Witterman, ATF. I talked to you on the phone earlier this morning, and this is Agent Wallace and this is Ken Janes. May we talk to you for a second?"

Wallace and Witterman were showing their identification, holding them up for her inspection one or two feet from her face, and thus temporarily blocking her view of Ken Janes. As I'd instructed, Janes stood in the background, showing no I.D., and hoping he wouldn't be asked to do so. If at all possible, Nancy Henry was not to find out that he was an investigator with the county Attorney's Office in Tucson.

Mrs. Henry seemed not to notice Janes's omission, and invited them all in. Wallace quickly picked up the conversation. Janes was impressed to hear Wallace sounding so professional, when minutes earlier he had been shivering and swearing at the cold.

"Ma'am, you know about the incident in Texas, when your husband was arrested on the weapon charge?"

"But I thought it had been dismissed. I thought it was dropped," Nancy Henry interrupted.

"It has been, ma'am. I was the agent working the case. Why we're here is to wrap it up. We want to be sure your husband got all his property back, and everything has been done properly."

"Oh, I see."

"Do you think everything has been returned to your husband?"

"I think so. He didn't say anything."

"We want to be certain he got everything back."

"I think he has everything."

"Does your husband always carry a weapon? Is that usual?"

"He does sometimes. He has to. Downtown, near the hospital where he works, there have been several muggings. I know he carries a gun for protection sometimes."

Janes studied her, and everything else, while there was the opportunity. Nancy Henry was attractive; she seemed a little nervous but that was to be expected. Some pictures on the wall showed two cute little girls less than ten years old. The house was furnished nicely; the furniture was nothing extraordinary. It looked like anyone else's house. He stood by, waiting for the right moment as Wallace continued his questioning. When he thought it was time, Janes asked a casual question.

"Mrs. Henry, did your husband get his briefcase back?"

"I'm not certain. I think he did. I'm sure he must have."

"Well, do you recall if he took a briefcase with him?"

"Let me think. He took a suitcase and his camera, and I'm almost sure he took his briefcase. I think he got everything back."

"That's good. By the way, how many briefcases does he have, do you know?"

"Well, he has two, but he doesn't use one of them. It's down in the basement; the handle on it is broken."

It had worked.

All three men knew what they had just been given, but their expressions betrayed nothing. Wallace deliberately controlled his desire to glance at Janes. Nancy Henry had no idea that the briefcase she thought was in her basement was in the ATF evidence room in Tucson.

To keep a silence from falling, Janes asked another question. "Can you tell me anything about his other briefcase?"

"Not really. I know it has his initials on it—PGH—but that's all I can tell you."

Wallace picked up the questioning, giving the impression that he was making small talk. Minutes later the agents stood up to leave, yet they moved very slowly toward the door. In the last series of questions Wallace established that Nancy Henry didn't know what her husband took to Tucson in his briefcase, or even that he had intended to fly to Tucson. When asked if she'd ever heard of either Terry Lee Cordell or Donald Vester, she answered that she hadn't.

As they were leaving, she volunteered, "You know, the more I think about it, I'm almost sure he got his briefcase back. I just can't say absolutely, but I think he did."

Once back in the car Wallace and Janes talked excitedly. They knew now that Patrick Henry had a second briefcase, one with his initials on it. And they were fairly certain that he had brought that briefcase home with him; that was why Mrs. Henry thought the authorities had given a briefcase back to him. As she was the doctor's wife, none of Mrs. Henry's statements could ever be used in court, but at last they could be sure what they were looking for. Dr. Henry had pulled a switch, and when they got to Dallas and El Paso they would try to prove it. For the moment, however, they had to turn to their second assignment in Baltimore.

Early the next morning, January 31, 1978, Ed Witterman drove Wallace and Janes to Hollins Street in downtown Baltimore. The houses all seemed identical—rows and rows of monotonous two-story buildings with nothing to distinguish them but concrete steps out front leading to a single door. Most of the buildings were old, their red brick blackened with dirt. The men climbed up one set of steps and rang the bell. This was the address given on Terry Cordell's driver's license.

"Someplace, somewhere back there in Maryland you're going to find the real Terry Lee Cordell," I'd told them. "I know he exists. Try like hell to find him, will you?"

They were in luck. An old man answered the door.

"Sure, I know Terry Cordell. He gets his mail here."

"Can you tell me how you met him, how that came about?" Ken James asked.

"Let me see now . . . yeah, I 'member that. I'm sitting out on the front steps, just sitting there, and he come down the street. Said 'You got a room to rent?' And I told him I did, but he said what he really wanted was a place to get his mail. Wondered, would I be willing to let him get his mail at my house if he paid me for it. I said sure; I can always use the money. That's the first time I seen him."

"Did he—" Wallace began, but Calvin Ingles wasn't finished.

"He come back later, wanted to know would I go with him to take his driving test. Said he'd pay me ten dollars if I'd drive him. An' I done it. Got paid ten dollars."

"Do you remember the kind of car he drove?"

"Vega. One a' them Vegas. Dark one. I'm not sure, but I think it was black. We went down and he took his test. 'Bout ten days later his license come here to the house. Then he come picked it up."

"Do you remember if he had a briefcase with him?"

"Yeah. He did. I don't 'member nothing much about it. Had it in the car when we went to get his license."

"Can you describe it, or tell us anything about it?"

"Nah. . . . It was new, I could tell that. Wasn't old or nothing like that. It was new. That's all I 'member. Wasn't banged up or nothing."

"Do you think you could recognize him?"

"Sure, He came around four times, maybe five. Young guy. 'Bout thirty. Wore nice clothes. Looked like an insurance salesman. I'd know him."

"Mrs. Ingles, I'm going to hand you this sheet. It's got six pictures on it, and I'd like you—"

"It's number three."

"You're positive?"

"Yep. That's him. That's Cordell."

"Do you remember if he got any other mail?"

"Yeah, my wife said he got a letter from the Social Security. Thought it was a card, but she wasn't sure. It was from the Social Security, though. She says he got a couple of things from the airlines. We got a letter here now. You want to see it? It's from a drug company."

"Yes. We'll look at it in a minute. Do you remember if he got any other mail?"

"Nah. Jest them. Weren't no more than five or six letters."

"Can you tell me when it was that you first met him? When was it that he first asked to use your address to get his mail?"

"Onliest thing I can tell you was it was summer. It was warm. I'm sitting on the step. 'Bout a year and a half ago. Something like that. 'Bout a year and a half."

After tape-recording a statement from Mr. Ingles and his wife, the agents thanked them for their help and left.

That afternoon Wallace and Janes telephoned me in Tucson. They had already called once, the night before to report on the Nancy Henry interview, and I had made them promise to call back as soon as they had something on Cordell.

"We found him," Janes began, without saying hello.

"Who? Cordell?"

"Yeah, and you're not going to believe where."

"Try me."

"Terry Lee Cordell is in the Henrytown State Mental Hospital, here in Maryland."

"A mental patient. Well, I'll be damned."

"At the Henrytown State Hospital," said Janes, putting emphasis on the first part of the name.

"Yeah, I caught it. I'll be damned," I answered again, trying to think.

"He's been a patient in mental institutions most of his life. He's considered hopeless. He'll probably always be in some kind of institution."

"Ken, get his medical records! Check to see who's treated him."

"We already checked the records."

"Good work. What do they show?"

"You guessed it. Terry Lee Cordell has been treated at the University of Maryland Hospital. He's been to their dermatology department three times. And you're not going to believe the next part." Ken paused, to be sure my curiosity was sufficiently piqued. It was.

Janes continued. "He was treated in 1974, before Patrick Henry got there, then again August 3, 1976, and then on September 14, also in 1976." He paused again, this time to let it sink in. It took a second or two.

"Ken, do you realize what this means? What you're telling me is, he's been preparing this whole thing since the summer of 1976. He came to Tucson in December of '77—that's almost a year and a half later. My God! No wonder we're having so much trouble. He's been preparing for a year and a half to do this."

"Yeah, but there's something strange." He told me about finding Calvin Ingles, and what Ingles had said about the mail drop and the driver's test. I was pleased to hear that Ingles had picked Patrick Henry, without any hesitation, out of the photo lineup.

"When did Ingles meet him?" I asked.

"He can't say for sure, just some time in the summer. All he remembers is that he was sitting outside on his steps when Cordell first walked up. But it was summer, and he says about a year and a half ago, which fits: summer, 1976."

"Beautiful. Nice going."

"Yeah, but here's the strange part. Ed Witterman got the Motor Vehicle Department to check their records. Terry Cordell applied for a learner's permit in July of 1976."

"So? What's the problem? I don't see it."

"Henry applied for the learner's permit in July of 1976, using the name Terry Cordell. But Cordell wasn't taken to the hospital for treatment until August. How did Henry know about Cordell in July? Where did he get that name two months before Cordell was even brought to the hospital?"

"I see what you mean. Maybe he just lifted the name from a file in the records. . . ."

"I don't think so. Cordell is just about his age. He knew who he was choosing."

"You're sure Cordell didn't visit the hospital between 1974 and August of '76?"

"There's no record of it."

"Wait a minute! Maybe Patrick Henry treated him earlier and then destroyed the record of that visit."

"That's possible, I guess."

"Sure, he could have treated him earlier in the summer and destroyed the record so Cordell's file didn't show any mention of Patrick Henry."

"That's possible. He has access to all records. He wasn't the treating physician for the August or September visits, but as long as Cordell was a patient in the Dermatology department he had access to his file."

"That's it. He took one of their patients and recreated him on paper. Are you getting all the records? Social Security, post office box, records from motor vehicles?"

"Witterman's going to follow up on all records. He's getting everything for us."

"Have him send me everything with Cordell's signature on it. I want to run handwriting analysis."

"We'll have everything."

"Can you believe this? He took a mental patient and lifted his identity. What kind of witness will Calvin Ingles make, Ken? Tell me more about him."

"He's an older man, not in the best of health. White, poor. He lives in a bad section of the city in what they call a row house. By the way, he lives near the university hospital. It's an easy walk. He'll make a good witness too; he's honest, real down to earth, and he's sure he can identify Cordell. I didn't tell him who Cordell really is."

"Good, don't. I don't want him to know."

Having given me the most important news, Janes then reported on his other activities in Baltimore. He and Wallace had interviewed the other doctors in the Dermatology department. Some of them had gone to the convention in Dallas with Dr. Henry, but not one of them remembered seeing him there after the first day. They'd joked about it, in fact. He did not attend any of the classes, and no one saw him anywhere else.

The most useful information came from Dr. Ira Berman, who mentioned that whenever there was an out-of-state conference or convention, he and Dr. Henry usually roomed together. But on this trip, they only shared a room for the first night. The next day Pat Henry arranged to move to a single at the Ramada Inn. When Dr. Berman asked if something was the matter, Dr. Henry told him that it wasn't anything against him personally, it was just a private matter of Dr. Henry's.

When asked if he remembered Dr. Henry's luggage, Dr. Berman recalled that as soon as they moved into the room, Dr. Henry had put his luggage in the closet and closed the door. He did recall, however, that he thought one of the items was a briefcase, although he could not be positive. He described it as being brown leather, with metal corners. He was unable to recall if it had initials on it. Dr. Berman admitted, as did every other doctor they interviewed who had attended the convention, that he hadn't seen Dr. Henry after the first day.

The next doctor they talked to was Patrick Henry himself. We didn't expect to take him by surprise—Nancy Henry would have told him of the visit she'd received, and Wallace, Janes, and Witterman had been at the hospital for several hours that day interviewing the doctors. Still, it was worth the effort. There was always the chance he inadvertently might say something. And besides, all the investigators were anxious to see the man for themselves.

Janes remembered the report filed by agents Rand and Lloyd when they arrested Henry, and he was particularly anxious to see the stare they had both described. "Looked right through me," Lloyd had said on the telephone. "Just like I wasn't there. He looks right at you, but he seems to focus someplace nine feet behind your back."

That was precisely what happened to Janes that day.

"The stare is the first thing you notice when he walks into a room," Janes told me. "He just stares right through you. Witterman started reading him his rights, and halfway through Dr. Henry says, 'Just let me say one thing. I do not wish to talk to you people. I have an attorney in Tucson. All questions should be directed to that attorney.' He sounded like a computer delivering a speech. we didn't ask him anything else. He didn't want anything to do with us."

The last doctor interviewed that day was Dr. Joseph Burnett, the head of the hospital Dermatology department. Wallace and Janes had spoken to him briefly, earlier in the day, to let him know their purpose in being at the hospital. On both occasions, Dr. Burnett had vouched for Patrick Henry. He considered him a fine young man and an excellent physician. That went along with the other interviews they'd done that day. None of the doctors had criticized Dr. Henry's performance as a physician, though several had admitted that they didn't associate with him.

Witterman, Wallace, and Janes were not there to argue or persuade anyone. They listened to Dr. Burnett and made mental notes that they would later commit to written reports on the conversation. Before they left his office, Janes asked

Dr. Burnett if it was possible to check the department's records for a person by the name of Terry Lee Cordell. What they wanted to know, he explained, were the dates on which Mr. Cordell had been treated.

Dr. Burnett sent for the file and checked it himself for the information. He did not let the agents look at the file, which was confidential, and they did not tell him why they were interested in Cordell. That was how they had obtained the treatment dates Janes had discussed with me earlier.

"Oh—one thing I forgot," Janes said as he was winding up his report. "When someone takes a driver's test in Maryland they record the license number of the vehicle used to take the test. Terry Lee Cordell took the test in a Chevrolet Vega Hatchback, license number ERJ-037. Well, I checked with the Maryland Department of Motor Vehicles. A Chevy Vega with that license number is registered to Dr. Patrick Henry and his wife Nancy."

I was exhilarated and so was Janes. We both felt we were on a roll. The next day he and Wallace were leaving Baltimore for Dallas and El Paso. Perhaps there they would find the answers to our biggest problem—the missing briefcase.

Ed Witterman subsequently obtained, and sent to us, all the records relating to the Cordell identification Dr. Henry had been carrying when he was arrested. There was an application filed with the Maryland Bureau of Vital Records for the birth certificate. All Department of Motor Vehicle records, Social Security administration records, and post office records were included. No library card records were available. Each record bore the signature of someone claiming to be Terry Cordell; they all appeared to be identical. Later on, the handwriting experts at the Arizona Department of Public Safety confirmed that impression. All the signatures had been written by the same person. But that person could not have been the real Terry Cordell. Records at the Henrytown State Mental Hospital had revealed that the real Terry Cordell was incapable of signing his own name.

While Janes and Wallace were busy out of state, we were not idle at home. Carol Eley prepared a forty-five-page memorandum on the law of attempted murder, citing cases from every jurisdiction in the United States that supported our position: that taking the briefcase with the tools and weapons to the scene of the crime was sufficient evidence to prove the crime of attempted murder. Federal law, state cases, different penal codes, and law review articles were cited. This put us in good shape legally. What we still needed, badly, was evidence. As always, that led me back to the briefcase.

I thought of the list found in Dr. Henry's notes. The cutters, the string, the stain, and the box had all been found in the briefcase with the broken handle. The batteries, presumably, were in a tape recorder somewhere. And the meat, also presumably, was missing because it had been eaten by Champo. The murder plan had said as much: "Feed dogs." No matter how I ran it down, the conclusion was always the same: there had to be traces of drugs or poison in the vomitus. Regardless of the lab analysis, there just had to be. I decided to recheck.

The ATF chemist, Daniel Garner, was certain of his findings. We were discussing them when he said emphatically, "I'm certain we're right. We checked for them both; there were no traces of either."

"Wait a minute," I interjected. "What do you mean you checked for them *both*? Both of what?"

"The two clear liquids in the briefcase. There were no traces of either in the material you sent us."

"You mean the acetone and the lighter fluid. But what about any drugs or poisons in the vomitus?"

"We weren't requested to check for those. Besides, this lab doesn't do drug analysis. You'd have to send it to the Drug Enforcement Authority. We were asked to check the substance for the chemicals in the briefcase. That's all. If you still want a drug screen, take it to a toxicologist. We just don't do that."

I was angry and happy at the same time. There had been a screw-up somewhere, but at last now there was still hope. As long as we still had our sample. "Is our sample okay? Did your analysis, whatever you did, damage it at all? Is there a chance of having it rechecked?"

"Yes, it's still good. What we do is put the whole sample in a beaker. Then we add the solvent, the pentane, which extracts the chemicals present. Then we evaporate the solvent. The dried residue that remains is what you have left. If there's any poison in there, you can still find it; there should be enough to check."

"Can you send the sample back to us immediately?"

"It's in the mail. I'll also send you a sample of the solvent."

We *were* on a roll! Now I was convinced of it. If we could show that the dog had in fact been poisoned, we'd have our "act in furtherance" of the intent to murder.

In terms of new information or evidence Dallas was a washout. Wallace and Janes spent most of their time re-interviewing agents and witnesses and rechecking information we already had. They visited American Airlines security to be certain that all flight information we'd previously obtained from them was accurate. In doing so they came across a computer printout showing how Terry Cordell had changed flights at the last minute, from the 9:05 to the 9:20. The printout gave the code number of the ticket agent who had made the change in reservations. But when the agent was shown a photograph of Dr. Henry and told about the disguise he might have been wearing, he was unable to identify the person or even recall the transaction.

The Dallas Hilton Inn and the Ramada Inn on the Central Expressway were both checked for their records of Dr. Henry's stay and for any additional information they could provide. At the Ramada Inn Wallace and Janes thought they might have found something. The day after Dr. Henry was arrested, a Dallas Lawyer who had been hired by the doctor called the Ramada Inn. He asked them to pack his client's belongings and hold them for pickup.

Wallace and Janes quickly located the bellboy who had done the packing and asked him about Dr. Henry's luggage. The young man just shrugged. He vaguely recalled a suitcase and camera case, but could not be sure if there was any other luggage.

El Paso proved more interesting. Routinely checking the lost luggage records at American Airlines, Wallace and Janes were able to locate the original teletype sent from Tucson by Randall Butler on the morning of the sixth. The teletype asked American to check all its baggage areas for a type-43 black briefcase bearing the initials "P.H."

What was important were the words hand printed on the top of the teletype: "Not at." This notation meant that the case in question had not been found in American's baggage area at El Paso.

Excited now, Wallace and Janes went looking for the agent who had printed those words. The writing was identified as that of Donald Lang, an employee who had recently retired. Wallace and Janes found him at home and showed him the teletype, hoping he wouldn't say he simply couldn't remember.

Donald Lang did remember. He had searched the baggage area the night the teletype was received and had been unable to locate the briefcase. Afterward he had written, "Not at" on the teletype.

Wallace and Janes were elated. As the one who had made the search for the briefcase, Donald Lang could testify that, contrary to the information on the delayed luggage claim in Tucson, the briefcase had not been located in El Paso at American Airlines. It was the break we needed.

Mr. Lang could see that they were pleased with his information. "I have to tell you something, though," he went on. "Just because I didn't find it, that doesn't mean that someone else couldn't have. Someone else could have looked later, and found it, and sent it on, without making any record of it."

Continental Airlines said the same. They had no record of having located the briefcase, but that didn't mean they hadn't. There was no way to check; records aren't necessarily kept when a piece of luggage is forwarded.

Frustrated and disappointed, Wallace and Janes prepared to come home. Then Janes had an idea. To prove his theory of the two briefcases, he would reenact the steps he was sure Dr. Henry must have taken.

Returning to the Dallas–Fort Worth airport, he checked his own suitcase and briefcase as baggage, but only as far as El Paso. When he and Wallace arrived there, Janes picked up his suitcase and left the briefcase behind in the baggage area. Then he checked the suitcase aboard their flight from El Paso to Tucson, which is what Dr. Henry would have had to do with the briefcase containing the gun, knife, and ammunition.

The demonstration was convincing: when they arrived in Tucson, Janes had a briefcase back in El Paso and, waiting down in the baggage area, a suitcase that was full—theoretically—of weapons and burglary tools.

Except it wasn't waiting. Down in the baggage area they

watched in disbelief as the conveyor belt slowly emptied of other passengers' luggage. Janes stood there, glaring at the belt, until it made its tenth unencumbered turn. He was furious. His briefcase was now back in El Pasco, and the suitcase he'd checked aboard the Tucson flight was lost. With Wallace razzing him every step of the way, Janes stalked to the Continental counter and filled out a delayed baggage claim.

When Janes and Wallace returned, we spent hours together analyzing the new information they had developed. By far the most exciting was that Dr. Henry possessed two briefcases, and even his wife didn't know he'd taken the one with the broken handle. This was important to know, but impossible to use in court. If I were to put Wallace or Janes on the stand and ask what Nancy Henry had told them, the defense attorney would object that their testimony was hearsay, and the objection would be sustained. Nancy herself could give the testimony, but there was no way I could compel her to testify against her husband. Under the law, I couldn't even call her to the stand. We had the information but still no way to prove it.

Taking a mental patient's identity and using it to help him commit a crime would be key evidence. Not only would it show how long and carefully Dr. Henry had prepared, but it would also support Christina Henry's testimony that he was devious and cunning. I would not try to put the real Terry Cordell on the stand. A simple description of his condition, offered by a psychiatrist, would be damaging enough to Henry's defense.

The information I liked least was the doctors' agreement that after the third of December no one had seen Dr. Henry at the conference. Off on his own for two days he could have been up to anything—for example, he could have made a preliminary run to Tucson and placed his briefcase in a safe spot where he could find it later. On the same trip he could have arranged to borrow a car or to have one left at the airport for him. We had never been able to find a cab or limousine driver who remembered him, and no car had been rented under any of his known aliases. He could have hitched a ride, of course, but perhaps on this preliminary trip he had set up a rental using yet another set of false I.D.

Personally, I didn't believe Dr. Henry had reconnoitered in advance. He seemed to be too much of a cheapskate to pay for two trips when, with careful planning, one would suffice.

The information from El Paso was the most provocative. Donald Lang's testimony about the lost briefcase was inconclusive as evidence, but invaluable in a different way. It turned our investigation in the direction of a new possibility: that there was only one briefcase after all, and Patrick Henry had never really been parted from it.

Instead of leaving a second, decoy briefcase in El Paso, perhaps he had simply concealed the one he was carrying in the Tucson airport, then gone to the counter and told Randall Butler it had been lost en route. The next day, when he returned to the airport, he went back to the Continental counter and reported that his case had been returned by another airline. Taking his word for it, Horace Smith had filled out the recovery information and "Terry Cordell" had signed the bottom of the form. *Voilà*: documented proof that Terry Cordell—that is, Dr. Patrick Henry—could not have carried weapons to 1409 East Broadway.

When we experimented to see if this kind of falsification was possible, we discovered that it was. In fact, it was easy.

Detective Janes went out to the airport and walked up to the Continental counter. He told the agent there that he had previously filed a delayed luggage claim, but now the bag had been returned by another airline. The agent produced the delayed luggage claim Janes had completed a few days before and together they filled out the recovery information. Janes signed it. Later on he talked to a supervisor and was told that the counter staff would probably be too busy ever to contact the other airline to verify the recovery.

"Off the record," the supervisor told Janes, "the chances of our verifying information like that is between remote and zero. And why should we? All we really need is your signature on the form acknowledging you got the bag back. Why would someone say they got it back when they didn't?"

Janes approached several other airlines and found the same system in operation. As long as the passenger had previously filed a delayed baggage claim, he could report the bag found and the form would be presented without question for his signature. Problems arose only when an airline was big enough to have its own luggage department at the airport. If American, for example, found a Tucson passenger's bag in another city, they would forward it to their own luggage department at Tucson International. The passenger would have to go there, not to the counter, to sign for the bag and get it back.

In other words, if American had found Dr. Henry's briefcase in El Paso and returned it, there would most likely be a record. Janes immediately went to American's luggage department and inquired. There was no record of their returning such a briefcase. This strengthened our growing belief that Henry had simply filed a false luggage claim—but we still couldn't prove anything. And we still had no idea where in the airport he could have safely concealed the briefcase.

We were back to zero: a theory and no evidence. Patrick Henry was a lucky son of a bitch, I thought. Even someone as devious and painstaking as he was could not have anticipated all the obstacles we would encounter in our search for solid proof. I gave him credit for dreaming up the false luggage claim; I just couldn't believe he had foreseen all the difficulties involved in proving anything about luggage movement one way or the other. I refused to give him that much credit.

It didn't matter, of course, what mark I gave Patrick Henry on his report card. Regardless of how I felt about it, his plan was working to perfection.

Less than a week after he returned from Baltimore, Ken Janes got a call from Christina Henry. She wanted to know how long she had to keep the sweepings from the nursery school.

"What sweepings, Mrs. Henry? I don't know what you mean."

"The ones Mr. Wallace asked me to keep. We've kept them since he told us, but if you don't want them, we'll throw them away. Is that all right?"

"What kind of sweepings?"

"They're from the school. Mr. Wallace told me to save whatever we swept up."

"When was this?"

"When he called that first time to say that Mr. Stevens wanted to see me. I told him the state inspectors were scheduled to inspect the nursery school. My mother and I were cleaning the place up and getting it ready. When I told Mr.

Wallace, he said to save whatever we swept up. I guess I forgot to tell you when you came over here and took everything.

"I'll be right there. Keep everything just as it is."

When Janes got to the school Mrs. Henry presented him with a cardboard box. Inside were approximately an inch of dirt, dust, lint, hair, and other sweepings. Janes asked for a newspaper and spread it on the floor, then emptied out the box's contents. As he knelt down to get a closer look, a blue-green capsule was the first thing to draw his attention.

"Where did this come from?"

Mrs. Henry looked down to see what he was referring to. "Oh, mother found that on the floor in the kitchen. The nursery school kitchen. It was behind a pipe."

"Can you show me?"

Mrs. Henry took him over to the school and pointed out the spot. It was behind a pipe that had been freshly painted. The linoleum floor was almost the same color as the capsule.

"Mother found it and put it in this cupboard here and that's where I found it," she explained. "It looked like medicine so she just didn't think she should throw it away."

Examining the capsule closely, Janes saw the word Roche stamped on it. He took the capsule and everything else in the box back to the office for further analysis.

When the vomitus material came back from the ATF laboratory, I had Janes pick it up and deliver it to the Pima County Coroner's Office to be examined by their toxicologist. The blue-green capsule was also submitted for identification.

This time I took no chances. I called the coroner's office myself and asked them to test specifically for the kind of drugs found on Dr. Henry at the time of his arrest.

I knew it would be at least a week before we could expect the results. On the fifth day I told myself to be patient; they would be calling soon. On the seventh day I couldn't wait any longer to know about the vomitus; I picked up the phone and dialed Dr. Louis Hirsch, the coroner.

"Randy, how are you? I was just about to call you."

"I'm fine, doc, thanks. Have you got any results yet on the stuff I sent you?" As I asked the question I'm sure I stopped breathing, waiting for his answer.

"No, there's a problem. The toxicologist needs more samples of the grass where the vomit was found. He wants to be sure that what he's picking up isn't a plant chemical. Can you send someone to get grass samples from several different places in the yard?''

''I'll get them to you right away.'' As soon as I hung up I called Ken Janes. The samples were at the laboratory in less than an hour. We would now have to wait even longer, but it had sounded encouraging: ''He wants to be sure what he's picking up isn't a plant chemical.''

Several more days went by. Each morning and afternoon Ken Janes or Carol Eley would invariably stop by my office to see if I'd heard anything. When the call came I didn't bother with pleasantries.

''What'd you find, doc?''

''The sample is negative. We can't identify any drugs or poisons in the sample. The capsule you sent us is chlordiazepoxide.''

''Damn it to hell. I was so sure.'' I had felt positive they would find something in the vomitus.

''Sorry. Do you want me to keep everything for court?''

I almost answered, ''You know someone who's going to court?'' Instead I asked him to keep everything and consider it potential evidence. The capsule was chlordiazepoxide, the same drug that was in one of the capsules Steve Rand took from Dr. Henry in Dallas. That was something. It had been found in the school, indicating that Dr. Henry had indeed been there. But, as always in this case, there was a catch.

Neither Mrs. Henry nor her mother could swear that the capsule had not been present on the schoolhouse floor prior to the night of December 5. Neither of them had cleaned behind that pipe for some time. They had painted not too long before Dr. Henry's appearance, and would probably have seen the capsule then, if it had been there—but even that they couldn't say positively.

I asked Mrs. Henry to find out if anyone in her family was on medication, and if so, what kind. I also asked her to call Mrs. Kempf, the woman from whom she had bought the schoolhouse, and ask her what kind of medication she had been taking during the last year she had lived in the house.

Mrs. Henry called back the next day. Neither her family nor Mrs. Kempf had ever taken medication in the form of that kind of capsule.

It was several days later that I ran into Dr. Hirsch. As

coroner, he often came to our office to meet with a prosecutor before testifying in court. He was on his way out the door when I stopped him.

"Hey, doc, isn't there a chance you could be wrong about that vomitus?"

"I doubt it. One test was inconclusive and the other was negative."

"Inconclusive? Which test was that?"

"The gas layer chromatography. Its graph was similar to the drug you were interested in, but not close enough for us to identify it. The second test was negative."

"Is there any way to get a more precise reading on the gas layer?"

"Not in our lab. The university has the equipment, but we don't. You'd need a mass spectrometer."

"You mean there's still a possibility? We've still got a chance at it?"

"It's worth a try."

"Do me a favor, doc. Find out the best laboratory in the United States for that kind of test. I don't care what it costs. I can't take a chance with anything but the best facility possible."

"I'll call you."

As soon as I could get to my office I called a friend of mine, Dr. Richard Froede, a forensic pathologist on the staff of the university medical college. He immediately suggested the Center for Human Toxicology at the University of Utah in Salt Lake City. "It's one of the best, Randy," he said. "If not the very best."

Dr. Hirsch called back with the same recommendation. At my request, his office mailed the evidence to Dr. Brian Finkle at the center in Salt Lake City. Then the wait started again.

I tried not to fixate on this particular piece of evidence, but it was difficult. We had nothing else, not one piece of evidence we could take to court to show that Dr. Henry was trying to follow through with his plan. We couldn't refute Henry's claim that he didn't have his luggage by standing up and saying, "But it's possible he had two cases. Or, he could have had one but hidden it someplace. . . . We don't know where or how, but it's possible." We needed proof.

During those days that we were waiting, no matter what I was doing my mind would turn to the Henry case. People would speak to me and I wouldn't hear them. It was especially unsettling to pull into my garage in the evening and realize I didn't remember driving home. And concentrating on a book or movie was out of the question. Yet from past experience I'd learned that this kind of preoccupation was very productive. It usually meant that the subconscious mind had joined up as a working partner in the investigation. The more I consciously thought about facts, ideas, images, and possibilities, the more data I was providing for my subconscious. If I was lucky it would eventually come up with some answers for me, probably at some totally unexpected moment.

As always, it was the briefcase that had me stymied. It was one thing to say that he had concealed the case for several hours while loudly complaining that it was lost. It was another to figure out where he had put it.

We had already surveyed the terminal once without finding any suitable hiding places. And the more I thought about Dr. Henry, the less likely it seemed that he would risk hiding the case in an unsuitable spot, where it might be discovered. He would certainly have known that airport security was always on the alert for packages and suitcases found abandoned in nonbaggage areas. Where had the briefcase been during those hours he stayed at the airport? What had he done with it?

The answer floated up around 3:30 one morning. I had been asleep, dreaming about the briefcase, then awake worrying about it, when suddenly I had the answer. It was so simple I was embarrassed.

On the delayed luggage claim Dr. Henry had deliberately described his briefcase incorrectly. He had told Randall Butler that his initials, P.H., were on the case. But they weren't. There were no initials on the case we had in evidence.

At first, when we had theorized the existence of a second briefcase, the initials had not presented a problem. We had assumed it was this second briefcase he had been describing. Later on, when we decided there was only one case, we still didn't think much about the initials. Perhaps he had removed them himself, to make the case more anonymous looking; later, in his nervousness at the Continental counter, he'd forgotten about doing so and described the case as it had always been.

But Dr. Henry was not a man to forget a precaution, and I should have known that. As I lay there, berating myself, another thought suddenly struck me. If I had been asked to look at the delayed luggage claim and choose the prototype of Dr. Henry's briefcase I wouldn't have selected illustration number 43. The edges on Dr. Henry's case were more rounded than squared, and the case opened in equal halves, more like the case in illustration 44 than 43. Type 43 was close; but not the closest.

Dr. Henry had described a case just slightly different from the one we had in evidence. Then, to make sure, he had thrown in the initials. Anyone searching the Tucson airport for the lost briefcase would have been looking for one bearing the initials P.H. Dr. Henry could have left the case in the baggage claim area, right out in the open, but anyone looking for type 43 with initials P.H. would have passed it right by. At 2:30, when he was ready to leave for Tucson, he had simply left the Continental counter, returned to the baggage claim area, and picked it up again.

That had to be it! I sat up, turned on the lights, and started writing frantically. Like the other theories we'd come up with, this one couldn't be proved. But unlike the other theories, this one gave me something I could use in court. We had the delayed luggage claim containing the description Dr. Henry had given. And we had the briefcase. At the very least I could point out the discrepancies to the jury, and hope they might begin to wonder if there wasn't a reason why he had lied.

It was the fact that I now had something, no matter how tenuous, to challenge the lost luggage claim that made up my mind: we would file charges. We would submit the case to the grand jury. Aside from the chance that the vomitus material might contain a drug or poison, most of the facts of our case had been determined by now. Those that were still unknown probably always would be, because there were no witnesses, no records, no trace evidence. Even if the vomitus tested negative, we could still continue the prosecution, basing our case on Christina Henry's testimony and on her father's, the "murder plan" on the stationery, and the surveillance notes. We might get trounced, but I didn't think so. If we could get in evidence just a few of the things Patrick Henry had done to his wife during their marriage we'd have a fair chance. One thing I knew we'd never get in was the time he'd instructed her to give the narcotic to the baby. Had she kept the capsule it might have been a different situation, but as it stood we had no proof.

Although the decision to proceed was made, it was clear that we were far from ready for a trial. The most important factor was that Mrs. Henry was emotionally unprepared. When I'd first mentioned that she would be our primary witness, she had almost come apart.

"Mr. Stevens, I can't! I can't do it! I can't be in the same room with him. I don't want to be anywhere near him. Can't it be done without me? I just can't be in a room with him."

Her fear of Patrick Henry had been obvious from our first interview. But it wasn't until the day she was hypnotized that I really understood the depth of that fear. Five times Dr. Lindsey or Dr. Russell had had to stop the interview and calm her down. When she'd looked up at her imaginary screen and thought she'd recognized Dr. Henry, she'd started to panic; the same thing had happened when she'd recognized his voice during the phone call, and at several other points. Her voice became loud and excited, then she began to shake and cry. The doctors had to stop and remind her she was at the police department and was safe.

"Christina, we can't make a case without your testimony. Without you we've got nothing."

"But they won't believe me. No one's going to believe what I say about him." She was utterly convinced of that, and I knew why—Patrick Henry had done an excellent job of cowing and terrorizing her.

"If we go to trial, Christina, they'll certainly try to disprove whatever you say. But we expect that; we'll be ready for them. That's my job, and I can do it. Your job is to decide that you can stand up to him."

"I don't know." Her face was full of fear, and she paused for a long time. "At the custody hearings it was frightening to be near him. He keeps staring at me. You'll see. It's the look on his face, the eyes. If he does that to me in the courtroom I won't be able to think. He looks at you—"

"When we go to trial—Christina, listen to me. When we go to trial, you're going to be able to stare him right in the eyes. From the first moment you're going to stare straight back at him, and he's going to know he's finished. You're going to meet his eyes, and hold his stare, and believe me, he'll know."

"I can't! I can't!"

"Yes, you can. You will. You'll be ready for him. I'll ge
you ready. You're going to look right at him and have n
fear."

"I don't know. I don't know. We've talked about him
Everything he's done. He was right outside our home. H
was in the school that morning, I know he was. Waiting fo
me." She was staring directly at me now, tears visible in he
eyes. "I'm so afaird of him. When he knows I've told yo
about him, that I've dared to tell you . . . he'll get me fo
that. He'll never forgive me for that." She looked desperate
as if she wanted to run away.

"That's why you don't have a choice."

She started as if she had been struck. Her voice wa
suddenly resigned. "I know," she said. "I've known it since
the first day I came to your office. If I told you everything
I'd have to go to court. I don't know how I will, but I'll try.'

"I'll have you ready, don't worry about that. When we go
you won't be afraid, you'll see."

She looked at me anxiously. "Mr. Stevens, just remembe
what I've been trying to tell you—he can fool anyone. He'
done it for years. He'll sit there pretending to be perfectly al
right, and he'll fool them. I've seen him do it over and over
He's a doctor; he knows how to act, how to be the perfec
person. They'll look at him and see the person he's pretending to be, and they'll believe him. You'll see, Mr. Stevens
He'll fool them. You'll see."

What I did see that day was that we would need months to
prepare Christina Henry mentally for the trial. Her fear and
almost total lack of confidence would take a long time to
overcome. Considering the nature of the case, she would
probably be on the witness stand for several days, being
cross-examined, attacked, and challenged on everything she
said. We had a lot of work to do, but I knew we'd have
plenty of time.

Dr. Henry was living and working in Maryland; my charges
would be brought in Arizona. Those two facts almost guaranteed him a year's grace between his indictment and the trial
He would not appear in court here voluntarily, and to extra-
dite him I would have to prove, first, that a crime had been
committed in Arizona, and second, that Patrick Henry was
the one who had committed it. Knowing how weak our proof

was, he would undoubtedly fight extradition all the way, from the lowest courts to the highest.

That was fine with me. We would use that time to prepare Mrs. Henry, to build up her confidence, and to dig up every piece of evidence that could corroborate what she would be saying on the stand. The dilemma was Dr. Henry's. Knowing what a faint trail he'd left he probably assumed, correctly, that we had very little physical evidence. And I was sure he knew how terrified his ex-wife would feel at the prospect of testifying. For a gambling man, the best strategy would be to waive extradition, demand an immediate trial, and watch our case fly apart in the courtroom. But I didn't think Dr. Henry would take that gamble. He couldn't be positive that some critical piece of evidence had not turned up. And his chances of successfully fighting extradition were too good; he wouldn't dare waive them. He'd fight us all the way.

On the seventh of March 1978, I presented the case to the grand jury. Ken Janes was the only witness I called. In grand jury proceedings hearsay testimony is allowed, so Janes was able to put the whole story on the record, including events he had not personally witnessed.

Deliberately omitting Christina's story about what had happened during the marriage, we began with Gene Zarr and the events at Tucson International airport. Janes narrated all the events leading up to the arrest in Dallas, then backed up to what Mrs. Henry and her father had seen and heard on the night of December 5 and morning of December 6.

I could see the jurors were enthralled. Janes finished up by revealing what he and Wallace had discovered in Baltimore— who the real Terry Cordell was, and how Patrick Henry, a physician, had used this mental patient to create himself a false identity.

When Janes stopped speaking there was dead silence. The jurors sat quietly, letting everything sink in. But after a while it occurred to them—as it had to all of us—that although this was an amazing story, there really wasn't any crime.

Slowly and carefully I explained the legal basis for the crime of attempted murder, but I could see they were still troubled. I talked about the precedent-setting California case, and how it defined the legal consequences of taking weapons to the scene of a crime. But I could still read it in their faces: "What's the crime?"

There was nothing more I could do. As a prosecutor my role before a grand jury is not to testify. My function is to present the evidence and explain the law. Once I'd given the jurors the best legal explanation I could, I advised them that additional witnesses were available if they wanted them. Then I formally submitted the case, and left the room with Janes so they could deliberate.

I was not optimistic, and was even less so when they called us back after only a few minutes. But the jurors surprised me. They had returned a true bill, allowing us to file an indictment in superior court. I don't believe they ever really understood the legality of the crime of attempted murder. But they had listened to everything Dr. Henry had done and figured that he had to be guilty of something.

No matter. That afternoon Dr. Patrick G. Henry was charged with Attempting to Murder Christina Bellios Henry. After a special hearing, bond was set in the amount of $250,000. All paper work was immediately sent to the Baltimore County prosecutor's office, notifying them of the warrant and the amount of bond.

On the tenth of March Dr. Patrick Henry was arrested on our warrant. He was subsequently released on a bond of $100,000, placing his home and another piece of property as security. Then he went back to work at the University of Maryland Hospital, and we began the long months of preparation for trial.

Shortly after the indictment was filed I received a phone call from a Michael Peat, who introduced himself as the associate director of the Center for Human Toxicology in Salt Lake City. He was the forensic toxicologist to whom our dog vomitus had been assigned for testing. In a very British accent he informed me that there was a problem.

"It seems the evaporation flask containing your samples shattered while in the mail."

"You mean that the sample was destroyed?" I couldn't believe our bad luck.

"Not exactly. I've examined the glass shards and there's a greenish, dry residue adhering to them in a couple of places. I don't know if that's going to be enough, but I'm certainly going to try."

A broken bottle. After all we'd been through, the bottle

broke in the mail. Michael Peat thought he could work with what was left of the sample, but if his results were positive, that broken bottle might make his analysis inadmissible in court.

Whenever evidence undergoes analysis, the burden is on the prosecutor to show that its integrity has been maintained from the time it was taken into possession until the time it was analyzed. This is called "establishing a chain of evidence," to show that the sample in question has not been changed, spoiled, altered, destroyed, or contaminated.

In such a case, the officer who seized the evidence would testify exactly what he did with it after taking it into possession. The property or evidence supervisor might be asked to prove that the evidence was not tampered with, or changed, while he held it in property. Then the chemist would be called to testify that he had done nothing that might have altered the evidence before he performed his analysis. If one of the witnesses in the chain testifies that he did do something that could have altered the evidence, there are problems. The judge might rule that the evidence was no longer reliable and prohibit the prosecutor from exhibiting it or mentioning it to the jury.

Already the chain of evidence on the dog vomitus was complicated:

> Ken Janes collected vomit-stained grass and dirt in the Bellios yard.
>
> Janes delivered scrapings to ATF Agent Lyman Schaffer.
>
> Schaffer sent scrapings to the ATF laboratory via United States Mail.
>
> Scrapings at ATF laboratory by Dr. Garner, opened by Robert Kopec, reg. mail 36709. The sample was washed with a solvent.
>
> Sample sent back to Tucson via United Parcel Service 276078.
>
> Sample picked up by Janes, delivered to Dr. Louis Hirsch at Pima County Coroner's Office.
>
> Dr. Hirsch hand carried sample to Toxicology section.
>
> Toxicologist Don Cash analyzed sample under Dr. Hirsch's upsvervision.
>
> Sample packaged by Frank Casillas, Coroner's Office, and sent via United States mail to Center for Human Toxicology, University of Utah, Salt Lake City.

I felt fairly confident that we could prove the integrity of the chain up to that point. How we would fare with a broken bottle was harder to predict. But this evidence, like Mrs. Henry's recollection under hypnosis that the briefcase handle was broken, was something we couldn't do without. I would worry about how to get both of them into evidence when we got to trial.

A week later Michael Peat called back. I had barely said hello when he announced his findings. "We've completed our examination. We used three separate procedures—high pressure liquid chromatography, gas liquid chromatography, and thin layer chromatography. All three were positive for the presence of chlordiazepoxide. Each method, independently, detected chlordiazepoxide, which, as you know, is a tranquilizer."

Chlordiazepoxide—the capsule found on Dr. Henry's person in Dallas, and the blue-green capsule found in the school. I'd been convinced all along that there had to be a drug or poison in the vomitus, but the fact that it was this particular drug was perfect.

During the many hours I had spent thinking about the case, I was often struck by the series of unlikely events and coincidences that had occurred. These were best recognized by asking a set of questions prefaced by the clause, "What if. . . .": What if Gene Zarr had not acted on his suspicions of A. Donald Vester? What if Frank Ramirez hadn't looked again and seen the wig protruding from Dr. Henry's coat pocket? What if Chuck Wallace hadn't taken time to compare the coded plan to the contents of the briefcase?

Now there were more "what ifs," occasioned by Michael Peat's findings. There had only been one chlordiazepoxide capsule left in the bottle Dr. Henry was carrying on his person. What if FBI Agent Rand had not stopped him when the doctor had asked permission to swallow some medication after he'd been arrested? What if Champo had not regurgitated the meat? What if Chuck Wallace hadn't told Christina and her mother to save the sweepings when they cleaned the school? For my own part, I had never challenged a chemist's findings before, but in this case I did so twice. What if I hadn't?

We had had an incredible string of lucky breaks. I just hoped it wouldn't be played out by the time we went to trial. That was when we would need all the luck we could get.

Christina Henry was making progress. We had invited her to work with us on decoding Dr. Henry's notes, and one day she came down to my office to look at the enlargements we'd made. To help her interpret his lists I brought out, for the first time in her presence, the briefcase and its contents. She glanced at the various items without comment, until she came to the double-edged knife and started to tremble.

Immediately I removed the briefcase, before she caught sight of the firecrackers. I was sorry to have upset her, but I had to gauge, from time to time, whether she was getting any stronger in her attitude toward Patrick Henry. Her reaction to the briefcase wasn't encouraging.

For a while we worked with the enlargements. Most of the words that puzzled us puzzled her too. In fact, she even pointed out that we'd been reading the word "oil" incorrectly.

Holding up the enlargement of the Ramada Inn stationery, she pointed to the *o*.

"If you look carefully," she said, "you'll see that there's another letter inside it. And the last letter, the one that looks like *l*—there's a movement just before that letter, so it couldn't really be an *l*."

Moving up close, I could see that she was right. There did seem to be another letter inside the *o*, and a movement before the *l* that we had not noticed before. After Mrs. Henry pointed this out, we understood even less than we had before.

Several days later Mrs. Henry called to say she thought there was another problem in the notes. Dr. Henry had listed all sorts of supplies and equipment, but there was no mention of the gun.

I told her we had noticed the omission also, but figured that when he wrote the word "box" it represented the metal box and its contents.

"No," she said. "The gun was too important a part of the plan. Pat wouldn't have left it out. I know him; it's there somewhere."

Thinking she might be right, I told her that she could take the enlargements home for the weekend to study them. She answered that she would be down as soon as possible to pick them up.

As I came into the office on Monday, Thelma said that Mrs. Henry had already called several times that morning. I called her back immediately.

"Mr. Stevens, I found it, I found it—the word *gun*. It's been right in front of us; we just didn't see it." I could feel her excitement. "It's there, it's there, you'll see."

She came down to the office just after lunch, still excited and proud of herself. Holding up the large photo showing the back side of the stationery, she pointed out the letters that we had thought meant umbrella.

"This doesn't stand for umbrella," she said. "Look—on the other side of the stationery umbrella is abbreviated 'umbr.' He wouldn't put it down twice. Now look again at these letters on the other side."

The word was the third down on that side of the page. As I looked at it, Mrs. Henry turned the photo upside down. There it was—"gun."

She was absolutely certain she was right. I was more skeptical, yet I had to admit that the word looked like *gun* when looked at upside down. But whether she was right or wrong, I was happy to see that Mrs. Henry was in there trying. She was so excited and pleased with herself that I couldn't help seeing the irony of the situation: the intended murder victim happy to find that her husband had written the word *gun* in his plan to kill her. But what mattered to me most was that she had looked at the murder plan without shrinking. In this small way, I thought, she had begun to stand up to Patrick Henry.

To conduct his defense, Patrick Henry had retained an attorney by the name of Harold Glaser, reputed to be one of the best defense lawyers in the state of Maryland. He had called once, to introduce himself, and we had talked briefly. Now he called to say that he was coming to Tucson for a few days, and we set up an appointment in my office.

After I hung up I called a criminal attorney named Benjamin Lazarow.

"Ben, I just wanted to thank you. I've got an attorney coming out here on one of the biggest cases I'm handling, and I already know his moves. Thanks to you, I know what he's going to do and say, even before he gets here."

Benjamin Lazarow was one of the best criminal lawyers in Arizona. During my second year in law school I had gotten a job clerking for him. After only a few days in his office I'd felt I should be paying for the experience of working with him.

"You stick with me," he said one day, "and I'll teach you the Jewish practice of law."

I had never heard that expression before, probably because Ben had made it up. I'd had no idea then what he'd meant by it, but I soon learned. And though I learned, I have always found it difficult to describe to others.

The best way I can define Ben's "Jewish practice of law" is to say that you must think, and then—really think. You must think before an event; you must keep thinking during the event; and you must think again afterward. In all matters, you must anticipate the actions of others. You must decide in advance what you think they will say or do. Then, if they do or say what you expected, you can read something in that. However, if they do not act or say as you expected, then you must determine why. And in the course of determining why, it is essential that you allow some degree of paranoia to enter into your mental processes.

Say you have a meeting with an adversary or someone you think is neutral. Prior to the meeting you should anticipate certain things that will occur and certain things that will be said. During the meeting you should observe and listen carefully. And if something occurs that you didn't expect—be alert, but show nothing.

If your adversary is not behaving as you expected, but seems to be driving toward the same objective you thought he would, things may be all right. But continue to stay alert. If things you had never considered start happening, watch out. Someone may be trying to *yentz* (screw) you.

When the meeting is over, go back over what occurred and look for ulterior motives. Review the actions and words. Are you reading them right? Are you sure? For added safety— worry about it for a day or so.

Ever since those days with Ben Lazarow I have devoted myself to the Jewish practice of Law. So I was ready for Harold Glaser. Days before he arrived in Tucson I told Carol Eley what I thought he would say, what he would wear, and even what he would smoke. She was amused but didn't take me too seriously. I explained that I wasn't really guessing. I knew what Harold Glaser would do because I knew what his objective was—to study his opposition, and to intimidate it.

Before he got there, I had to decide what impression I wanted to give him. He probably thought of Tucson as a cow town—maybe I should play the hick. Or maybe I should present myself as a typical western prosecutor, an inexperienced young attorney putting in time before going into private practice.

I quickly decided that both of these would be mistakes. Why? Because if Glaser was as good as the grapevine said he was, he would be thinking ahead too. He wouldn't meet with me until he'd checked out who I was, how I worked, and how many years experience I had.

I had already done the same for him. After his introductory phone call I had contacted four colleagues in Maryland—two of them state prosecutors and two of them federal. "Tell me about Harold Glaser," I'd said.

After that I had Ken Janes and Chuck Wallace talk to the police and law enforcement agencies in Baltimore. From these calls, I learned his approach, his method of pretrial dealing, his trial tactics, his degree of preparation, his cross-examination ability, his effectiveness with juries, his trial record, and his reputation in the legal and law enforcement community.

Almost unanimously he was rated excellent. One prosecutor said that he didn't trust him, but further questioning revealed that Glaser had wiped the floor with him in a trial a few weeks before. One federal officer said, "He's the F. Lee Bailey of Baltimore." This was not a man I could con into believing I was a novice. I would, however, create the image I wanted him to have.

The day we were to meet, I rolled up the sleeves of my white shirt and loosened my tie. I did not ask Thelma to hold my telephone calls after he arrived, or to tell people not to disturb me. I wanted him to feel that I hadn't thought enough of his visit to put on a suit coat, and that I was too busy to really spend much time. I wanted him to feel that I wasn't impressed with him one bit.

When he presented himself at the front desk, I deliberately made him wait for several minutes. I knew that if he was sharp, he would never sit down. He'd stand no matter how long he had to wait.

No high-priced criminal attorney would ever sit down in a prosecutor's waiting room. The minute they sit they become just like all the witnesses and law enforcement people who stream in and out of the office. By staying on their feet the defense lawyers convey that they're too important to sit— they've got things to do, and you'd better not make them wait like everyone else.

The only exception to this rule is Ben Lazarow. If someone makes him wait he laughs and sits down. He knows the game, and he makes his adversary feel silly for playing it. And somehow—I still haven't figured out how—he makes the other guy feel guilty for making him wait.

I knew I couldn't make Glaser wait too long; that would make too clear what I was up to. Seven or eight minutes seemed right. When I went out to greet him, I saw just what I had expected: he was wearing a very expensive suit, a gold pocket watch with a gold chain and fob, and was smoking a big, expensive cigar. He reeked of success, he reeked of importance, he reeked of the Eastern establishment—which was exactly what he wanted me to notice. He was also standing up.

He came back to my office and quickly took over the conversation. I had heard differert versions of his pitch many times in the past, but he was really good. He went for twenty minutes, nonstop, trying to scare the hell out of me.

"Randy, you know, I've tried cases all over the United States and it's a wonderful, wonderful experience. This case is going to be a wonderful experience, and I'm looking forward to it. I haven't been to Tucson for years. I went to college here and I haven't been back since. You know, I try cases in federal and state courts all up and down the East Coast and throughout the Midwest. I imagine you try cases all over too, don't you?"

He knew, of course, that the answer was no. I work for the Pima County Attorney's Office, and that's where I try cases. The question was designed to make me feel inferior.

"I seem to be involved in a lot of cases lately, a lot of cases in the Baltimore–Washington area. A lot of scandal cases, lots of them. When they get in trouble, I don't know why, but they always seem to come to me."

I listened patiently until I thought he had finished; then I looked directly at him and said, "Have you finished yet?" But he wouldn't be hurried.

"No, no, no," he said, "we don't have to discuss the case

yet. We don't have to get into that yet. We've got plenty of time to discuss the case.'' And off he went again. He wasn't by any means finished. He went on to give more and more information about his career and his activities. He bragged about representing Mafiosi on the East Coast, and notorious figures well-known to almost anyone in the United States. He finally finished by telling me he was involved in a bribery case involving Marvin Mandel, then the governor of Maryland. He was just about finished when I interrupted again.

"All right, Harold, let's get down to it. You're here be-cause you want to see who your opponent is. And I'm talking to you because I want to see who mine is. And if you're worth a damn, you already checked me out and you know I've checked you out.''

"Well,'' he hedged, "I've made a few inquiries, if you call that checking.''

"Let's get right down to it. You represent a doctor and he's practicing medicine and if he gets convicted of a felony, any felony, he's finished as far as his career goes. And I've got serious charges. I think your guy is an animal, dangerous as hell, and I'm not going to reduce my charges. So there's not going to be a plea agreement. You and I are going to court. It's as simple as that.''

Without hesitation, he switched to a second tactic. "Well, Randy, if we're going to court, we're going to court. But that doesn't mean we can't be friends. I always like to deal on that level; there is no need for us to be antagonists. In fact, I'd like to take you and your wife out to dinner.''

I stopped him. "Harold, we're going to war. And I'm not going to be friends with you. I'm not going to deal with you; I'm not going to socialize with you. When you walk out of this room, that's it.''

I thought I detected some annoyance, but he quickly switched to yet a third approach. "Well, Randy, why don't you do this for me. Why don't you give me the name of someone who used to work for you, some good prosecutor who's left here to go into private practice. He might enjoy trying this case with me. I'd love to have somebody like that on board. It would be a marvelous experience for him.''

I answered. "You're not listening. I'm not helping you. I'm not giving you anything. We're going to war.''

He tried a few more remarks, but the air was thick, and he

concluded the meeting. I walked him to the front desk; I don't remember if we even shook hands when he left.

Back in my office I immediately reviewed the meeting mentally. Glaser was certainly a total pro. And one who left no ploy untried. His attempt at being "friends" was an excellent tactic, one that was hard to resist. It was hard to be rude to a man, hard to reject a social invitation to dinner, hard to keep from recommending a friend in private practice who'd proabably love to try a case with someone as good as Glaser.

But if you let yourself respond you've been co-opted. Friends don't fight. Glaser knew that. Become friends, and you, as prosecutor, begin to feel unfair if you don't at least offer to negotiate. Become friends, and you begin to feel that you should at least discuss reducing the charges.

When Glaser saw I wasn't buying, he had tried another route. If he and I couldn't be friends, then he would take as his associate someone that I would have to respect. Someone whose friendship with me could perhaps be exploited. Friends, Glaser? I thought to myself. No way. Not in a million years, buddy.

It was on the twenty-sixth of October 1978 that I saw Patrick Henry for the first time. He appeared in the company of Harold Glaser and Ron Sommers to surrender himself to the jurisdiction of the Pima County Superior Court pursuant to the indictment filed against him and the outstanding warrant. Before we left court the judge would set a date for the trial to begin.

Dr. Henry would not have been in court at all that day if it hadn't been for Bates Butler, the U.S. attorney in Tucson. Months before, Bates had lodged a federal charge against Dr. Henry for trying to check a weapon aboard an airplane without notifying the proper authorities. Because that was a federal charge, it didn't matter that Dr. Henry lived in Maryland rather than Arizona; he was obliged to appear in Tucson whenever the U.S. attorney decided to proceed against him.

That federal charge had been the ace up my sleeve all along. Ever since posting bond in Maryland, Dr. Henry had been fighting extradition. But if Bates Butler proceeded against him, he would have to come, in person, to Tucson. Once here, he would be arrested by an Arizona law-enforcement officer and would thereafter be subject to the jurisdiction of Pima County. Extradition would no longer be necessary. He would have to appear for trial in Tucson or be declared a fugitive.

The strategy worked just as I'd hoped. Once we had our state indictment for attempted murder, the U.S. Attorney's Office began proceedings on the weapons charges. In due course, Dr. Henry was obliged to come to Tucson to appear in federal court. He was on the courthouse steps, on his way to a taxi, when Ken Janes stepped to his side and arrested him on the state charge.

Now, almost a year after the attempted murder, Patrick Henry and I stood on opposite sides of a courtroom, waiting to learn when our "war" would begin. Trying not to be obvious, I examined him closely, trying to store up as many impressions as I could.

Patrick Henry was just as everyone had described him: tall, very handsome, well built—and strange. Throughout the entire proceedings he wore the slightest of smiles, more of a smirk, really. He seemed nonchalant about what was happening, but several times I caught him staring at me. Remembering what I'd told Harold Glaser—that I considered Patrick Henry an animal, and dangerous as hell—I could guess what he was thinking, but nothing showed on his face. Aside from the smirk, he was absolutely expressionless.

Harold Glaser entered a Not Guilty plea to the charge of attempted murder and a trial date was set in January 1979. My next order of business was to get that date changed. In January I would be prosecuting another major case, one that meant a great deal to me personally: the murder of an undercover police officer who was a friend of mine by a heroin dealer named Rufus Junior Mincey.

Eventually Patrick Henry's trial was rescheduled for a date agreeable to both sides: May 21, 1979.

We all knew that the trial would be a battle; it would be several weeks of controlled warfare. The outcome was so important to both sides that nothing less than an all-out effort was called for, and both sides would undoubtedly give just that.

If the doctor was acquitted, Christina Henry's life would be in jeopardy again. She had committed what Dr. Henry considered the ultimate crime—she had run from him. Not only that, but by cooperating with us she had exposed and humiliated him. He would never tolerate this, never. No matter how long it took, or how much it cost, he would get even. None of us doubted this. Ken Janes, Carol Eley, Chuck Wallace, and everyone else familiar with the case—we all knew the danger Mrs. Henry was in. And Christina Henry knew; she knew far better than we did.

I was shocked to learn that Patrick Henry's medical license had not been suspended after his arrest. But that shock was nothing compared to my reaction upon learning that it probably wouldn't be suspended even if he were found guilty. This meant that we would have to put him in prison for as long as possible. Otherwise he would resume his medical practice after the trial and quickly rebuild, financially. And with enough money, anything is possible.

My own safety and the safety of my family had also been a consideration once I discovered what Dr. Henry really was. I knew it was only a matter of time before he turned his obsessive hatred toward me as well. This was confirmed for me by the psychiatric reports I received after Dr. Henry's breakdown on May 17, four days before the trial date.

On that day Nancy Henry committed her husband to the Sheppard and Enoch Pratt Hospital, a mental institution in Maryland. She did so after several weeks of observing him go into deep, depressive moods. He would neither talk nor eat but would sit and stare mindlessly at a wall for hours.

In the hospital Dr. Henry was treated by a clinical psychologist, who administered numerous psychological tests to him over a two-day period just after he was admitted. The purpose of the tests was to determine his mental state, and to reveal whether or not he suffered from mental diseases or disorders.

Since the trial was officially delayed because of the breakdown, our office was entitled to see the hospital's psychiatric summary. The clinical psychologist's report on those tests was part of that overall summary.

Of the hundreds of papers and reports we encountered during the investigation, those five single-spaced pages were the most welcome document we received. They confirmed Christina Henry's description of her ex-husband's bizarre behavior. The psychologist had caught it all: the obsessive hatred, the sadism, the anger, the determination to get even—they were all there in the report. The following are excerpts:

> He spoke of the arrest and subsequent investigation by the prosecution and pressing of charges by his former wife, with a great deal of anger—probably the only display of emotion readily observable during the interview.

> "I am not accustomed to openly aggressive behavior. I tend to hold things in and to say I'll get you later!" [Dr. Henry said during examination].

> His tenacity is something he respects in himself.

> Again, there are indicators of continuing obsessive hatred for his first wife . . . someone he would like to treat in a sadistic manner . . . he feels that he must protect himself on his own, cannot rely on help from others, and must "settle the score later on."

> Women are pictured as disgusting people who think they have some sort of control over him.

> His stories (composed for a psychological test) are well constructed and coherent, but the content tends to be sadistic and filled with a combination of hatred and feelings of hopelessness.

> The T.A.T. reveals a man in a state of great turmoil, obsessed with hatred and disgust. . . .

> Dr. Henry remains dangerously preoccupied with his obsessions.

> I would consider him in dire need of psychiatric care.

He was committed on the seventeenth day of May 1979. After being hospitalized for twenty-three days, he was discharged on June 8. By that time he was no longer the person who would neither talk or eat, the person who would stare at a wall for hours at a time. Once again, he was the promising young physician.

The discharge summary stated:

> Compared to the state in which Dr. Henry arrived at the hospital, his condition on discharge is much improved. It should be noted that his behavior and his level of functioning is somewhat in contra distinction to the psychological tests obtained and only with continued outpatient treatment will these seemingly disparate assessments be integrated.

> With continued outpatient therapy and proper use of medication, Dr. Henry's prognosis is felt to be good.

The discharge summary specifically noted that his psychiatrist diagnosed him as latent schizophrenic. This would explain some of his conduct, but not what the psychologist had seen. Sadism, anger, obsessive hatred, disgust toward women, the desire to get even—these are not the common symptoms of schizophrenia. Something else was there; something the doctors couldn't explain. But whatever it was, Dr. Henry was free again. With medication he could function normally.

After reading the discharge summary I thought of one of Christina Henry's warnings to us: "He can fool anyone. He's a doctor; he knows how to act, how to be the perfect person." Dr. Henry was like two different people.

A new trial date was set for the sixth of September 1979. After being discharged from the mental hospital, Dr. Henry received outpatient care under another psychiatrist. He was required to see the doctor weekly, and was kept under medication. He also resumed his medical practice. It took Dr. Henry no time at all, after his release, to convince his psychiatrist that he was a fine young physician, and a danger to no one. In a letter to the judge, the outpatient psychiatrist wrote:

> . . . at no time did I feel that Dr. Henry posed any danger to himself or others.

> I very strongly feel that incarceration for this patient would be most harmful, not only to himself but to those whom his medical expertise could be benefiting. I be-

lieve that the greatest degree of rehabilitation would be accomplished by allowing Dr. Henry to continue his practice of medicine. . . .

Mrs. Henry was right. If her husband could fool his professional colleagues, what would he do with a jury? And the jury would only have Christina Henry's testimony; they would never know what the psychologist had found. That evidence was all inadmissible under the doctor-patient privilege.

As the second trial date approached, I tried to determine Glaser's defense. Relying on the Jewish practice of Law, I came to a few conclusions.

Glaser couldn't possibly use insanity. I would slaughter him if he did. The legal test for insanity in Arizona is the traditional M'Naughton test: knowing right from wrong, and knowing the nature and quality of one's acts. Dr. Henry had known very well what he was doing. For eighteen months prior to his attempt, Dr. Henry had taken one step after another to avoid being caught. His planning, his preparation—all this had been done while he practiced medicine and lived with his new family, without the slightest hint of any mental problems. There was no way he could claim a straight insanity defense.

There was another, and possibly more important reason: if he did claim insanity, I would be permitted to show the jury the psychiatric summary from the mental hospital. It would substantiate everything that Christina Henry had to say.

There was also a chance that he would lose his medical license if he claimed insanity. Insanity was not the route Glaser would take. It had too many drawbacks, both legally and practically.

Now I really concentrated, trying to see the case not as a prosecutor, but as a defense attorney. I put myself in Glaser's shoes. How the hell do you get out of the web of evidence woven by the prosecutor? Taking all the evidence the state has, how do you give the jury a reason not to convict?

Glaser would know, long before the trial, what I could get in evidence and what I couldn't. He would know that he could not stop me from proving the creation of the second Terry Lee Cordell. The driver's license, Social Security card, library card, birth certificate, all would be shown to the jury. The same was true of the Ramada Inn stationery—the murder plan. No legal maneuvering could keep the jury from seeing it. Although Glaser would try to get it suppressed, by claiming the search of Dr. Henry by the Dallas FBI agents was illegal, he would know that that evidence would not be suppressed. The same with the briefcase: he'd claim it was illegally opened and searched, but he would know that he wouldn't win that motion either. Both searches were good, legally.

The jury would eventually have all that evidence before them. The question was, how to explain away the murder plan? During the twenty-some months we had worked on the case, I'd kept that plan where I could see it every day. I'd read it over and over, and I could think of no other meaning for "MT" than "Murder Tina." I felt confident there wasn't any other word that would fit. It amused me to think of what Dr. Henry had to be going through trying to come up with some other plausible meaning. The only possible words were actually funny: Select window, tape, plunger, thr, open, find Tina—Meet Tina, Marry Tina, Mug Tina. It had to be Murder.

In the final analysis, Glaser would have to admit that Dr. Henry had come to Tucson to murder his wife. The evidence of his intent in coming to Arizona was too strong to ignore. The defense would have to be exactly what Ron Sommers had told me over the phone almost two years before: that Patrick Henry came to murder her, but the airlines lost his luggage and once he got to Tucson he changed his mind. All he did was go to see his child, to see how the boy was being raised.

That, in its basic form, had to be the defense. It would be embellished and improved upon, but that was it—just exactly as Dr. Henry had planned it in the event he got caught. The delayed luggage claim made it perfect.

To counter Mrs. Henry's testimony, Glaser would have to destroy her on cross-examination. He would try to make her look like a crazy, vindictive bitch. If he would make the jurors hate Christina, they would understand why Dr. Henry had been driven to the brink of murder. If they disliked her, if they felt she was making up some of the things she was saying, they would sympathize with him.

Dr. Henry's new life would provide a perfect setting from which Glaser could work his defense. The doctors in Maryland would testify that he was an excellent physician, conscientious, hard working, facing an unlimited career. Nancy, the new Mrs. Henry, would add a most important ingredient. She was Dr. Henry's wife now. They had lived together for years, and she had never seen Pat behave as Christina said he had. She would swear that Pat was a wonderful, loving husband; a perfect father for her two children.

The jurors would be very interested in her testimony. She lived with the man; she would know if he was insane or dangerous. Nancy would be the witness to destroy Christina's credibility. People don't turn craziness off and on. Surely, if the new wife hadn't seen any of this bizarre behavior, the old wife had to be dreaming it up.

There was something else Nancy could do, something just as dangerous to us as her other testimony: she would arouse sympathy. The jury would be made to see that if they convicted Dr. Henry they would be destroying Nancy and the children. They would be ruining a family who were completely innocent of anything. It was possible that Nancy Henry could turn the case on us.

Glaser had another advantage. Without using insanity as a legal defense, he could tell the jury about Dr. Henry's breakdown. He would claim the doctor was crazy when he made the decision to kill; he would claim he was "obsessed" during that time. The recent breakdown would only make this contention more believable. Under these circumstances I would not be allowed to bring in the psychiatric summary. All I would be able to do was challenge him on cross-examination.

Finally, Dr. Henry would probably claim he came to his senses when he got to Tucson. He couldn't do it. He was a physician; he just couldn't take a human life. I could visualize his performance on the witness stand; done correctly it could be devastating. If he could fool the jury, he'd go free.

The other attorneys in my office didn't think we had a chance, although Chuck Wallace was beginning to lean our way. On separate occasions I told both my father and father-in-law about the case and they both had the same response: "What's the crime? I don't see where he committed a crime." Even after being told the law of attempted murder, they didn't think I could convict.

Personally, though, I didn't have the slightest doubt—because Christina Henry was ready.

The opposition would be toughest on her. Carol Eley and I

had spent hour after hour with Mrs. Henry, letting her know in advance how Glaser would portray her, trying to prepare her so there would be no ugly surprises.

Glaser would undoubtedly try to establish, we told her, that she was the one who had destroyed the marriage. She was the one who had married a doctor, deceived him, left him, and now wouldn't let him see his child. Glaser would insinuate that she married him for his future wealth and then ran out on him. Even today, he would announce, she didn't have a real job, but was getting $300 a month in child support while living at home with her parents. She would be the lazy, money-grabbing, deceitful bitch. Meanwhile, Dr. Henry would be the model young man, working, studying, supporting his new wife and family. Glaser would contend that Christina was fabricating it all, making up absurd, bizarre stories. It would all fit together—she was the cause of everything.

But I had a surprise for Harold Glaser. What neither he nor Ron Sommers knew was that, during the year we had been preparing for trial, Christina Henry had remarried. By the time the trial started in September they would have to think twice about attacking her on the stand in front of a jury. You just don't do that to a madonna, a woman who's in the seventh month of a pregnancy.

PART THREE

The Trial

THE TRIAL was just what we had expected—a battle. Harold Glaser fired off the first gun in his opening statement to the jury. Wadding up a copy of the indictment, he threw it into a wastepaper basket. These charges against his client meant nothing, he said, they were "just another piece of paper."

Fortunately, the decision was not up to him, but to the judge, Ben C. Birdsall. The judge would be the one to decide whether there was sufficient evidence that Dr. Henry had proceeded far enough toward his goal as to constitute attempted murder. If he decided there was, Judge Birdsall would then allow the jury to decide if Dr. Henry were guilty. So before we even got to the jury, Judge Birdsall was the man we had to convince.

Glaser's opening statement contained another jolt, although I was prepared for this one. There's no need for all this fuss, Glaser told the jury. The state doesn't have to spend all that money, bringing in witnesses from all over the country, from Timbuktu and everywhere else. We admit Dr. Henry came to Tucson to murder his wife. We admit it; we don't deny it. But the evidence will show that, once he got to Tucson, he changed his mind. He couldn't do it.

It was a clever move. In acknowledging Dr. Henry's intention to commit murder, he was trying to imply to the jury that much of the testimony they would be hearing was unimportant. I had a great deal of evidence to show how thorough and cold-blooded Dr. Henry's preparations had been. But Glaser was already trying to focus the jury's attention on the weakest part of the prosecution's case: what was there to prove that he had actually carried out acts in furtherance of that intent?

During the defense's opening statement, Glaser had made

217

statements that I knew would not be borne out by the evidence. In a voice just loud enough for Glaser to hear, I asked the court reporter to make me a copy of his statement. It always nags at an attorney when the other side requests a copy of his opening. All through the trial he finds himself wondering what mistake he might have made. Naturally, once he heard me, Glaser ordered a copy of mine.

During my opening statement I related, chronologically, the events of the fifth and sixth of December 1977. I covered the incident of Dr. Henry at the airport, the opening of his briefcase, his arrest in Dallas, the discovery of the murder plan, his disguise, and, finally, what Christina Henry and her father had seen and heard on the morning of the sixth.

I told the jury that Dr. Henry had poisoned the dog. This was solid evidence, I said, that he had never abandoned his murder plan. He had only been unable to carry it out. Telling this to the jury so early was a gamble. Glaser and Sommer were going to fight to keep that evidence out, and if they succeeded, the case would undoubtedly end in a mistrial because I had already mentioned it to the jury. But I really had no choice. If that evidence was not permitted to go to the jury, I probably couldn't convict anyway. Without that lab test on the vomitus I had no case.

Normally, legal questions concerning the admissibility of evidence are decided prior to the trial, but that was not possible in this situation. The witnesses whose testimony was needed were all chemists from out of state. It might have been possible to assemble them all in Tucson prior to the trial, but I must admit I didn't try very hard. Psychologically, it is harder for a judge to declare a mistrial once the case has been under way for a while. A lot of time, money, and inconvenience are involved. I hoped that if the admissibility of the lab test was a close call, the judge might be swayed by that fact.

After my opening statement, the court took a recess. Glaser and I happened to meet in the hallway outside. As he walked by he muttered, "You've got a job with my firm, any time. I'll make room for you." I had to smile. His compliment might have been genuine, but it was definitely another attempt at co-opting me. All during the trial, he never stopped.

As I called the first witness, Gene Zarr, Gene Weber, and FBI Agent Rand, Glaser began his performance. After I had questioned each witness, it was Glaser's turn, but he really had no interest in their testimony—or so he pretended to the jury. He would ask only a few questions, or none at all. Then he would announce in a loud voice, apparently directed at no one in particular, "I really have no more questions for this witness. It wasn't necessary for him to testify; we stipulate to all this."

This testimony was killing him, and we knew it, but you would never have guessed it by watching Glaser. He seemed bored and slightly irritated, as though the prosecution was wasting his time and that of his dear friends, the jury.

At the first moment when the jury wasn't present, I requested the judge to instruct Glaser to stop making these speeches. The judge so admonished him, but that night, as I thought back on it, I knew I hadn't acted quickly enough. I should have cut him off the very first time. If I'd been on my toes, I could have drowned him out with an angry objection before the jury could hear what he was saying. I couldn't help wondering if his professed admiration for my opening statement had softened me. Did I wait to object until the jury had left because I thought he didn't know better, and I didn't want to embarrass him? Whatever the reason, I should have nailed him but I hadn't. I made a stern mental note to myself: quit listening to Glaser's B.S.

However, Carol Eley had gotten in a good shot for our side. During the recess after the opening statements, Glaser walked up to her and said, "I'll bet you never expected that—admitting that he came here to murder her."

Without hesitating Carol answered, "Oh, yes. Randy said that was what you'd do. We'd known for some time." Before Glaser could respond, she walked away.

When Agent Rand testified, I had him describe all the events that occurred in Dallas at the time of Dr. Henry's arrest. After he identified each of the items of evidence taken from the doctor, I asked him to describe the defendant's clothing, especially the underwear.

Standing in the courtroom was a full-sized mannequin dressed in Dr. Henry's padded undergarments. At my instruction, Ken Janes had prepared this exhibit before the trial, and now I gestured toward it as Agent Rand identified the items one by one.

The effect was eerie. The mannequin looked like a mummy,

but much more sinister. As Rand and I went over the items, we could see the jury registering the amount of time and attention Dr. Henry's painstaking disguise had required.

Knowing Glaser wouldn't dare object—that would have been inconsistent with his pose that none of this evidence was important—I offered the underwear in evidence just as it was, on the mannequin. Glaser did not object and the judge allowed the exhibit in evidence.

I had told Janes to remove the mannequin's head before he brought it to court. Now I stood it up on its feet, against the wall behind me, and it loomed there, headless, during the remainder of the trial.

The next witness was Christina. Although she was remarried and had a new name, she was using her old name for the trial because she didn't want Dr. Henry to know what her new name was. As I called her, I glanced over at Glaser. He knew, and I knew: Mrs. Henry's testimony, and her ability to hold up on cross-examination, was the crux of the whole case.

We had spent almost two years preparing to corroborate as much of Christina Henry's testimony as we could. Since she was the key to the whole case, we had focused at least half of our investigative efforts on proving she was telling the truth.

Our trial strategy was to put Mrs. Henry on the stand, have her tell what had happened on the morning of the sixth, and back it up with some, but not all, of the bizarre stories from their marriage. Then we would have to stand back and let Glaser try to rip her to pieces on cross-examination.

It was important that she not hit the jury with all the atrocity stories about Patrick Henry. She could have talked for days about his incredible behavior, but since most of it could not be corroborated with other independent evidence, the jury might end up not believing any of it. For this reason we decided to hold back on some of her testimony.

I couldn't wait to let Glaser tear into her on cross-examination. I'd discussed my strategy with Mrs. Henry so she understood what was going to happen and why. It is a strategy I've used for years in rape cases. When the accused rapist's attorney cross-examines, usually he will yell, he will intimidate, he will insinuate, and he will attempt to make a liar out of the victim. If he's good, the jury will begin to disbelieve the victim.

After the victim leaves the stand, I immediately call a series of witnesses who testify, independently, to the truth of the victim's testimony. As my questioning goes on, I begin to seem a little angry—not at the witness, but at the defense attorney, for insinuating the victim wasn't being truthful. The more areas of the victim's testimony that I can corroborate, the better the tactic, and the madder I get at the defense attorney.

Eventually the jury gets angry too. They begin to feel that the defense tried to trick them, even to deceive them. I emphasize this possibility, during final argument, by pointing out that the defense had received, in advance, the reports and statements of the corroborating witnesses.

This compounds the defense attorney's crime. Not only did he embarrass and humiliate the victim, but he tricked the jurors, knowing all along that the victim was being truthful. After all, he had read the statements of the other witnesses long before the trial started. That means, I angrily point out, that all the defense attorney's antics—his yelling, his insinuations, his outrage—all of this was a big fraud. In the end his credibility is destroyed.

As a tactic this is devastating—but it can also be devastating to the victim unless she's thoroughly prepared. Christina Henry was. I had told her which areas of her testimony would most likely be challenged, and what Glaser would hope to achieve by attacking those areas.

The louder he gets, we told her, the more he yells, the more he insinuates, the better for us. I also told her not to look to me for protection. I would not object to his questions unless they were totally out of line. Knowing this, she wouldn't suddenly fear I was abandoning her; she would know that it was all part of the strategy we had agreed on together.

Mrs. Henry would be on her own during cross-examination. We did not help her prepare answers to the most likely questions. That would have been improper, and would not have served our own cause: Mrs. Henry's honesty always came through when she spoke in her own words, and I was sure the jury would be affected by her.

Instead we gave her the most simple and the most effective advice: answer Glaser's questions without getting mad. If she let herself get angry, we explained, she would be giving Glaser exactly what he wanted. If she shouted back at him she would be showing the jury that she really was the shrew her husband claimed she was. Whenever she felt herself getting mad, she was to stop and tell herself that Glaser was getting what he wanted. That would help her regain control.

When we thought she was ready, we arranged a little run-through.

"I was talking to one of the other prosecutors yesterday, Christina," I said one day. "He's never met you, but he knows all about the case and he's convinced you're lying. He thinks you're a vindictive bitch, out to ruin your ex-husband and take him for everything he's got."

She was shocked and hurt. "But why would I make up such things?" she said. "No one would do that just for money."

"He thinks you want to make sure Pat never sees his kid again," I told her. "Now, this guy has just gone through a divorce himself, and I'm sure that's part of it. But he's a hell of a prosecutor. If he disbelieves you, I'm a little worried about what the jury will think."

Several days later, I told her that I was considering something: it might be a good idea to let this prosecutor question her.

"He says he can prove you're lying. Why don't you think about it for a few days and let me know?"

"I don't have to think about it," she said. "Let him ask me anything he wants."

I made the arrangements. A few days later I escorted her to the office of Tom Reed, one of the best prosecutors in my office. He greeted her politely but with obvious coldness. Then they sat down and he went at her for half an hour. At times he was downright insulting. At first she backed off, scared and nervous, but the longer he questioned her, and the ruder he got, the calmer she became.

Satisfied she could handle herself, I said, "Okay, Tom, thanks." He broke out in a big grin, put his wedding ring back on, and said to Mrs. Henry, "I hope you'll forgive me—he made me do it."

The whole experience had been arranged to give her confidence. We had scared her, put her under pressure, let her worry over it for a few days, and then given her the experience of undergoing questioning by someone intent on proving her a liar. And she had handled it beautifully. We

wanted to watch something that would explode, but I
don't remember the exact word, whether it was an explosive or firecrackers. Just that it shouldn't be very powerful because if it was, he couldn't watch. That is all I
remember about that.

As Christina was talking I could see that several jurors'
mouths were hanging open—in shock and disgust, I hoped,
not in disbelief. At one point I caught Dr. Henry glaring so
intently at her that anyone could have seen the obsessive
hatred he felt. At that moment I wished, more than anything,
that a juror would turn and look at him, but none did, and he
regained his composure as quickly as he'd lost it.

Q. Was there ever—were there conversations about
the type of weapon or anything similar to that?
A. Yes. There was a knife that my husband had from
before—before our marriage—that was about this big
[indicating] and sometimes he would say how you
could—he could—or he could degut a person is the word
he used, by pushing like that [demonstrating] and going
up in one move.

She answered the questions slowly, carefully, pausing to
think to be certain she was accurate. When she could, she
tried to give his words, or exactly what he had showed her. She
had not been rehearsed, and she sounded much as she had
during our first interviews. The jury was seeing her as we had
seen her, and I felt sure she was making an impression on them.

When she described the alligator incident in Florida, however,
and the time he growled like an animal when she was pregnant,
knocking her down and terrifying her, I could only guess at
what the jury was thinking. Several of them turned and
looked at Dr. Henry, as if unable to imagine that the handsome young man at the defense table could possibly be the
person Mrs. Henry was describing. If they were having trouble believing her, they would find the next area of questioning even more difficult.

Q. All right. We'll go to Pat's camera. Was there
anything unusual about photography and Pat's camera
and what happened during the course of the marriage?

A. I'd say it was very unusual because it was more than a hobby. It sort of started like a hobby, I think. I remember I bought him a set of photography books one Christmas when we lived in Mobile because he started talking about it and he expressed interest in it. He always had some interest, so it started like a hobby, something you would want to do for fun.

Later, things changed because he started to think of that camera—I know this sounds incredible—but he started to think of it as alive. He would sit with it on his lap like this [demonstrating] and touch it like this [demonstrating]. He was methodical about that camera, very meticulous about every tiny aspect of it.

I don't think it's wrong to say it was an obsession.

Q. Did he frequently take pictures of you?

A. Yes.

Q. Were they unusual pictures and were they unusual circumstances?

At that, Mrs. Henry explained how he took pictures constantly, how he used the glass paperweight to create distortions, how he had kicked her in order to get a picture of her screaming, and finally how he had photographed her while she was pregnant and vomiting.

Having heard that her husband considered his camera alive, that he petted it, and that he liked to take pictures of her morning sickness, the jurors had to be wondering if she could possibly be telling the truth. I paused in my questioning, let a few seconds pass, then leaned across the table and took a large manila envelope from my case file. Standing slowly, I took the envelope to the clerk and asked her to mark, as exhibits, the envelope and the photographs and slides inside it. Although I didn't look, I'm certain that every set of eyes in the courtroom were glued to what I then carried to the witness stand for Mrs. Henry to identify.

When she had done so, I walked to the jury box and handed around the eight-by-ten color photographs we had made from the slides. Several of the jurors reacted visibly to the grotesque images. But the payoff came when I asked Mrs. Henry to read from the slides the captions written in her husband's handwriting: "Tina Distorted" and "Tina Making Chunks." Several jurors turned and stared at Dr. Henry in disbelief. Sitting upright in his chair, he stared straight ahead, completely expressionless. I could guess at the fury and anger he was really feeling, but nothing could be read in his face; he was making sure of that.

However, after the recess which followed, Dr. Henry's behavior was noticeably different. Either he had realized his ice-cold demeanor was inappropriate, or his attorneys had told him so. Whichever it was, he loosened up and acted more human, moving around more and occasionally whispering to his attorneys. But Mrs. Henry was not reassured. During the recess she had taken me aside.

"Mr. Stevens, didn't you see the way he was looking at me?" she said. "You could just see the hatred! You could feel it! He's going to get me for what I'm doing. He'll never forget this. He'll never forget."

Before we had ended the direct examination, Mrs. Henry had told the jury various incidents from her marriage and recalled what she had seen or heard the morning of the sixth of December. Her testimony included the details she had only been able to remember when under hypnosis.

This was a gamble we had decided to take. Several weeks before the May trial date, she had been taken back to Drs. Lindsey and Russell, who gave her full recall of her experience under hypnosis. Now, in court, she described the broken handle on the briefcase, the moustache, and the sneakers. The jury listened closely but had no idea why the broken handle was significant. And we had no idea if her recollections under hypnosis would eventually be declared inadmissible.

For Harold Glaser there were no surprises in Christina Henry's testimony. Under rules of criminal procedure, he had been entitled to have all our witnesses' statements before the trial, and to interview the witnesses if he wished. We had given him Mrs. Henry's statements, as well as the tape recordings made before, during, and after the hypnosis. He had also spent several hours questioning Mrs. Henry before the trial, asking her in particular to describe in detail the incidents involving Dr. Henry and the baby.

Glaser had been a gentleman that day, probing for as much information as possible to avoid surprises during cross-examination, but doing so politely. I knew he would conduct himself quite differently in front of the jury, and I had warned

Christina not to be lulled into a sense of false security by his earlier restraint.

And sure enough, although Glaser started his cross-examination quietly, as the hours went by his voice began to rise until he was almost shouting. Pregnant or not, Christina Henry had to be destroyed. He ridiculed, he overstated, he did everything he could do to make her testimony sound absurd. His manner implied that he didn't believe one thing she had to say.

But Christina was ready for him. She didn't get excited, didn't try to argue, and didn't become defensive in her answers. During recesses we cheered her on, reassuring her that Glaser's attacks were eventually going to backfire. Because of her condition she tired quickly, but nonetheless she held her own.

> Q. [By Mr. Glaser] And he starts talking to you— this is during his internship I believe you said—about torturing people and taking them out to the swamps and pushing in their eyeballs and everything else. How long after he first told you about it did you remain married, until you left him in New York?
>
> A. I remember him first mentioning the swamp stories in New Orleans.
>
> Q. When would that have been?
>
> A. '72, I guess that would have been the year.
>
> Q. . . . but it wasn't until '74 that you left him, is that correct.
>
> A. . . . that is correct.
>
> Q. Here you're married to some guy who is a screwball. He's telling you, I'm going to take somebody out in a swamp and push out eyeballs and things of that nature, and you saw him beat up a cat so badly that the cat never walked right again. He's doing—coming back home after you're first married and saying you messed up again, you did not tell this doctor to shave, and you stayed two and a half to three years afterward in your marriage, is that right?
>
> A. It would have been two, I think. Yes, that's true.

Glaser had hit her most vulnerable area—the question we had asked ourselves many times, the question that couldn't really be answered unless one knew and understood the Bellios family. If Patrick Henry was such an animal, why hadn't Christina left him sooner? It was everyone's question. We had warned Mrs. Henry that this would be one of the major areas of Glaser's cross-examination, and when we recessed for the weekend, I told her to come back on Monday expecting to discuss it again.

When cross-examination resumed, Glaser produced several slides from the vacation trip to Florida. They showed Christina swimming and playing in the water. None of them showed any alligators. Pointing out the small waves created by her swimming, Glaser tried to suggest that she had imagined them to be an alligator. Mrs. Henry had to admit, under his careful questioning, that she had actually seen no more than something low in the water making waves, and a tail when it splashed. He did not ask questions that allowed her to repeat what Dr. Henry had said to her as she crawled out of the water, nor did he let her mention that there were other slides that did show the alligator. In some of the jurors' minds, at least, he had probably created doubts about whether she was telling the truth about the incident. But that was all right. We had a surprise waiting for Glaser; it just wasn't time to spring it yet.

As we'd expected, Glaser next moved to the same line of questioning he'd been following the Friday before.

> Q. I asked you, if you remember, the end of Friday, if you were married to a man who is talking about taking people out to a swamp, you're not even pregnant at the time, torturing and mutilating people out there, why did you wait two and a half years before you left him?
>
> A. There were several reasons I did that. One of the reasons was that in my family divorce is a very bad thing. My father is from Greece. He is an older man. I knew that if I said anything about these things back then, it—it would be such a shame and a disgrace, as it really did turn out to be for him. But there were other reasons too. I didn't know as much then maybe as I know now. I didn't have—
>
> Q. How old were you when you were in Louisiana?
>
> A. Let me see. Well, that's '72, this is '79. It was seven years, I'm thirty-four. Twenty-seven.

Q. You were twenty-seven? Had you gotten your Bachelor of Arts degree at that time?

A. Yes I did.

Q. Which included two years of nursing?

A. Well, I was in nursing first, so I switched.

Q. You had some experience in the world, I believe you said you were Miss Romper Room in Tucson for a year and a half.

A. Yes, I did.

Q. You had other jobs?

A. Yes.

Q. But you mean to say your lack of experience at that time wouldn't have made you able to see, from your testimony, that your husband was completely off the wall?

A. No, I don't think I meant it that way—when I said my lack of experience.

I didn't mean that I hadn't been in the working world or that I didn't have any education.

I just meant that perhaps I was more sheltered than a lot of women might be. And maybe I was—I tended more to let him steer the whole thing, than maybe I should have. Maybe it comes from my background.

Mrs. Henry's testimony and the simple way she delivered it was obviously hurting Glaser; he quickly moved to another subject. Later on he approached it again from a different perspective.

Q. Here he is a doctor in general rotation, he's an intern in a hospital, that he goes to almost every day of his life. Part of the people are pediatric, children; he is with old people, young people; he comes home and is talking to you about torturing people, taking them to the swamp, and you just go along with it, is that right?

A. I don't think it is quite fair to say it that way. Going along with it isn't right.

Q. Okay then, I—

MR. STEVENS: Excuse me. I don't believe she finished her answer.

THE COURT: You may finish your answer.

THE WITNESS: I don't believe to say I was going along with it would be telling the whole story.

I had to listen to it—but that doesn't mean that I believed it was right or good.

Dr. Henry had handed his attorney more slides illustrating their happy family life. He was carefully selecting what he wanted us to see. But the doctor made a mistake, and Glaser didn't catch it:

Q. Your husband thought that was a nice picture, he took the picture.

A. He took a picture. He was the only one who took pictures.

Q. He took the picture of you preparing the foodstuffs for the animals.

A. He took a picture of me feeding the animals.

Q. It doesn't sound like somebody who goes around beating, kicking cats or beating dogs.

MR. STEVENS: Objection.

THE COURT: Sustained.

MR. GLASER: I'm sorry.

Q. [By Mr. Glaser] I'll show you Defendant's exhibit one for identification, and ask if you can identify that. Read it first, then we'll put it in.

A. It says 'At Tina's birthday, Pineville, Louisiana '72.'

Q. When is your birthday?

A. July 28.

MR. GLASER: Your honor, I would like to offer Defendant's exhibit—

THE WITNESS: Am I allowed to say something else about the picture?

MR. GLASER: Sure.

A. I think that's the picture that says "Happy Toad Day" in the picture, on the cake.

Q. "Tina's birthday"—that's where it says "Happy Toad"?

A. On the cake, right.

Q. On the cake?

A. Right.

It was the first time I saw Harold Glaser thrown off guard. He looked closely at the photograph of the birthday cake, saw that she was right, and had no choice. He had to offer it as an exhibit. The jury had heard everything; he didn't dare not offer it.

Late in the afternoon of the second day Glaser decided to gamble. After hours on the stand, Christina was beginning to lose some of the control we'd taught her. It was being chipped away by Glaser and by exhaustion. Waiting until the last hour before we recessed for the ay, he asked Mrs. Henry to tell the jury about the things she claimed her husband had done to his child, the things she had told him during the pretrial interview in my office. The things I had deliberately omitted from the direct examination. As he instructed her to discuss these incidents, he gave the jury a look that said, "Wait till you hear this. You thought her stories were wild before? Just wait."

One by one he led her through the stories. He made sure she related the "blue arm incident," the "blanket incident," the night Dr. Henry threatened to smash in the baby's crib, and his discussion of sexual conduct with infants. Glaser's tactic was not only to bring out the stories that were hardest to believe, but also to emphasize that Mrs. Henry had never told anyone or done anything about them. She had gone to a doctor only once. She had remained with her husband for months after these incidents. Glaser bore down hard on her for that, but tired as she was, Christina held her own.

Q. If you're interested in your baby's welfare wouldn't you have reported such unusual behavior to the child's doctor?

A. I'm glad you asked me that.

It came up many times during the marriage that my husband told me he was the doctor and nobody was going to believe me anyway about other things. This is something I was very sensitive about, and he knew the doctor so even if I had, I didn't have any proof the doctor would even have believed me, so that's why I didn't say anything about that at that time.

And a few minutes later:

Q. After your education, at your age, wouldn't a rational person have packed up after he went to work and scooted out of the house?

A. Mr. Glaser, I think I'm a rational person, but I think I should explain some of the other things that made—make—made me feel this way. I was very subjugated and kept under my husband's—I don't want to say domineering personality, that's not the right word. It was like he had a psychological hold on me, and he worked on this, too. I was very afraid of him, but he did this very gradually until I really did feel that if I had said that to somebody, they would either think I was making it up or that something was wrong with me—because as a doctor, right, he is practicing, so who's going to believe me if I say something like that and I didn't have any proof. That's how I felt. So if you ask me why I didn't say sometimes certain things, that's why, partially.

Q. When you say he had a psychological hold over you, what did he do, did he hypnotize you or something?

A. No, I don't mean that. I mean that's one facet of his personality. He's very good at finding out what makes people tick and how to have a psychological hold on you. Very good at it. And I know it from personal experience quite well.

Q. Mrs. Henry, if all this is true as you say, what difference would it have made to you whether somebody else believed you or not when it came to protecting your life and your child's life?

A. I think I indicated that was primary in my mind when I left, and planned to leave.

Glaser cross-examined Mrs. Henry for three days. Despite all the sarcasm, the ridicule, and overstatement, I sensed that at least some of the jurors weren't buying his contentions. Christina Henry's message, the point she was trying to make to the jury, came through most clearly in an answer to one of Glaser's questions.

Q. Am I correct that he didn't talk to you much, he just took pictures?

A. I told you, no, he talked to me. I tried to make clear before, when we talked in Mr. Steven's office—

that his periods of silence were real and deep. They
would last two to three days.

They started in New Orleans, but became progressively
worse until after the baby was born, but he wasn't
always the same. I know him, and I know he had almost
two personalities. He's two different men.

Christina Henry had made that point with me repeatedly
when we'd talked; I'd told her to be sure to register that point
with the jury, and she did: "He's two different men."

Some of the jurors would believe her. All they had to do
was look at the handsome young doctor sitting at the defense
table, and then at the padded dummy standing behind me. It
was headless because I wanted the jurors to visualize Dr.
Henry wearing that outfit—no other face, just his.

Carol and I thought Christina had made a favorable impression on the jury, but that view was not shared by everyone.
Several people thought she had been destroyed; others didn't
believe her; most weren't sure what to believe. I was concerned,
but I knew that most of them hadn't seen her testify the entire
three days.

The next series of witnesses were people who could substantiate bits and pieces of Christina's testimony.

Mr. Wright Thomas, the principal of the school where
Mrs. Henry had taught, and his wife, were called to the
stand. Neither Glaser nor Sommers knew what they were
going to say. Their names were listed as witnesses, but we
hadn't taken written statements from them so there had been
nothing for the defense to read.

On the stand, the Thomases told the jury what they'd told
Carol Eley over the telephone. They were at the Bellios home
and Dr. Henry had shown slides. They remembered the slide
of Christina in the water with the alligator. Audrey Wright
said she had asked Christina how she could have possibly
gone swimming knowing there was an alligator in the water.
She remembered that Dr. Henry had answered for Christina.
He told everyone that she hadn't known it was there when she
went in the water. Mrs. Wright also remembered Dr. Henry
laughing as he answered.

When shown the picture that Glaser had dwelt on—the one
with no sign of an alligator—Mrs. Thomas was emphatic.

That was not the picture she had seen that evening and not the picture she was describing.

Mr. Thomas told the jury that he recalled seeing a full-grown alligator swimming toward Christina.

Trying to cross-examine them was difficult. They no longer lived in Tucson. They had not seen Mrs. Henry or her family in years. Before we contacted them, they had not heard anything of what had happened between her and her husband. They had been questioned before they knew the significance of what they were asked to recall. There was no possibility that Mrs. Henry or her family had refreshed their memories before Carol had called them.

The most Glaser could do was show disagreement between them. He drew a diagram of the scene and asked them each to show the position of the alligator. One said it had been on the right; the other said on the left. I could have cared less. Both said it had been coming right for her.

Mrs. Henry's mother and sister were called next. They testified to everything that they had witnessed personally.

Karen told how she had sat at the dinner table while Dr. Henry discussed murder and torture. She had also heard him threatening to smash in the head of the baby's crib. Glaser countered with the suggestion that she would swear to anything to help her sister. Disregarding our warnings, Karen became furious at Glaser, right in front of the jury. Two recesses were taken but they did not calm her. She remained upset and angry at the insinuation that she and her sister were not telling the truth.

Glaser's strategy with Athena Bellios was excellent. He did not question her integrity. Rather, he concentrated on her love for her daughter and grandson.

> Q. [By Mr. Glaser] Mrs. Bellios, even at that time and later on, you would do everything that you could to insure and to help your daughter to keep her son from being taken away.
> A. Yes, I wouldn't want him to take him away, knowing everything.

If the jury believed Christina Henry's testimony, they would understand what her mother was saying. If not, they could assume what they wanted from the question and answer. Mrs.

Bellios had told the truth. Under no circumstances did she want her grandson turned over to Dr. Henry.

William Bellios was next to testify. It was his chance to act, to protect his family, and it had been a long time coming. For months he had been in close contact with our office. He and I met several times to discuss the case and the chances of getting a conviction. His inner turmoil was always apparent, and one day we discussed it.

"What I do, Mr. Stevens? I don't know. This thing goes on and is not over. I won't live much longer, I am old man. I know that. But I cannot die before this is over. Who will take care of them? He don't leave them alone. That Pat, he don't stop. If I die what will happen?"

"Mr. Bellios, we've got a good chance at him. Our case is getting better. I think we'll get him." I firmly believed what I was telling him; I felt sure we could convict.

"And if you don't, what will happen? He go free. He get away with this. He don't leave Tina alone."

"But we're going to get him. He isn't going to go free."

"I don't know. I have gun. Sometimes I think to myself maybe I should do something. I cannot die before this is over. And I think, 'What they do to me if I kill him? What they do? Huh. I am seventy-three years old, what can they do to me?'"

"But you can't think like that. That goes against everything you are, everything you believe in."

"But what I do? Leave my family like this? Every day, every day, this is what we talk about. No day passes when we don't talk about this. Tina, she is sick with fear. My wife, she is not well. She worry all the time. I don't sleep at night. Don't sleep. Take my gun and walk around house at night. If he come to my house I kill him."

"Mr. Bellios, you've got to hold on and save your health. I need you. I need your testimony. If you get sick, or if something happens to you. . . . You're the only other witness to what happened that night with Champo. I need your help. You're the one who knows what time it was. You've got to keep your health. If you keep up this worry . . . it's not good for you. Not at all."

"I don't know. Something must be done. I cannot let this keep on. I don't know what I do."

"What you're saying is that you don't have confidence in

me. You've got to give me a chance, give me a chance to convict him.''

My words didn't mean much. As long as there was a danger to his family William Bellios would carry his burden. I had the distinct feeling he had decided to see what we could accomplish before he did anything.

When he took the stand and began to testify, he spoke just as he had during the interviews.

A. . . . I know something is back in carport because the fence divide the carport with the yard, but I don't go out in that yard.
I tell the little dog, ''Stop. Don't do that. Stop it.''
But the little dog is still barking.
. . . Dog, you know, he is barking. I call him and he come to me and go back to the fence, and come to me, and go back to the fence three, four times.
But I don't see anything in the yard and I close the door and lay down on the bed, but I don't turn off the light.
Q. [By Mr. Stevens] Then what's the next thing that happened, Mr. Bellios?
A. . . . And the time comes, you know, six o'clock which every day, six o'clock, I go out and feed the little dog and pick up the paper from the front yard of the house.
And on the way out to put the food in Champo's plate, in other words, he—he never jump. He sleep on ground. Every morning he jump and come to me on account of his food, he want his food.
But this morning he still on the ground. He shake his tail, but he don't get up.
So I put the food on the plate and I go in front and pick up my paper and I come back.
The little dog still on the ground. Well, I say, probably he don't feel good, the dog. I don't give him much thought.
Q. When you went out to go to work, did you see anything else about Champo?''
A. Well, as soon as I go out to work, I go there to pet the little dog.
I say, ''What the matter, Champo? You don't feel good today?''

. . . on the way there I see vomit in the yard. On
the ground, soupy-like. That's when I say to myself,
"That's the reason the little dog is sick. He vomit."

I would have bet anything that every juror listening believed him. Glaser was too smart to challenge that testimony.
He asked no questions.

William Bellios had been essential. If it was decided that
the chain of evidence had not been maintained, the chemists
would not be permitted to testify to the drugs in the vomitus.
In that case, Mr. Bellios's testimony would go a long way
toward proving that something had happened to the dog that
morning.

Later, in the hallway outside the courtroom I went to tell
him how well he'd done, but I could see that he was ill. His
face was colorless, his head was down, and I think he was in
great pain although he denied it when I asked him. I offered
to have someone take him home, but he wouldn't hear of it.
He wanted to remain, just to sit, in the hallway near the place
where the trial was going on, the place where his family's
future was being decided.

He returned the next day, but was not allowed to enter the
courtroom. As a witness in the case, he was excluded from
court except when he was testifying. Ken Janes, the lead
investigator in the case, was the only exception to that rule.

"Why? Why I can't listen?" Mr. Bellios said angrily.
"They are deciding what happens to my family. I already
testify. Why can't I listen to everyone else?" He looked and
sounded even worse than the day before. Again I asked him
not to stay, to go home instead and try to relax. But again he
refused.

Later that afternoon, his wife finally convinced him to see
a doctor. The doctor called her as soon as he'd completed the
examination. "Athena, your husband has had a massive heart
attack. There's been a lot of damage to the heart. He needs to
be hospitalized immediately."

Despite his protests, William Bellios was placed in the
intensive care unit of St. Joseph's Hospital on the afternoon
of September 12. The doctors weren't certain he would make
it through the night.

*   *   *

The next day's witnesses were the chemists.

A month or so before the trial I had had to confront the problems I faced with the chain of evidence. Counting people who had done nothing more than wrap the vomitus for mailing, there were at least fifteen witnesses who would have to be called to testify, many of them from out of state. But there were already out-of-state witnesses who would have to be brought in from Baltimore. The cost was becoming prohibitive.

Worrying me even more than the cost was the thought of what would happen if one of the witnesses in the chain didn't remember exactly what he had done—or if he remembered something that might have contaminated the evidence. In checking, we didn't find any indications of that, but once a witness was on the stand, anything could happen. I finally concluded there was only one thing to do—bluff it.

Glaser was coming to Tucson for the trial. His fee was the same whether the trial was long or short; every day away from his Baltimore office he would be losing money. Perhaps that would give me an edge.

When Glaser called from Baltimore several weeks prior to the trial, he asked me how long I thought it would last.

"Well, let me see. Adding up all the witnesses I've listed it seems to me that my case will last . . . five or six weeks. Right around there somewhere."

"What? How could it possibly take that long?"

"There's a lot of witnesses I have to call."

"Who? There can't be that many."

"Well, there's the chain of evidence on the dog vomitus; that's quite a few right there. I'm not taking any chances; I'm bringing them all in. And there's a hell of a lot of people from Baltimore—driver's license, Social Security, records from the hospitals, Calvin Ingles. All those people have got to be talked to."

"Wait a minute. You don't have to bring them all. I'll stipulate to some of their testimony. You're going to get it in anyway, why bother bringing them all in? I'll stipulate to the people from Baltimore."

"Well, that ought to cut it down a couple of days."

"Who's in the chain on the dog stuff?"

"Everyone who had anything to do with it. Mail clerks, secretaries, doctors, chemists. . . . You name it, I've got them coming."

"That'll cost you a small fortune."

"I know it, but I don't have any choice, we've got too much invested already. I'm not taking any chances. I'm bringing them all."

"We can stipulate to some of that."

"I don't know. I don't want to get to court and have problems with the chain. I've got them all located and ready. I just don't want any problems."

"You've got them all located?"

"Yeah. They're not happy about it, but they'll come."

"Send me the list and I'll stipulate to everyone but the chemists. I want the chemists, but the rest you don't need to bring."

"I don't know, Harold. I'll send you the list, but I want to think about it first. I don't want any last-minute problems."

He called back a week later and we agreed to stipulate to everyone's testimony but the chemists'. One phone call, a little bluff, and the county saved thousands and I didn't have to worry about Glaser breaking the chain somewhere.

The first chemist was Dan Garner, from the ATF laboratory. He identified the two chemicals in the briefcase and the drugs found in the small bottle taken from Dr. Henry when he was arrested. He was asked to identify, in particular, the capsule containing the chlordiazepoxide. He was also asked to explain the procedures he'd used with the vomitus, and to make clear that his procedures wouldn't have changed or altered any drugs that might have been contained in it.

Ron Sommers, Glaser's associate, had majored in chemistry as an undergraduate. He questioned the chemist extensively, carefully pointing out that not one examination of the physical evidence taken from the school linked anything to his client. Having clearly established that for the jury, he challenged the procedures used to examine the vomitus and the way the evidence was packaged and stored, implying that the material could have become contaminated. Fortunately, the evidence procedure in the ATF laboratory could not really be challenged. It was too professional.

Don Cash, formerly the toxicologist with the Pima County Coroner's Office, was called next. He had been flown in from Wisconsin. I limited my questioning to the capsule he had examined, the one found in the school, and the examination he'd performed on the vomitus material.

I wanted him on and off the stand as fast as possible to avoid lengthy cross-examination. He had been able to identify the chemical in the capsule, but not the drug in the vomitus. His tests had been negative, something I preferred not to hear him testify to on the witness stand. But Ron Sommers wasn't about to let him get away quickly. He challenged the procedures used, the types of instruments available in the laboratory, the way the vomitus was packaged when it was mailed to Utah, and then questioned him about the possibility that the capsule could have contaminated the vomitus material.

While Sommers cross-examined, it occurred to me, again, how incredibly lucky we'd been. The vomitus had lain in the yard for thirteen days before Ken Janes collected it, and during that time it had rained. Don Cash's analysis had involved the use of yet another solvent, chloroform, thus weakening the original sample even more. He'd ended up with a quantity that couldn't be identified with the instruments available to him; they were not capable of analyzing such minuscule amounts.

As hard as he tried, Sommers was not able to prove that there had been any contamination. Ken Janes had delivered the capsule in a separate plastic bag. The capsule had been removed, analyzed, and returned to the bag without contact with any other material.

There was more good news that day: William Bellios had survived. He was still in intensive care, but he was going to make it.

I should have known he would live. That tough old man would never let go while his family was still in danger.

The receptionist called to say that Michael Peat was at the front desk. It was just after 8:30 A.M., an hour before he was to testify. When I went out to the front desk to greet him I recoiled in shock. Michael Peat was the toxicologist of toxicologists, known to be one of the best in the country. Unfortunately, instead of being tall, slender, gray haired, and dignified, Michael Peat looked like the last of the Berkeley hippies.

As we shook hands I tried to conceal my dismay. He was at most five feet five inches tall, with a beard so thick that only a glimpse of his cheeks was visible, just under the eyes.

His hair was long, much longer than his beard, and it seemed never to have known a comb. He wore a corduroy suit that, after hours of travel, looked as if it had been packed in an accordion. Over one shoulder was a sort of knapsack, which served as his suitcase.

I didn't know what to say. I would have thought there was some mistake, but I recognized his voice right away. He was Michael Peat. Walking back to my office, my mind was racing. No jury will believe he's a chemist. They couldn't. A potter, maybe, or a furniture maker, but not, under any circumstances, one of the best toxicologists in the United States.

When we sat down across from each other in my office, I noticed something I had missed—his eyes. They were alert, keen, intelligent. I had the feeling that he was aware of what I was thinking, but he didn't say anything. I also had the feeling that he was amused.

As we talked over the next forty-five minutes, I found myself fascinated by him. Unquestionably, he was brilliant. He was a total master of his field, and it was obvious that he loved what he did for a living. What really sold me on him was his confidence in his findings—there was no doubt whatsoever in his mind. His credentials, his British accent, and even his appearance would intrigue the jury. I had been totally wrong; he would be a terrific witness.

The jury loved him. They listened intently as he gave his background: in 1969 he had earned a chemistry degree from Oxford Polytechnic in England (the equivalent of a master's degree in America); from 1969 to 1973 he worked as a forensic toxicologist at the Metropolitan Forensic Laboratory of the London police department. After that he had spent two years as a lecturer in forensic medicine and toxicology at the University of London, and had left that position to become associate director of the Center for Human Toxicology at the University of Utah.

His examination of the vomitus had taken a week, he explained, and had involved such specialized techniques as gas liquid chromatography, high pressure liquid chromatography, thin layer chromatography, and gas liquid chromatography using an electron capture detector.

I was certain no one in the courtroom knew what he was talking about. I knew I didn't, but that wasn't important. He had instantly established his credibility, and if he said he found drugs in the vomitus, the jury would consider that a fact. I felt so confident that I simply asked him to give his results without explaining any of the tests. He told the jury that all of his examinations of the vomitus indicated the presence of chlordiazepoxide, the active ingredient of Librium.

Ron Sommers tried to cross-examine him on the sufficiency of the sample he had had to work with. Michael Peat answered that he worked in micrograms and nanograms (which he explained, was ten to the minus nine of a gram). Seeing that he was in over his head, Ron wisely backed off, asked a few more general questions, and sat down.

We were over our biggest hurdle and going strong.

Ken Janes and Chuck Wallace were two of the last witnesses to testify for the state. Wallace related everything he had done from the time he first became involved in the case. There was no serious cross-examination.

Likewise, Ken Janes testified to all his activities since the case began. In the months just before the trial, he had developed some new information. When the ATF released to us the clothing taken from Dr. Henry in Dallas, Janes had discovered that the workshirt with the name "Herman" on the pocket had a laundry mark. Using that, he was able to locate the laundry in Baltimore, have them check their records and determine that the shirt belonged to the University of Maryland Hospital.

Examining the inside lining of Dr. Henry's coat, the one he had worn buttoned up to the neck on the plane, Janes found a pocket not readily visible. In it were the moustache and goatee that Randall Butler and Fred Edmond had described, and that Christina had seen under hypnosis. The "bushy kind" of moustache she described could have been the combination of the moustache and the goatee.

As I had done with Wallace, I led Janes through each step of his investigation. The screen door from the nursery school was even brought into the courtroom and made an exhibit; Janes was asked to demonstrate for the jury what he had found, and how it was possible for someone to get through the screen to unlatch it. He was asked to explain the method used to enter a building with glass cutters, tape, and suction. He was then asked to interpret the plan, its words, and what we had determined the notations meant. The jury listened intently as he took them step by step through Dr. Henry's deviousness. When he described the notations dealing with the box, I thought I caught a faint smile on Patrick Henry's face. The notations that appeared on the ''Acne Gel, Benzac'' paper were pointed out to be the bus schedules and rates from Tucson to El Paso and then from El Paso to Dallas. Had he not flown out of town, he was prepared with a bus schedule and a map of Texas.

Ken Janes was also able to explain one more of the keys found in the briefcase. Wallace had already explained three of them; Janes had discovered that one of the two remaining was a key to the University of Arizona Medical College, which gave access to the student lounge. In the lounge were lockers with combination locks, which, Janes explained, could have been why Dr. Henry brought a combination lock in his briefcase.

On cross-examination, Glaser had Janes pinpoint the time Dr. Henry had been last seen at the airport, and the minimum and maximum times Janes had determined it would take to walk from the airport to the Bellios house. As we had determined, it couldn't be done in less than two hours. Glaser then had him explain in detail all the efforts we had made to check on rental cars, taxis, and limousines. He was using our evidence to prove that Dr. Henry couldn't have been at the Bellios house until much later than 3:30, when Champo had started barking.

Next he had Janes go through all the investigation procedures and examinations conducted with the nursery school. Janes had to admit that nothing had been found to prove anything against the doctor.

From left field, Glaser then began a series of questions I hadn't expected. If Dr. Henry really wanted his ex-wife dead, he was asking, why did he leave town on the sixth? At that point no one suspected him of anything. Why didn't he simply hang around for another day, waiting for a better opportunity?

Glaser's point was well taken. Dr. Henry even had airline reservations for the seventh, a day later. Why didn't he stay in Tucson and finish what he'd begun? Very cleverly Glaser was interpreting Dr. Henry's action as evidence that he really had changed his mind.

Fortunately, I was able to stop him before the jury grasped what he was getting at. He was asking Janes to guess why Dr. Henry had or had not done certain things, a procedure to which I quickly objected. Dr. Henry was the man to whom those questions should be directed, not Detective Janes. Only Dr. Henry could explain what he had been thinking.

My objection was sustained. I knew, of course, that Dr. Henry was very unlikely to tell us the truth about why he'd left town, but I had long ago developed a theory of my own. Like so much else in this case, it was just a guess, unsubstantiated by proof. But it fit the facts better than any other theory, including Glaser's, because if Dr. Henry really had been innocent when he left Tucson, why had he left wearing his disguise?

My own hypothesis had been put together during one of my midnight think sessions. If Dr. Henry had called his ex-wife from inside the school at 9:30, he could have been watching from the window as she grabbed Stevie and ran out the back door to her mother's apartment. Mrs. Henry was certain that she had screamed as she ran, and she had confirmed this under hypnosis.

Seeing her screaming and running to her mother could have panicked him. He couldn't have been positive she had figured everything out, but from her actions he would probably have guessed that she had. That meant he had to get out of town quickly. If she called the police and described him, he could even be stopped at the airport. So he needed to change his looks, but without going back to his own regular appearance. What he did was eliminate the facial hair. Mrs. Henry had seen something "bushy" on his face that morning; it was gone by the time Zarr and Weber saw him at the airport. Thus he looked neither like Patrick Henry nor like the man who had been spotted on East Broadway that morning. There was a final bit of evidence that fit this theory: the only window from which he could have seen her run across the yard was the window whose shade had been tampered with.

Having been halted on one front, Glaser now launched an attack from another direction. Turning to the capsule of chlordiazepoxide that had been found in the school, he made much of Janes's admission that it had not been turned over to investigators until we had been on the case for several months. Expressing wonder at our great good luck, Glaser

clearly implied that the capsule could have been falsely sup-
plied as evidence either by us or the Bellios family.

Later on, during redirect examination, I was able to clear
up that issue in the minds of the jury. Janes explained that
none of the Bellios family had been told, at that point, about
the drugs that had been found on Dr. Henry, therefore they
wouldn't have known what drug to plant. Nor would the
investigators, for that matter. The capsule tied Dr. Henry to
the drug found in the vomitus—but it wasn't until weeks after
the capsule was turned over to us that we had sent the
vomitus to Michael Peat, the first toxicologist who had been
able to identify all its contents.

Having established our innocence, I pretended to be furious
at Glaser's insinuations. They were vile; they were underhanded. In my own mind, of course, I had to admire him. It
was his job to tear holes in our case, and he wasn't missing a
thing. But neither was I. I remembered what I had said to
Glaser when we first met: "Your guy is an animal, dangerous
as hell . . . we're going to war." And war it was. I was
determined to put Dr. Henry behind bars not only for what he
had attempted to do, but to prevent him from doing what it
was obvious he would do if he were set free: attempt to kill
Christina Henry again.

When Ken Janes stepped down the prosecution rested. We
had tried to show that Dr. Henry came to Tucson with intent
to murder his ex-wife; that he had brought weapons and tools
to the scene of the intended crime; and that, by drugging
Champo, he had committed acts in furtherance of his intention.
Now it was up to Glaser to persuade the jury that we were
doing his client wrong.

He began by calling Dr. Joseph Burnett, the head of the
Department of Dermatology at the University of Maryland
Hospital. Dr. Burnett testified that Patrick Henry was an
excellent young physician. He had performed so well, in fact,
that in his third year he had been made the chief resident,
which meant he taught other doctors, interns, and medical
students.

Offered in evidence was an ariticle Dr. Henry coauthored
with Dr. Burnett which had been published in the prestigious
American Medical Association *Archives of Dermatology*. Ac-

cording to Dr. Burnett, Patrick Henry had done "99.9 percent of the work."

Even after he had been charged with attempted murder, Dr. Henry had continued to perform his duties exceptionally well. Dr. Burnett testified: "Dr. Henry's conduct of himself during the mounting pressure of his legal difficulties was amazing to me, far better than Nixon's, far better than what I have seen with people under stress. Far better than I think I could have done."

I didn't question Dr. Burnett about the breakdown that Dr. Henry had suffered prior to the first trial date. I preferred to emphasize that while Dr. Henry had been performing so well at the hospital he had also been creating a new identify for himself. Dr. Burnett confessed himself "utterly amazed" at the story of Terry Lee Cordell. He had no idea that Dr. Henry had used a patient's records to steal his identity. I could only hope that the jury was making the connection here: as Mrs. Henry had said, her ex-husband was two people. Dr. Burnett had seen one; Terry Lee Cordell had experienced the other.

Then Dr. Terry Hayden, a dentist, was called to testify. He had been at the Public Health Service Clinic in Mobile with Dr. Henry. He testified that Patrick Henry worked hard and was extremely conscientious about his patients. During the few occasions he had seen him socially, he had noticed absolutely no strange behavior. When he finished I asked him a few questions, but didn't think his testimony was really significant.

Glaser's first important witness was the director of the Drug Information Center and Poison Control consultant at the University of Arizona, Keith Likes. In addition to those duties, Dr. Likes was also an associate professor in the College of Pharmacy.

When Glaser asked him how chlordiazepoxide would affect a small animal, Dr. Likes replied that Librium would act as a muscle relaxant and that the chances of its making a dog vomit were "very, very slight." Librium would not irritate the gastrointestinal tract but would, in fact, calm it. When I questioned Dr. Likes, however, he admitted that the amount given and the substance given with the drug could cause the reaction to vary. Then I asked him how much time would pass before a drug like Librium took effect. He responded that it would probably reach its maximum effect in three hours. With that information I next asked a hypothetical question:

> Q. [By Mr. Stevens] If in a situation you wanted to go ahead and feed some—feed a dog this substance, you're going to have to wait for about three hours for it to take effect, is that correct, so you're certain you have got the results you want?
>
> A. Yes, that's correct.

My next series of questions established that if the dog was showing the effects of the drug at 6:00 A.M., then the drug had most likely been given several hours before. The jury could see what I was getting at: Champo barking at 3:30 and barely moving at 6:00. In the end, Keith Likes's testimony helped our case more than it helped Dr. Henry's. I should have called him as a witness for the prosecution.

It was the next series of defense witnesses who were the most dangerous.

Nancy Henry was the backbone of the defense. As she took the stand, the courtroom grew as silent as it had for Christina Henry.

A petite woman, with a pixie haircut and a southern accent, she seemed tiny, almost frail, as she sat in the witness chair. She spoke softly; jurors and spectators strained to hear her. The microphone had to be adjusted and moved closer.

Nancy Henry was questioned by Ron Sommers, but it would have been much better if she had been allowed to make a speech. She knew what she had to do, what she had to tell the jury. She knew very well the importance of her testimony. When asked to describe her husband's relationship with her children, she began to sob midway through her answer.

> Q. [By Mr. Sommers] Tell the jury, if you would, what kind of a father Pat's been to the children.
>
> A. Pat is a marvelous father. . . .
>
> THE COURT: Mr. Bailiff, will you get the witness a glass of water?
>
> THE WITNESS: Patrick is great with kids. . . .
>   [crying]

THE COURT: You take your time in answering the
                 questions, and if you get to the point
                 where you need a recess, you tell me
                 so, and I'll give you a rest.
THE WITNESS: Yes. No, Pat is a very good husband
                 and he's very good with the children.
                 In fact, he's marvelous with them.
                 They literally just worship the ground
                 the man walks on. He does every-
                 thing he can in his spare time to be
                 with them and do things with all of
                 us.

She was crying and talking at the same time.

Later, when Sommers asked her to characterize her own
relationship with Patrick Henry she broke down completely.

    Q. We have got some strange characterizations and
I'm going to ask you about them, Nancy.
    First, after your marriage did you notice any change in
Pat's personality? He courted you but how was he toward
you since that time?
    A. To be honest with you, I went through a very
difficult divorce before, and Pat has been my Rock of
Gibraltar. He's my entire life.

At which time she broke into sobs again and cried for
almost a minute. Judge Birdsall was about to call a recess
when Nancy Henry, the tears streaming down her cheeks,
looked up and pleaded with us. "He's my life. My whole
life."

Several jurors were in tears. I couldn't blame them—even
though I suspected her of deliberately acting overemotional, I
too felt sorry for her. And I believed her. Our investigation
had disclosed that her first husband had been a military man
who was a heavy drinker, and who often mistreated her. She
had wanted a savior, and I didn't doubt Patrick Henry's
ability to play that—or any—part. Even if she had spotted
signs that something wasn't right with her husband—and I
suspected she had—I doubted that she'd even say anything. If
her marriage was fairly happy, or even marginally happy,

she'd overlook as much as she could. Her new life was far better than anything she had ever known before.

To me, the interesting question was, why had Dr. Henry decided to play this role of loving husband? Perhaps it was because he genuinely cared for Nancy Henry and her children. But I doubted it. My own suspicion was that his transformation was part of a long-range plan, the plan I was sure he'd formulated the day he finally realized that his wife Christina wasn't returning.

I'd always felt that he had decided to kill her as soon as she left. The actual plan had required some time, but the intention had been alive for years. Knowing that he would be the prime suspect, he had decided to create the perfect defense—to become a model of decency, to become the last person people would consider capable of doing such a thing.

I'll probably never be able to prove this theory. But I find it very interesting that Dr. Henry began seeing Nancy shortly after Christina left him; that he and Nancy were married six days after his divorce became final; and that when he returned Christina's property before he remarried, he kept the pistol and the key to the Volkswagen.

Ron Sommers asked Nancy Henry a series of questions concerning the things Christina had told the jury. Nancy emphatically denied ever seeing any of the sort of behavior Christina had described. As she told the jury of her courtship and family life, she described her husband as one who sent flowers, brought perfume, took her out to dinner frequently and was totally unselfish with her and her children. The man she described was the antithesis of the person to whom Christina Henry had been married.

To counter the photographs we'd put in evidence, Nancy Henry described how she and Patrick often took pictures using glass prisms, obtaining "gorgeous" results with flowers. According to her testimony, if she or the children "happened to be sitting around" Patrick would sometimes take distorted pictures of them also. She found nothing "bizarre" about that. She and Pat had a perfect, loving marriage.

I knew there was another side to Nancy that the jury wasn't seeing. Nancy hated. As a witness she was excluded from the courtroom, but this tiny, frail-looking woman sat in the hallway each day, glaring at me, Carol Eley, Ken Janes, or Christina Henry as we walked by. It upset Christina and

Carol but I expected it. After years of being a prosecutor you find that the defendant's immediate family will often dislike you intensely. I've been yelled at, screamed at, and threatened many times; wives, mothers, and sisters are the worst at this.

In Nancy's situation, she had to hate us all—we were taking everything away from her. We were listening to Patrick's crazy ex-wife and believing her spiteful lies. We were helping that woman keep Patrick's son away from him. Nancy did not know what we knew about her husband. She didn't know anything of his first marriage—only what Patrick Henry had told her, and he certainly wouldn't tell her what we knew. She had not read the psychologist's evaluation of her husband's hatred of women. She didn't know what Dr. Henry had brought in his briefcase, or why he had brought those particular things. She didn't know why the knife was sharpened on both sides. And if we had told her any of these things, it wouldn't have mattered. She wouldn't have believed us.

I was not rough with her on cross-examination; I did not raise my voice or show any particular emotion. She had done nothing to anyone and did not deserve to be mistreated.

I had only one objective in my questioning—to show that Christina Henry was telling the truth. Knowing her hatred for Christina and knowing she would never agree with anything Christina said about her husband, I asked my most important question:

> Q. Christina Henry has told us that she thinks that he is two people, two different people. Would you agree or disagree.
>
> A. I would totally disagree.
>
> Q. She says he can be one way and then another way.
>
> A. That is something that I have never seen, absolutely never seen. Patrick has always been exactly like I have said he has been.

I asked nothing more about the two Patrick Henrys. Instead, I returned to my seat, pausing for a moment to glance pointedly at the padded dummy behind the prosecution table. My next questions were designed to show that this "marvelous" husband and father had, in fact, kept many secrets from her.

Q. Do you—do you know what preparations wer
made before he came out here?

A. No, other than I know—know about going t
Dallas for the convention.

Q. Do you know what he brought to Tucson?

A. No, I don't. I don't know everything that—no,
don't.

Q. Did you know what he was going to do when h
got to Tucson?

A. No, I didn't.

Q. Did you ever know what the specific plans were
how he was going to do the different things?

A. I have no idea whatsoever that any of it, perio
[*sic*]."

And then, my final question:

Q. You knew nothing of what happened in Tucson, o
the morning of the fifth or sixth of December 1977, di
you?

A. No, I did not.

MR. STEVENS: Thank you very much.

In a way, I thought Nancy Henry might have helped us
Like Dr. Burnett, she had seen the man every day and neve
suspected that he was planning a murder in his mind.

Finally, on Friday afternoon, September 14, Dr. Patricl
Henry took the stand. We knew he was under medication, bu
his composure could not have been entirely due to drugs. H
did not seem nervous, nor did he seem outraged. He wa
perfectly cool and emotionless.

Harold Glaser questioned him for hours that afternoon
Glaser started with Dr. Henry's childhood, then went throug
all of his schooling, including his medical training. Patricl
Henry stated that he had worked his way through college an
medical school. His mother had loaned him money onl
once, and he had repaid it.

He described his first meeting with Christina, how they'
started dating and eventually married. According to hi
testimony, their marriage had been excellent, without majo
problems or difficulties. He was totally shocked when Chris

tina left him, and shattered by the loss of his infant son. He had tried very hard to get his family back together, but Christina had refused even to consider it. The loss of his son, in particular, became unbearable.

Glaser then took him through each of the incidents that Christina had described to the jury. Dr. Henry, of course, remembered them very differently. He had indeed cut his arm reaching under the bed for the cat, but he didn't beat it or become upset. The stories about the swamp simply were not true, they were "nonsense." The child's arm had turned a dusky color one day, but he had certainly never made a comment about a heart defect. The baby had tangled himself in his blanket once, but hadn't been in any danger.

Yes, he was a judo enthusiast and had practiced the art for years. But it was "absurd" to think he would have used a judo throw on his wife during her ninth month of pregnancy. It could have been fatal to both Christina and the child. He couldn't imagine how she and her mother had come up with such a story. He had never threatened her with a knife either. And the ridiculous story of how he had played "werewolf" when she was pregnant was just that—ridiculous. He might "have played with her, but it certainly never reached that kind of roughing up, that she described."

The alligator slides, which had been seen by people outside the Bellios family, were more difficult to explain. But Dr. Henry was ingenious:

A. [By Dr. Henry] The slides of Tina in the scuba gear were interspersed with pictures of the alligators. I thought at the time that it was a funny thing to say. This is Tina and these are the alligators. We are out in Florida where you people expect you're going to be swimming with alligators if you're out in the water. It was meant to be a joke. It was a kibitzing thing rather than a serious thing. I'm really amazed the people took it seriously, to believe there were alligators in there. I wouldn't have gone in there myself if there were alligators. It was the way the slide show was presented.

Q. [By Mr. Glaser] Can you give a reason why, even though Mr. and Mrs. Thomas have the alligator doing different things in their testimony, that they remember—

that they would remember that you showed the slide with alligators.

A. There was a ripple in the water on that picture and I probably teased them and said, "Here is an alligator right here." I think that's what they remember. They crossed in their minds the ripple in the water and the others I had taken of full-grown alligators at the alligator farm and I think their imagination did the rest. That's the only thing I can figure out.

When he was questioned about another area of his ex-wife's testimony he answered a little less cleverly. I only hoped the jury realized how incongruous his answer was.

Mrs. Henry had given me the letter she had received from her husband after she left him, the one in which the clipping about the kidnapped child found in a swamp had been enclosed. I had offered it as independent evidence of Patrick Henry's fascination for swamps. It was damaging enough that Glaser wanted to counteract it with some explanation.

Q. Why did you send that clipping in the letter?

A. I think I was heartsick about losing my child at that time, and I tried everything else I could think of to get Tina to come back and she wasn't interested.

I sent this clipping in the hopes of jarring her into her senses and bringing my son back.

Q. Did you plan—was that a threat to her and were you planning on kidnapping the child?

A. Goodness, no. I wouldn't—I wouldn't send her a warning like that if I were going to be kidnapping the child. I wouldn't warn her. No.

Q. Have you any intentions or have you ever had any intention of harming your child?

A. Never. I loved him more than my own life.

I was delighted with these answers. He hadn't offered any reasonable explanation for sending the clipping; no normal person would send such an article to "jar" someone "into her senses." I especially liked his remark that if he had been planning to kidnap the baby, he wouldn't have sent a warning. "I wouldn't warn her" showed his way of thinking.

I wanted more than anything to cross-examine him quickly,

before he had a chance to realize his mistake. But Glaser knew how damaging these answers had been. Quickly he went on to questions that Dr. Henry could answer easily, and he continued his direct examination all afternoon. There was no way he would submit his client to cross-examination until they had had a chance to confer on those earlier answers.

It was a Friday, and Glaser carefully built the image he wanted the jury to take home with them that weekend. For the next two days he wanted the jury to remember Patrick Henry as a bereaved father, shattered by the loss of his child. The one subject he never got around to covering were the events that had taken place in Tucson on the fifth and sixth of December. The jury went home for the weekend without having heard the words "attempted murder" all day.

On Monday Glaser was ready to tackle the big stuff. Under his questioning Dr. Henry explained how losing his child had almost caused him to have a nervous breakdown. So concerned was he that he had spent hours in the medical library researching the effects on a child of losing a father and of being raised by a woman without a man. He read over a hundred and thirty articles on the subject. The more he read, and the older the child became, the more distressed he felt.

In the meantime, his ex-wife refused to let him see his son. He wrote over and over, trying to persuade her to let his parents bring the child to Baltimore for a visit. But she steadfastly refused. He went to court to get better visitation rights, but couldn't. To see his son he had to come all the way to Tucson, and even then Christina wouldn't allow him to be alone with Paddy. She insisted on being present.

At last he decided he had no choice. He would kidnap the child. With that in mind he had begun the creation of Terry Lee Cordell. He would use Cordell to get his son back, not to commit murder.

After eighteen months, he told the jury, he had obtained all the necessary identification. But by then, he explained, he'd been forced to face the fact that he couldn't do it—there was no way he could keep the authorities from suspecting him and reclaiming the child.

Now he was desperate again. But when he received the invitation to attend the dermatology convention he'd had another idea. The only way to get the child permanently was to murder Christina. Then, as the surviving parent, he would get custody. He began to make his plans.

During this part of his testimony—the tale of woe, as I called it—I leaned over to Carol Eley and whispered, "His performance would go a lot better with violins in the background." I wasn't buying one word of it, and I hoped the jury wasn't either. But there was no way to tell.

Glaser took Dr. Henry right through all the evidence we had spent months collecting, studying, and analyzing. The legal term for this tactic is "drawing the sting." By going into our evidence, Glaser was hoping to minimize the damage it could do. It was the same tactic he'd used against my first witnesses: admitting certain things so that the jury would assume none of this evidence was really important. There was just one problem. His tactic worked, all right, but on the wrong person—his client.

Glaser held up a copy of the murder plan and asked Dr. Henry to explain what each word or phrase stood for. The doctor complied, but much too eagerly. There was something wrong in his attitude. He showed no remorse, no embarrassment even, as he reviewed his list of tools and weapons. Instead, he took the jury through the various steps of his murder plan like a cook discussing a favorite recipe. He protected himself on a few important points, but for the most part he seemed unself-conscious and even proud—proud of his ingenuity, his thoroughness, and his cleverness.

I had sat impatiently throughout his earlier tale of woe, but now he had my complete attention. For one thing, I wanted to know how close we'd all come to deciphering the plan. But as curious as I was, I was astounded that Dr. Henry was discussing these matters so coolly. He seemed to feel he had somehow been given immunity by Glaser; and that he could finally take credit for his clever scheme because it didn't matter anymore.

Fascinated, I watched him in the witness chair. He looked like the doctor in a public service advertisement: handsome, poised, intelligent, well dressed. Yet he spoke the words of a cold-blooded murderer:

Q. [By Mr. Glaser] What did you do?
A. [By Dr. Henry] I made arrangements for a private room.

Q. Why did you do that?

A. Because this was the time when I was formulating the plan to murder my former wife and I wanted to make sure that I could come and go un—unnoticed rather than rooming with somebody.

Q. The no. 6 is a boy scout hunting knife. You have heard testimony about that. The blade was sharpened on both sides and—

A. I didn't have a great deal of faith in my ability to cut glass. I had tried cutting the glass experimentally at home in Baltimore and found that to really effectively do this you have to tap the glass from the inside after you make the cut. Tapping it from the outside greatly raises the risk of shattering and not following the cut marks.

So I brought this tool as—for routing. I envisioned I might have to rout out the putty or the wood.

Q. What murder weapon were you planning on using again?

A. The Iver Johnson pistol.

Q. Now, the next item is a plumber's plunger with a detachable handle. Explain to the jury why you took that.

A. The plunger was for the purpose of attaching to the glass.

As I indicated, the glass had to be cut first before it will break. I anticipated using Super Glue to hold this plunger tightly enough that I could hold the broken pieces of glass if it was going to work that way.

Q. What were the two pairs of gloves for?

A. To avoid leaving fingerprints.

Q. Why did you have two pairs?

A. In case they ripped. Sometimes they rip very easily. I didn't want to rip one and not be able to get another one.

Q. I'm going to show you the homemade blackjack, and it's some metal, I believe the testimony was a chain with a handle wrapped in gauze.

Where did you get the metal ingredients for it, in Baltimore?

A. In Baltimore. I found this laying on a road. It's a chain from the back of a pickup truck where the tailgate

lets down; there is a little pin that goes into the back
tailgate to hold it on.

Q. You took that item and you wrapped it up in—it
looks like adhesive tape.

A. It's cloth adhesive tape.

Q. What is that for?

A. This isn't a blackjack at all. It's a tool used for
weakening the crystalline structure of the glass.

Q. What do you mean by that?

A. That when you cut glass there is a little round glass
cutter that you make the cut in the glass with. The glass
doesn't fall out until you tap it. This is designed for
tapping without making a clanging noise. It's heavy.
You could look at it like a hammer.

Q. Was that going to be used in torturing anybody?

A. No.

Q. We have looked at the green metal box. What was
that for?

A. To contain the metal tools in tight enough proxim-
ity to each other to where they—outlines wouldn't be
visible in an X-ray machine. I didn't know for sure if
they outline packages through X-ray machines. I knew
they did for people going on the plane. I wanted to be
prepared if they scanned the luggage for guns, so I
packed all the metal tools together tightly inside the little
metal box.

Q. That included the gun?

A. Yes.

Q. What about the stain?

A. The stain was something I needed to color the edge
of the moustache. This was written before I actually
obtained the sample of Clinique.

Q. Where did you buy the stain?

A. I didn't buy it. I was planning on getting it at one
of the drugstores. That is where I got the Clinique, at the
conference. This is a stain used by black people to stain
white spots darker. This is the type of stain I was
looking for.

Q. All right. The next thing that looks like it says
cutter.

A. Yes.

Q. What kind of a cutter were they? The glass cutters you mentioned?

A. No. These were not. So much of this stuff was preparatory. I didn't know what I was going to find when I came to Tucson.
I envisioned I would need some cutters to cut the telephone wires.

Q. You have got "1, 2, 3" on the exhibit. You see that?"

A. Yes.

Q. The two lines, 1, 2, 3, and the box, 1, 2, 3, and the picture and the word box. Describe those.

A. Detective Janes described what that is for. It's easy if you match up the box with the diagram. You can see that each of the lengths on the original piece was part of the regular box.

Q. Is that what you were going to use to mail—

A. Yes.

Q. Underneath that you see P.O. and this says wallet. I can't read that, what does that say? It says camera plus something plus wallet.

A. It's my initials, umbrella, camera plus wallet, my wallet—that's what I used because I didn't have a scale in my hotel room. I calculated using a hanger. It would take the weight of a camera case, my wallet, and some other things to make the precise weight of the box. This is what I needed in order to tell the postman at the post office, P.O., how much stamps I was going to need.

Q. Did you go to the post office?

A. I went to the post office and brought stamps in that amount of money.

Q. Activity?

A. Activity means to notice any activity in either the neighborhood or the houses, who was around and that sort of thing.

Q. If you noticed the activity, if there were activity, what were you going to do?

A. Well, obviously, I couldn't come out and kill somebody when there were people around. So I had made this flight arrangement for the following night. I had a whole—another day to use if I could. I was going to be surveilling the house until I had my opportunity.

Q. You have route, neighborhood, route, phone, changing place.

A. This is things I was going to check out in the neighborhood.

Routes by which I could leave. A location of a telephone that I could call a cab from. And a place to get my clothes, to get out of that suit and put my checkered pants on so I could look like a normal person again.

Q. Then underneath you have 1409, select window, tape, plunger, et cetera. Go right down.

A. This is fairly straightforward. This is the murder plan.

Selecting a window which would be my—my preferable way of entering. There was a time when the Bellioses had been—somebody started to break in through one of their windows and the attempt failed because something about the windows, they were difficult to break into. I remembered that and that's why I would have preferred to have entered by way of a window. That's why I put this in the plan, although I was reticent if it would work or not.

Q. All right. And now you have a plan here, it says one o'clock route. Well, excuse me.

Thru-open, find T., M.T., out front.

A. Find Tina, murder Tina, and get out by way of the front window or doorway.

Q. What then?

A. Route 1. This is written out in terms of a preferable time, which would have worked only if I had kept my original flight, but which I missed, but this other route takes the route to the nearest place where I could change. That gives me a certain amount of time.

Q. Suit.

A. Went through that already.

Call a cab. Mail the package. Two fifteen airport. This assumes that everything had gone by that schedule. I could have changed my flight to an earlier flight.

Q. Two fourteen, out evening, Dallas; is that correct?

A. This would be my leaving for Dallas.

I didn't know about anyone else, but I thought his answers were frightening. He was describing how he intended to go to

Christina's house in the middle of the night, put on rubber gloves, cut the telephone lines, get into the house, and murder her. But as he testified, he talked and acted as if he'd been asked to describe how to remove a wart.

I had to admit, though, that he hadn't entirely let his guard down. I had always wondered how he would explain the double-edged knife. His answer—that it was a routing tool—was one that had never occurred to me. Later, when Glaser asked what the firecrackers were for, he answered that they were to create a diversion if he needed one. That was ingenious, too.

And he'd explained away the note "Feed dogs" by saying he'd meant to make friends with the animals, not poison them. We'd found an apple turnover in the briefcase, and he claimed that that was what he'd planned to bribe them with, not with "meat," as written in the plan. The apple turnover wasn't used, however, because he had never even seen the dogs. They hadn't showed up the whole time he was there.

Dr. Henry had prepared himself well for the trial. But I consoled myself by recalling that he was capable of stupid mistakes too—like keeping the briefcase and its contents, keeping the murder plan, keeping the wig and padded underwear. I knew why he'd kept those things, though. If he wouldn't throw away a piece of green sandwich meat, he sure as hell wouldn't throw away his carefully assembled murder tools—especially if he planned to try again.

Next Glaser had his client explain what happened when he arrived in Tucson. Dr. Henry told how he had missed the original flight, due to heavy traffic in Dallas, and how he had taken the later flight that required him to fly via El Paso. Once in Tucson, he learned that his briefcase had been lost. Without the briefcase, it was impossible to carry out the plan.

As he explained to the jury what he had done at the airport during those hours, he added a piece of information that we had not heard before from Randall Butler: he had insisted that they search the airport for his luggage. In fact, he had demanded that they search everywhere. That piece of information would help us.

When it became clear that his briefcase wasn't going to reappear that night, he decided to use the time by walking to the Bellios house. He wanted to see his son at least. He arrived at 5:00 A.M. and saw that Mr. Bellios was already up. Having nothing else to do while he waited, he made notes of everything he observed that morning. It was a habit he'd had for years, writing things down. All he wanted was a chance to see his son, to see how he was being raised, how he was being treated.

Q. [By Mr. Glaser] Then what?
A. Then I moped around and walked around the streets for a while. Nothing happened. I began wishing I had never come.
Q. Why was that?
A. Well, because when I was walking on this street here and I saw my former wife and my son, I was—I was overcome and—with emotion about seeing my son there and seeing her there, and I determined that I couldn't go through with it.
Q. Couldn't do it?
A. I couldn't—couldn't ever do it. I knew that I couldn't at that point.

At this point Dr. Henry seemed on the verge of tears. Collecting himself, he explained that he then decided to leave, but was curious why the nursery school wasn't open. He thought it might be a phony, a scam to make his wife look better during the custody hearings. That was why he had called her that morning and asked for information about the school. He hadn't called from inside the school, but from a pay phone nearby. He had never gone inside the school; he couldn't have, because the key was in his lost briefcase. Afterward he walked downtown and took a limousine to the airport.

Backing up, Glaser returned to the previous testimony to reinforce its effect on the jury.

Q. Why didn't you stay and kill her?
A. I changed my mind. Like I told you before, when I saw her out there, I knew I couldn't commit a murder. The only thing on my mind was to get the heck out of town and get back to where I belonged.

Glaser then proceeded to the question of why Dr. Henry had left town in disguise. The answer was simple: because he had lost the key to his briefcase and therefore couldn't change.

Back at the airport he'd gone to the Continental counter, told them his name was Cordell, and asked about his lost luggage. The agent checked under the counter, found the briefcase, and returned it to him. As soon as he had it, he went to the American counter, where he encountered Mr. Zarr. He checked in, then realized this was his chance to change back into his own clothes. He got the case back from Zarr but when he got to the men's room he couldn't find the key. Later on, when Mr. Weber asked him to open the case, he'd had the same problem. He hadn't committed any crime, but he couldn't open the case without a key. That was why he'd let them keep the briefcase. He knew he hadn't violated any law while he was in Tucson, so there was no reason not to let them inspect his belongings.

As I listened to this testimony I was waiting for the kicker. That key had been found on Dr. Henry when he was arrested in Dallas and the defense, which had seen Agent Rand's inventory, knew it had. I would have loved to jump Dr. Henry about that during cross, but I had the feeling I wouldn't get the chance.

Sure enough, at the end he added a postscript. The key, Dr. Henry said, had been in his pocket all the time. But it was mixed in with all the safety pins and loose change he'd been carrying, and in his nervousness he'd missed it.

While he was on the subject of the safety pins, Glaser asked him what their purpose had been. I wasn't surprised to hear that, just as there was another reason for the knife and firecrackers, there was another reason for the pins. They were to hold up his oversized pants. Walking into town he'd had trouble with the pants, so he'd stopped at a convenience market and bought the safety pins. He didn't remember which store, or where it was located—just that it was somewhere on Park Avenue, the street that runs most of the way to the airport.

Wallace had checked each all-night store on that street, and no one remembered an oddly dressed man in a wig. Yet Dr. Henry assured the jury that he had bought the pins as an afterthought, strictly to help hold up his trousers.

Listening carefully, I caught one small error in his presentation. Several times he used the word "preparatory."

Legally, if his acts were still in the preparatory stage, no crime had been committed. I wondered if he had picked up the term in his legal research or from Glaser—either way, I'd get him for it later during final argument.

Something else occurred to me as he testified. Although he seemed to talk freely about his preparations, he rarely gave us anything we didn't already know. For example, he didn't remember why he had written the word ''oil,'' or what the fifth key was for.

I could ask him about those items on cross-examination, of course, but that was just what Glaser wanted me to do. Suppose I asked him if ''umb,'' turned upside down, meant ''gun.'' He would deny it and I would look like the victim of a wild imagination. Damn! Unimportant as it might seem, I had worked for months on that murder plan, and I was dying to ask him about it. But thinking ahead, as Ben Lazarow had taught me, I knew I'd get burned by that line of questioning. In final argument Glaser would point to it as yet another example of the absurdity of the state's entire case.

After wading through much of our best evidence, Glaser finally indicated he had no more questions. Dr. Henry had explained the entire story to the jury. Now it was my turn.

I'd waited almost two years for my chance at Dr. Henry. I had been dreaming my questions for months, concentrating on areas that would cause Dr. Henry trouble. I'd written them all down; then, the week before the trial, I'd thrown out those that could be answered easily and added tougher ones. During the trial itself I had kept jotting down more questions as the different witnesses testified, especially the defense witnesses.

Cross-examination questions are a lawyer's best tool for determining the truth and putting it on the record. The best questions are designed to force certain answers from the witness. Even the tone in which the attorney speaks can be useful. Glaser was a master at displaying anger, disbelief, ridicule, sarcasm, and surprise in his cross-exams. Now it was my turn.

When I started my cross-examination of Dr. Henry I had several hundred questions accumulated. However, to cross-examine effectively you don't read questions from a list. You fire them at the defendant in rapid succession, constantly changing the subject. That means you have to remember the questions on your feet, while still paying close attention to he answers you're receiving. The answers to cross-exam questions are often the undoing of a criminal defendant.

I started by asking Dr. Henry what documents he had been given before the trial. I made him answer specifically: he was told each state witness's name, then asked whether he had been given that person's report or statement. He had to admit that he had been given every witness's statement. Agent Wallace, Detective Janes, Christina Henry, Mr. and Mrs. Bellios, Karen, the FBI reports, ATF reports, the chemists—he had them all. The only testimony that had surprised him was that of the principal and his wife who had seen the alligator slides. What I wanted the jury to understand at the outset was that Dr. Henry had had in hand for some time all the materials he needed to prepare for my cross-examination.

That established, I turned to the lost luggage claim. Glaser had entered it earlier as evidence supporting Dr. Henry's statement that his briefcase had been lost. I now took the original form and asked Dr. Henry to identify it, as the delayed luggage form he had caused to be filled out on the morning of the sixth. After he did, I produced a photographic enlargement of the same form, five times the size of the original.

The enlargement was then placed on an easel so the jury could see it easily. Then I took the doctor's briefcase and put t on the floor, right in front of the jury. Dr. Henry watched me intently, but I couldn't tell if he realized what I was about to do. I wanted him to sit and squirm before I began my questions, but he showed no signs of nervousness.

With the two exhibits clearly visible to the jury, I asked Dr. Henry about the way he'd described his briefcase to the airline. Why had he said it had initials on it? Why hadn't he picked type 44? Did he really think type 43 more accurately described his case? The jurors could see for themselves that it didn't. In my questioning, I tried to make clear that he had: deliberately described the case inaccurately so he could hide t out in the open. Whether or not the jury believed me, I hoped I'd at least cause them to question the validity of the lost luggage claim.

When I moved on to other areas Dr. Henry's memory became clouded. He had responded fully to all of Glaser's questions, frequently going into great detail. Now he was

suffering memory lapse. To jog him out of it, I decided to use
the same tactic I'd used with Nancy Henry—hatred for
Christina. I would pose a question by quoting Christina
knowing he was bound to answer the opposite. It worked
better than I could have prayed for—and his answers had to
have had an impact on the jury.

Q. [By Mr. Stevens] Christina's testimony about you
striking the cat and causing the injuries is false?

A. [By Dr. Henry] Yes, it's false.

Q. You never told her about what you would do if
anybody crossed you?

A. No.

Q. Is that false?

A. That's all false.

Q. You never mentioned to her what would happen if
anything or anyone ran from you?

A. No, I didn't. That also is false.

Q. That's false. I see.

How long was it after she left that you came after
her?

A. I don't understand the question.

Q. Tina left in April 1974. How long was it before
you came back after her?

A. I never came back after her.

Q. What were you doing here on the sixth of December 1977?

A. This is not—what was I doing on the sixth of
December?

Q. What was your reason for coming here?

A. I came here to murder my wife.

Q. That's three years, almost four years, after she left,
is it not?

A. Yes.

Q. Four years and you came back—you were still that
mad?

A. No, I wasn't mad. I was disturbed, very much so.
I was frustrated. I was not mad.

This is not a vengeance. This was not a vendetta sort of
thing at all.

Q. Just an elimination?

A. That's precisely what it was, yes.
Q. Just going to eliminate her?
A. Yes.

He was as cold as anyone I've ever seen. He showed not he slightest indication of remorse, embarrassment, or shame. 'd have given anything to know the jurors' thoughts when he "marvelous husband and father," the "outstanding young physician" coldly explained that this was not vengeance, not a vendetta, just an elimination.

Satisfied that he had damaged himself, I picked up on his statement that he had been "disturbed . . . frustrated." This was a reference to his primary defense: that the loss of his son had made him so distraught that he was willing to murder his wife to get the child back. It was essential that we prove to he jury this wasn't true.

In the courtroom was a special calendar that I had had my office make up. It was a large piece of posterboard showing he years 1974, 1975, 1976, and 1977. When Detective Janes had testified, I had had him write down significant dates on he calendar: the date Dr. Henry went with Calvin Ingles to get his driver's license; the dates he obtained the other identification (birth certificate, Social Security card, and library card) for Terry Cordell; and the dates the airline reservations were made. On the calendar, the jury could clearly see that Dr. Henry's preparations had begun eighteen months before he came to Tucson.

When Christina Henry testified, I had her write on the calendar the date of their divorce and the dates of the subsequent child custody hearings. She was asked to write them with a different color pen than Detective Janes had used. Now I used the calendar to challenge Dr. Henry's story.

I put the calendar up on its easel and turned to Dr. Henry. Did you tell the jury, I asked him, that you didn't decide to kill your ex-wife until you'd lost the final custody battle? The jury had heard Glaser say that in his opening statement, and they had heard Dr. Henry say it when he testified on direct examination.

Dr. Henry looked at the calendar and knew he was caught—he knew what I was about to do to him. He had described to the jury in detail all the legal battles he'd gone through and how he had always lost. Now he was caught.

The calendar showed clearly that Dr. Henry had begun creat‑
ing Terry Lee Cordell months before the first custody hearing.

Dr. Henry did the only thing he could do—he succumbed
to amnesia again.

Q. [By Mr. Stevens] Before the hearings here in
Tucson in 1976, before you had gone to court, you
began creating—going to Calvin Ingles and creating Terry
Cordell, didn't you?
A. I don't remember.
Q. Well, July 7, 1976, Cordell applies for birth
certificate. July 15 Cordell applies for learner's permit.
Then your hearing is down here in August. You didn't
even wait for the hearing, did you?
A. I don't remember, Mr. Stevens. I do not remember
the events these timings were.
Q. Isn't it true you never even waited for the results of
the hearing before you began preparations?
A. That's not the way I remember it at all. If that's
the way you have proven it, then that's the way it was,
but I did not recall it being that way, no.
Q. When you began to get identification, what were
you going to do?
A. I didn't know.
Q. Did you just think, "I would like to be somebody
else for awhile?"
A. I may have done that, yes.
Q. Isn't it true that as far back as the summer of 1976
you began to create the ability to come and kill your
wife?
A. No.

His convenient memory lapses didn't matter. The dates on
the calendar exhibit were right in front of the jury. What Dr.
Henry would not remember, the jurors could see for themselves.
What he would not answer the exhibit did.

I had to be sure the jurors understood that the creation of
"Terry Lee Cordell" was the first step in his murder plan and
not just the beginning of a kidnap scheme, as he'd claimed.
So I switched the questioning to the absurdity of the idea that
he could reclaim his son in that way.

Q. Well, what else could you do if you flew to Tucson under the name Cordell?

A. Could steal the son, kidnap my son.

Q. Take him where? Back to Baltimore?

A. Possibly, yes.

Q. Where would everybody look for Patrick Henry, Jr.?

A. In the home of Patrick Henry, Sr.

Q. So that didn't make sense.

A. Except I had another identity. He could have been in the home of Terry Cordell.

Q. In the home of Mr. Ingles?

A. No. Mr. Ingles was no longer the address of Mr. Cordell. Terry Cordell has a post office box. Everything was—

Q. If they came to look at Patrick Henry, Sr.'s house, they would find the child.

A. No.

Q. Why wouldn't they?

A. Not if I had obtained another residence.

Q. How would you practice medicine? Who would you be when you went to work during the day?

A. I don't understand the question.

Q. How could you possibly give up your identity and keep the child?

A. I think this is one of the main reasons I didn't go any further with that plan. It would have been too difficult.

Q. How could you possibly have given up your own identity and sequestered the child?

A. Could have hired somebody to take care of the child.

Q. Was this one of your thoughts?

A. It was probably one of my thoughts, yes.

Q. On the twenty-third, when you made the reservations, isn't it a fact that you knew then you were going to murder?

A. I don't recall. It's too far back for me to remember that specific date.

Q. How long have you been preparing for this trial?

A. I don't understand that question, either.

Q. You have had twenty-some months and you don't recall what you were planning at that time?

A. I would like to answer your question, but I can't.

Q. Haven't you gone back and thought, "Where did
start this whole thing, where did I begin it?"

A. I think my mind was so distraught, I preferred no
to even try and think about that.

Q. That's something I would like to ask you about.
How is it your mind was so distraught but nobody
noticed?

A. I'm a very stoic person, Mr. Stevens. I don't show
my emotions as easily as many people.
I suspect many people didn't suspect that anything was
going on inside my mind because I tried to prevent it
being noticed.

Q. You could go to work, take care of patients, come
home, play with the kids, and at the same time be
planning preparations for a murder, couldn't you?

A. Could I?

Q. Did you?

A. I apparently did.

Q. Christina says you're two different people. Is she
false about that also?

A. Yes, she is. Not two different people, but I can—
can hide my emotions when I need to.

Q. This is not a question of hiding emotions. I'm
asking you about carrying on, pretending to live a regular life, seeing patients, coming home to a wife, new
wife and two kids, but in your mind you're preparing a
murder. That's not emotions. It's two different people
is it not?

A. It's not, no.

Q. Is there any way that you could have brought that
child out there and hidden the child from authorities?

A. Yes.

Q. How?

A. Under an alias name I could have rented an apart
ment and I could have hired somebody to take care of
the child at the apartment.

Q. Was that one of your thoughts?

A. It was.

Q. Why did you veto that one?

A. I don't remember why. I think it was too involved
for me. I don't recall.

Q. This is at the same time you're writing technical articles for medical journals?

A. Yes.

Q. Was your thinking messed up then?

A. With respect to the articles, no. I think my irrational thinking began much later.

Q. When did it begin?

A. I couldn't tell you precisely when it began. It was sometime not long before I went to Dallas.

Q. There is no easy way to hide your child, is there, if you grab him and kidnap him?

A. Easy way?

Q. Easy way. Convenient way.

A. Nothing is easy.

Q. But can you come up with one plan that would allow you to grab the child and bring it back so that it could become a part of your family?

A. You're asking me to postulate a plan.

Q. I'm asking you what was going through your mind in June, July, August, September, October, 1976.

A. I couldn't tell you what was going through my mind at that time.

I hoped the jury was seeing through his story. There was no way he could have brought his son back to Maryland to live with him. It takes, at most, ten to fifteen minutes to figure this out, yet Dr. Henry said it had taken eighteen months for him to realize that the plan wouldn't work.

Yet the jury might have been reacting very differently to the testimony. This was a complicated case and they were coming into it cold, without the months of preparation we'd had. I remembered my own reaction the day Bates Butler and Chuck Wallace had first told me about Patrick Henry. I hadn't been sure myself if a crime had been committed, and maybe the jury felt the same way, in spite of my opening statement.

Another possibility was that the jury was simply incredulous. They had come into the courtroom expecting to hear some run-of-the-mill case, but instead the prosecutor stands up and tells them one of the most incredible stories they've ever heard. Then the defense attorney stands up and says half of that story is true, but. . . . Then, over the next few days, they

hear about the alligator, the werewolf, the swamps. Wha
were they thinking?

Each day the judge reminded them that they were not t
discuss the case with anyone, not even their families. When
thought of how often I had gone over the case with Eley
Wallace, and Janes, I felt sorry for these jurors who had t
sort it all out on their own. I had deliberately selected th
smartest jurors available. I could only hope that they wer
following us and understanding—really understanding—wha
we were doing.

Dr. Henry had told a lot of lies during his testimony.
couldn't accuse him of that outright, but I could—and did—
convey my skepticism to the jury by ridiculing his story.

When he got to the Bellios house that morning, I asked
had he noticed anyone else running around dropping capsule
that could have drugged the dog? I had him tell again how h
had planned to throw firecrackers as a diversion, all the whil
frantically routing putty out of the window frame with hi
double-edged knife. As if asking him to reconfirm his choic
of murder weapon I said, "You were going to be chivalrou
and go ahead and shoot intead of stab, is that right?"

Already thinking of my final argument, I asked, "Did yo
think about the fact that when anything happened to Tin
everyone would look at you?"

For once, I received an honest answer: "Yes, I did. That i
why I made so much preparation."

Having led him into admitting his degree of preparation,
then asked if he had thought about who was going to find th
body the next morning. If he was so concerned about his son
why hadn't he considered how the child would feel when h
found his mother murdered?

And what about the ammunition? Why had he brough
extra ammunition for the gun? His answer was candid, bu
scary.

"I don't know. I just came prepared with it. I anticipate
maybe I would have to fight with somebody, contend wit
somebody. I don't know who." If the jury was listenin
carefully, it had just heard him admit that he had bee
prepared to shoot Mr. and Mrs. Bellios if they got in his way

One lie I particularly wanted to expose was the one abou
not having the key to the briefcase. I wanted to show tha
he'd left Tucson in disguise, not because he couldn't get t

his other clothes, but because he'd committed a crime and didn't want to be recognized. I hoped to trap him on this by asking an innocuous question.

"Now, on the morning of the sixth you were wearing a stocking cap, is that correct?"

"No, it is not. I wasn't wearing the cap then."

Again I asked him and again he denied it, this time more emphatically. Our eyes met and I knew he had anticipated me.

A stocking cap had been found inside the briefcase. He wasn't wearing one at the airport or aboard the airplane, yet from her first interview with Agent Wallace Mrs. Henry had said she saw a close-fitting cap pulled down on his head. Dr. Henry had removed the cap sometime after she saw him and put it in the briefcase. He had to have had the key to open the case. If he had admitted to wearing it that morning, I could have caught him lying, right in front of the jury. But he was too smart. Long before the trial, he had seen the inventory and realized the significance of the cap's being found in the briefcase. He couldn't explain it, so he denied he'd been wearing it.

He also denied that he'd been wearing the black and white sneakers Agent Lloyd remembered and Mrs. Henry had recalled under hypnosis. What he had been wearing he couldn't remember, he said, but it wasn't sneakers.

His footwear wasn't significant. He just wanted to cast doubt on Mrs. Henry's other testimony, especially her recollection of the stocking cap.

Dr. Henry was parrying my cross-examination well. It wasn't till the end of the first day that he made a mistake.

I was asking him what he had seen when he got to the house that morning. He answered that he'd seen Mr. Bellios in his apartment, reading the newspaper. At first that idea didn't mean much to me—then it clicked.

As nonchalantly as I could I said, "Where were you when you saw that?" I got his answer, then moved on quickly. I asked a few more questions, then came back to lock him in, to tie him down specifically so he couldn't change his answer later.

Q. Is it your testimony you didn't see the dog at all?
A. No, I didn't see the dog at all.

Q. Did you see Mr. Bellios come out?

A. No. Oh, wait a minute. I may have seen him com out because I did notice when he drove off in the car.

Q. Well, you told us that you saw him with th newspaper. Was that always when he was inside?

A. Inside, yes.

As soon as we recessed, I grabbed Detective Janes. "Ke go back to Christina's house and walk everywhere you ca up and down the sidewalks, everywhere, and see if it possible to see in to Mr. and Mrs. Bellios's apartment window I don't think it can be done, but I need to be sure."

He was back in an hour. "There's no way anyone coul see into that window," he reported. "I tried every wa possible and it can't be done."

I asked him one more question. I thought I already kne the answer, but I needed to hear it confirmed. "Where woul he have to have been to see into that window?"

"Inside the nursery school," he answered.

Later, that evening, I went to the school myself and walke around. I checked all the angles and Janes was absolute right. Dr. Henry had to have been standing either in th school, which he had denied, or in the back yard, where M Bellios would have seen him. In court that day I had aske Dr. Henry where he had been standing when he saw into th house.

"Out on the corner of the street," he had answered.

Dr. Henry, you're in trouble, I thought to myself. I ju hoped he wouldn't catch on before I could get him.

The next day, I didn't go near the subject when I starte the cross-exam again. I questioned him for twenty minut before going back to Mr. Bellios and his newspaper.

Q. Did you see him read the paper?

A. I couldn't see that well.

Q. Did you testify yesterday you did?

A. I testified I saw him in there with the newspap holding the newspaper. He appeared to be reading th newspaper but he could've been shuffling it or doin some other thing with it. I didn't see him clearly.

Q. You saw Mr. Bellios reading the paper sometim that morning in his apartment?

A. That was my interpretation of what I saw.

Q. Tell us, what could you see, what was he doing?

A. I just told you I saw him moving around the apartment. The lights were on and I saw a newspaper in his hands.

Q. How did you know it was him?

A. He was tall and lanky. He was the only male person in the family. I saw his outline.

Q. How did you know it was a newspaper?

A. It looked like a newspaper.

Q. Can you see through the window enough to see that it was a newspaper in his hand or something like that newspaper?

A. I don't recall how clearly I could see. I could see at least the outline of him with what appeared to be a newspaper.

Q. He had the lights on?

A. The lights were on, yes.

I then asked him to step up to a large aerial photograph taken from the police department helicopter. It was four feet by four feet large, and showed the nursery school and the Bellios house, as well as the apartments in back of 1409. I wanted to lock him in even tighter before I sprang the trap.

Q. Would you step out to [State's Exhibit] 56 and put your position on there when you saw Mr. Bellios with his paper in his apartment.

A. I can't recall now whether I was up here or over here. But it was one of those positions.

Q. Put one of the two positions—

A. Put what?

Q. Put one of the two, or put them both where you think you may have been.

A. I put them both. I put one X here and one here.

Q. What color are you putting them in?

A. In black.

Q. These are the positions where you think you might have been when you saw Mr. Bellios reading the newspaper?

A. Yes. I was circling the house and I could have been in either one of these positions to see that, I believe.

And then, the trap:

Q. If I were to tell you that you can't see into that apartment from anyplace but the school, would you disagree with me?

A. Yes, I would.

Q. Look right here. Right there the shed blocks any view. There is no way you can stand here and see anyone in that room.

A. Yes, there is. Right here I can see from this corner all the way across the back yard.

Q. It's your testimony that you could see from here, the X that you have placed on 56, you could see into that apartment?

A. Yes.

Q. And you could see Mr. Bellios?

A. I could see what appeared to be Mr. Bellios inside the apartment.

Q. Didn't the shed get in the way?

A. I don't recall. You're asking me to remember something that [happened] at the time when I was extremely upset and disturbed, and it's two years ago. And I just can't specifically remember what you're requesting me to remember.

Q. I'm asking you to remember what you just testified to.

Where were you when you saw him?

A. I don't remember. I had to be one of those two places, I assume.

Q. Now, Dr. Henry, the other place you placed an X on here, testified you stood, would be where you placed the X on the walk over here by Broadway.

A. I'm just postulating that. I don't know what I could see. I'm just guessing right now.

Q. Well, give us any other area where you could have been to see into that window.

A. As you indicated, I could have been in the yard of 1403 and seen it, too.

Q. Were you?

A. I don't recall.

Q. You don't recall if you were in the yard of 1403?

A. No, sir.

Q. Don't you remember if you— Wouldn't you remember if you got in the yard and walked around back here?

A. I don't remember now that I did, no.

Q. Do you have a memory lapse on what happened that morning?

A. I have difficulty with that period of time because of my state of mind that I was in, yes.

Q. Well, you recalled practicing with the glass, did you not?

A. That was in Baltimore. I remember that, yes.

Q. When did the memory difficulties start as far as your recollection today?

A. I couldn't say.

Q. Did you get into that school that morning?

A. No, I didn't.

Q. Did you carry the key for that school?

A. No, I didn't.

Q. When you came to Tucson was the key to the school in your briefcase?

A. Yes, it was.

Q. How did you know you weren't in the building?

A. I don't have a total memory lapse, just some specific details. I recall not going into the house because I didn't have a key.

Q. If the only way you can see into this apartment to see a person is by windows in the back of the school, could you have been in there?

A. "If" is a big word. I can't agree with you. You're asking me to postulate something you're trying to make me say and I can't do.

Q. Did you hear the testimony about the door?

A. About the door being torn apart?

Q. Screen door.

A. Yes, I heard the testimony.

Q. You heard the testimony about the envelope, the shades, the toilet seat.

A. Yes, I heard all that.

Q. But that wasn't you?

A. That wasn't me, no."

The point was made; he lost his memory only when the truth conflicted with his false testimony I would emphasize this to the jury in the final argument.

If only I could have been allowed to tell the jury what I really knew about Dr. Henry's memory! When Dr. Henry was hospitalized at Sheppard and Enoch Pratt Hospital, the psychologist had tested his memory I.Q. Her report stated:

> He felt that he had become obsessed and described in detail the year in which he had made arrangements. including developing an alias for himself prior to his trip with the intent to murder.

> The Memory I.Q. is 143, a very superior performance for both verbal and visual memory.

> Dr. Henry appeared to be almost hyper-vigilant to detail.

He was lying through his teeth, and my hands were legally tied. No wonder prosecutors get old quickly.

With Patrick Henry's testimony the defense had rested. But the prosecution wasn't finished yet. Both Dr. Henry and his wife Nancy had accused Christina of fabricating much of her testimony. As a rebuttal witness I was calling Janis Tyler, Christina's only close friend during her marriage.

Mrs. Bellios and Karen had both testified to scenes they had witnessed and conversations with Christina in which she'd described her husband's behavior. But they were relatives. Janis Tyler was the only person outside the family to whom Christina had confided, years before, some of the incidents about which she was testifying now.

Mrs. Tyler had visited the Henry apartment the morning after Dr. Henry had threatened his wife with a knife. She told the jury that Christina had related this scene to her, then sat there crying, trying to decide what she ought to do if her husband went into a rage again, as he had done the night he threatened to smash in the head of the baby's crib. Mrs. Tyler remembered clearly how Christina had trembled in fear.

Having told the jury everything she recalled of that conversation, Mrs. Tyler was asked to describe Christina's physical condition after the baby was born. She described how her friend's health had deteriorated, then said that she had offered Christina money to see a doctor. Christina had refused, Mrs. Tyler said, because she was afraid Patrick might find out.

Mrs. Tyler was a hard witness to cross-examine, but Glaser did his best. He began by establishing that everything Mrs. Tyler had told the jury came from conversations with Christina Henry. Then he asked Mrs. Tyler if she had ever seen Dr. Henry mistreat his wife, go into a rage, or even yell at her. Mrs. Tyler answered that she hadn't. When she tried to point out that she never went to their house when Dr. Henry was there, Glaser thought he had something.

Q. Oh, she wouldn't let you come in when he was there?
A. No, he forbid it.
Q. Oh, he forbid your coming in, he didn't like you?
A. After the little remark about the flowers. . . .

Glaser wisely changed subjects before she could explain the "little remark about the flowers." He then had her draw a diagram of the building in which they had lived. Then he had her show how the two town houses were separated by a single wall. Just as she had not seen Dr. Henry do anything inappropriate to his wife, she had to admit that, living right next door, she had not heard anything either.

Then Glaser tried to get her to admit that Mrs. Henry could have told her all these stories so that she could be a witness during the divorce proceedings, but Mrs. Tyler made it emphatically clear that until now she had never been contacted by Mrs. Henry or asked to be a witness in any proceeding.

Mrs. Tyler was then permitted to step down. She was the only witness we had been able to come up with in Mobile. Carol Eley and Ken Janes had flown out there, partly to interview Mrs. Tyler and partly to canvass old neighbors of the Henrys. They were looking for people who could substantiate even the smallest bit of what Mrs. Henry had told us. But they found no one who was willing to cooperate.

I had particularly wanted them to interview the woman who had been Dr. Henry's secretary at the Public Health Clinic. But she had disappeared from Mobile. Several months after Christina left Dr. Henry the secretary had suffered a nervous breakdown. Now she had moved away, leaving nothing behind that we could use to trace her.

The next rebuttal witness was Jerry Lloyd. He had been flown in from Dallas solely for the purpose of confirming that Dr. Henry had been wearing black and white sneakers when taken into custody.

Ken Janes was the final witness in the trial. He took the stand to explain that it was impossible to see into the Bellios apartment from either of the two places Dr. Henry had marked on the aerial photograph. The only places from which one could see into the apartment were the back yard of the house or the school, or from inside the school itself. We hoped this would suggest to the jury that Dr. Henry had been lying on cross-exam, and that perhaps he had been in the school after all.

When Glaser questioned Janes he focused on the possibility that Dr. Henry could have been in the back yard of the school, rather than the school itself. I hoped the jury would realize that if this had been the case, Dr. Henry wouldn't have had to lie on cross-exam.

Janes also described his investigation in El Paso, and how he was unable to locate anyone who had found the briefcase there and sent it on to Tucson. The teletype with the notation "Not at," was explained, but it was also pointed out that the briefcase could have been returned without a record being made. It all sounded skimpy on the stand, but I was counting on the jury to see that some uncertainty existed, and the lost luggage claim did not constitute proof that the bag had indeed been lost, found, and returned.

With Ken Janes's testimony, the state rested its case.

When all the witnesses have testified, when all the evidence is concluded, it is time for final argument. In a bitterly fought criminal case, final argument is the most dramatic and competitive moment. Each lawyer turns directly to the jury and attempts to persuade them of what the evidence has shown. Some lawyers find this a good time to perform. They may yell, plead, cry, beg—any extravagance is permitted as long as it is within the rules.

Although both lawyers are limited in what they may say to the jury, the prosecutor is much more so. He has to focus strictly on the evidence as presented; he may not express any opinion about what the defendant may do in the future if he or she is found not guilty. In this case, I could not tell the jurors how certain I was that Dr. Henry would try to kill Christina again.

Somehow I would have to try to convey that anyway. But I would have to be very careful. Invariably, the lawyers for both sides come very close to the line as they fight to get the jury to interpret the evidence and the law in their favor. But if the prosecutor crosses the line, if he is the one who goes too far, the judge can declare a mistrial. Even if the judge does not, the case is certain to be reversed later on, when it is appealed to a higher court.

I was expecting an Academy Award performance from Harold Glaser. In fact, I was looking forward to it. My own method would be quite different. Instead of becoming overly emotional, I would make an appeal to logic and reason. I would relate the evidence shown and then discuss the law. In Arizona, final argument is the first time during the trial that the lawyers are permitted to argue the law as it applies to the facts. I would show how our evidence proved what the law said had to be proved.

Then it would be time to attack the defense. Final argument is the prosecutor's only chance to speak directly to the jury and comment on and expose the defense's tactics. Without resorting to invective, I would expose the defense case for what it really was, a sham and an attempt to take in the jury. No mercy is shown either the defendant or his attorney. It must always be kept in mind that the defense attorney is poised and waiting to rip apart every witness or piece of evidence that the state has produced. And if it is appropriate, the defense attorney will not hesitate to brutalize the prosecutor.

The final challenge is to keep the jury from realizing just how vicious each side is willing to be.

The prosecution argues first. I began by relating the story of the investigation, showing the jury how and when each piece of evidence was obtained. I made it clear that the Bellios family was not privy to anything that we found until long after they themselves had been interviewed many times.

For almost an hour I recounted the facts we had proved, and argued that they proved beyond a reasonable doubt that Mrs. Henry was telling the truth. She had been telling the truth all along, I argued, yet for three days she had been verbally assaulted on the witness stand. She had been accused of making up her testimony. Yet not once had the defense proved she was lying. When I felt that this point had been amply made, I asked the jury to consider her testimony, analyze it any way they cared to. In the end, I said confidently, they would find she was telling the truth.

I then turned to the defense's case:

> With any crime that is committed there is a legal defense. With any crime. In this one, there are three good defenses that could be used.
>
> Attempted murder. First defense—the one he worked on for so long. First defense, the automatic: I didn't do it. It wasn't me. Alibi. That wasn't me in Tucson, no way.
>
> You might think about this. Had Frank Ramirez not looked down, it would have been beautiful. If he had not looked down and seen the hair sticking out of the pocket, there is no way we could have found him. Cordell coming in and Vester going out. Perfect alibi. Worked on and prepared.
>
> You can accept his testimony if you wish to. He didn't think about this until the last minute. Or you can see the long preparation. But alibi is the first defense and it's the best. That's why I asked him, "Didn't you know as you prepared, that if anything happened to Christina, everyone would look to you?" " 'Yes, I did.' " Everyone would be looking to him. Why? What happened here? There is no way, no way we could prove it, had he not been caught.
>
> He's at that convention. He's in a private room. There is nothing at the airport to show that his name was used, that he ever took a plane anywhere. The alibi was worked on and created to allow him to get away. When you talk about a mind that anticipates doing a crime and getting away with it, he worked for months and months before he even began to put it into effect.
>
> Or, if you take his testimony of the last couple of days, he just happened to have Mr. Cordell created by then.
>
> Alibi would be great. If Christina had been killed and we looked backwards we'd find nothing. But it fell apart

when he was caught. And he was caught under the worst of all circumstances—with his intent in his own writing, and he was caught with all the tools he needed to carry out that intent.

So alibi just cannot work in this case. In fact, it begins to work against him. It shows you how beautifully planned this thing was. Alibi no longer is of assistance to him, it's now detracting. It shows that this is not somebody who is doing a crazy, irrational act, somebody that's distraught and loses his train of thinking, and goes off the deep end for a couple of days.

This is a man who prepared and prepared and prepared. And, not one person had an idea of what he was doing. Okay, alibi is out.

What else? Insanity. That's a possibility. Not in this case. And the judge is not going to tell you it's no defense in this case.

Why? In Arizona, and almost every other state, the only people excused for their crimes are the people who don't know what they are doing. And that's the wisest way, and the way it should be. The only ones who are excused are those who do not know right from wrong. If someone does a crime and he is at the time—by mental disease or some other reason—he just doesn't know what he is doing, then he is excused and he should be.

What's the trouble we have with honest, decent people? What's the first thing we say whenever we read a newspaper and see a horrible crime committed? What do the good people say? What's the first thing you say? He must be sick! That's the first thing you say. But that's not sickness under the law.

Only those who are unable to know what they are doing are excused. So there is no insanity defense. It will not be given to you, and you'll get an instruction on that from the judge: anything short of legal insanity is not sufficient.

What's left? A defense called abandonment. Abandonment. Abandonment is a proper legal defense. It is: "All right, I intended to do it and I was going to do it, but I got to a certain point and I just—I just couldn't do it." That's the defense called abandonment.

Now, let's back up a minute and go to the defendant's

opening statement by Mr. Glaser. Do you remember how that occurred?

Mr. Glaser stood up and said, "I don't know why the prosecutor is wasting his time on this and so on and so forth. I'll stipulate. I'll put it right on the record, my man intended to commit a murder. I want to tell you that." However, in the next breath—"He changed his mind." "There is no reason to bring in all these witnesses, the FBI agents from Timbuktu and Afghanistan. There is no reason to bring all these people from Baltimore. We're going to admit all that."

That's exactly what you saw. It's a proper defense, but let me show you something.

What has he admitted? Is there anything truly being admitted? Here's what we could prove, and here's what he says I admit.

You can't deny this, we had found Terry Cordell. We had found Calvin Ingles. We had found the phony address, driver's license, Social Security card, birth certificate, post office box, all of that done and we were accurate. Detective Janes was.

The preparation and all of that, we had it. I ask you to go into the jury room and check me on it, check my logic and reasoning all the way through. Check Mr. Glaser, also. Don't let us act or raise voices or do anything else. Logic is what is persuasive.

There it is again [pointing to enlargement of murder plan]. No matter how hard Mr. Glaser might like you to, no matter how hard you might work on it, you will not get any other definition for "MT" other than murder—Tina.

So I've got all the preparation, everything he did in Baltimore. I had his plan and I had the tools. Did he really say anything when he said, "We admit it"? There is no other explanation, so nothing was truly admitted to you. That made my task easier because the burden of proof is on me. Here it is, Mr. Stevens, prove all of that. So I proved it.

But the point is, this is how the abandonment defense was prepared and begun. It is—well, I did it. I had that intent, I was going to, and everything, but I got here and couldn't do it. Not only that, I lost my suitcase, I couldn't have done it.

If Mr. Glaser had said anything different to you, if he had said there was no intent to commit murder, he would have no credibility with you, obviously, because there is no explanation for that note and the knife and the gun and all the other things. He would lose his credibility.

He has no choice but to say exactly what he did. "We admit this." That's why you heard the admission.

Now, the question is, did he abandon it? Here again is where the second area of law comes in.

I spoke to you about a second area. A person can abandon. If a person thinks—I'm going to kill him, and he makes the preparation, arranges for the planning, the devising, obtaining and arranging for the means of commission, and then they stop and say, this is ridiculous. They can do all the acts of preparation. They can gather up the tools, they can buy a gun, they can make the plans, make the reservations—that's preparation. You can stop. And, you should be allowed to. That's what we hope in our society. All of us reach that point at some time where we think of something and then realize this is ridiculous, this is asinine.

In that case, if a person stops before he starts to act it out, he is not responsible. He had committed no crime.

But if he stops because he is forced to stop, if something intervenes, then it is no excuse. That law will be read to you.

The law does not reward the unsuccessful criminal.

Voluntary abandonment of an attempt which has proceeded beyond the mere preparation into an overt act or acts in furtherance of the commission of the attempt does not constitute a defense. You are not allowed to try, and then be prevented from doing it. Once you have gone so far, once the slightest acts in furtherance are committed, then that's it.

So the defendant must contend—I didn't do anything in furtherance of it, I stopped before I did anything. That's why all the argument on whether the dog was poisoned. Obviously, that's horribly damaging to the defendant's case. That's a long way past, a long way past mere preparation.

The surveillance. That's why Dr. Henry said, "I ha
nothing to do and I thought I would just walk around.
That's past mere preparation.

How many times did you hear him use the word
when he testified—preparatory? Twice. That's why yo
heard it. Not with the dog poisoned, no way.

The judge is going to tell you what the law is tha
applies in this case. And one of the first things that yo
will see missing is what is obvious. No two people ma
settle their disputes, arguments, or disagreements b
murder.

You will not hear Judge Birdsall tell you that if tw
people have had a horrible marriage and they are havin
custody fights, they don't like each other, they despis
each other, they may settle it by murder. You won't hea
that.

There is no justification for his coming to Tucson t
murder her. No matter what his testimony, if you believ
all of his testimony, which you are allowed to do, if yo
want to, and you may disregard everything Tina said
which you are allowed to do—that does not justify it
and you will not hear that it does. It can't be. We are no
a society that allows it. He has other recourse.

By the way, that's what I wanted to show you. Th
story is: everything went against me. Now, let's go bac
to Mr. Glaser's opening statement, go back to the open
ing statement and you will recall—everything is goin
against him. He's paying alimony and this and that.

He was not paying alimony. That's a mistake, unin
tentional. Unintentional.

He went to court and he lost and he didn't know wha
to do and he got despondent and so on and so forth. He
didn't wait to get to court. That's why he would no
answer those questions for me.

When did you start creating this? I don't remember.

Question: Well, when did you go to Calvin Ingles? I
don't remember.

It wasn't until August that they went to court and
decided this. He started preparing before and that's why
he would not answer my questions.

There is no legal justification for murder, but how
would you at least think better of him? Well, he is a

distraught father who has had his child taken away from him unjustifiably. His wife sneaked away. She won't let him see it. She won't let him visit. He's truly a devoted father, loves the child, and wants to see him. Would you think better of him? Would that at least explain what he is doing out here with this [pointing to briefcase and contents]?

That is the nonlegal defense. That's who I am, that's what caused me to be here. I went through all the court battles, I had the custody things going on, I kept losing, I kept losing. I wanted my family together. That's exactly what you heard. That's exactly what was contended. That's exactly why you had Christina's testimony.

Part 2—Who he really is. If you remember my opening statement, I never mentioned anything about their relationship. Because I wanted you to consider the case— you can decide the case on the facts that I have talked about right now, but if you truly believe that the defendant is telling the truth, then match that with Christina's testimony.

The analysis of her testimony is what I would ask you to do. It sounds unbelievable. This man is obsessed with taking weird photographs. That this man has a thing about swamps and degutting people. That this man would do the strange things he did, and tell her, "I'll get you or I'll get anybody if it takes me forever."

What was the most important thing she tried to tell you? He is not who you see. He is two people. He is two people.

You see right now a young man, a professional man, he makes a good appearance as he sits here politely. But he is not what you think.

When you analyze Christina's testimony, balance it. What does Dr. Burnett tell you? He had absolutely no idea of the creation of the identity, no idea he had taken a patient and duplicated him.

Nancy Henry. He's a good father, good husband. No idea of what was going on, no idea of the planning.

Is he two people? Was Christina right?

Go back, if you will, and you can do this as the triers of fact. Go back, if you will, to the day he took the stand and Mr. Glaser asked him the questions about what happened out there that morning. The man whom you have seen for a couple of weeks explained to you what was on his mind, what he was going to do, and if that didn't scare you, if that man who can sit there and discuss: "I need the cutters because I wanted to cut the telephone lines. I practiced in my garage tapping glass so I could break the crystalline structure of the glass. I remembered they had had that problem, that difficulty with the window once before and I anticipated it."

That's an entirely different person than the person you see before you, than Dr. Burnett thought he was, and Nancy and the rest of them . . . Maybe Christina is not crazy. . . . Maybe there is some truth in it.

Mr. and Mrs. Thomas. No contact whatsoever with Christina. We contacted them first. How did they come up with the crazy story about the alligator? Was it put together? Was it manufactured? If it was to be manufactured, you would tell Mr. Thomas, "Your wife said the alligator is over here. You put it over on this side." No. You take it as you get it. You take the testimony as it comes. You don't correct it.

Janis Tyler knows part of it, she knows part of the things, Christina's mother knows part, her father knows less. Karen knew parts, and you noticed that it would be so easy to say to Karen, "Now, here is what has been testified to. Your mother says that she went there and he was growling and she grabbed Tina. That's what she testified to so get that straight."

No. She's not told any of that. That is why you can take the testimony and analyze it any way you want to.

How do these people come up with the story? When did all the stories start? And this is only if you want to believe that he is who he tells you he is, the father who is distraught.

Then you can get into this with the second part of Tina's testimony if you choose to. You can balance it by what he did. He said, if it took him forever he would get even. Well, three years and nine months later there he is.

He said, "Don't ever cross me." He had an obsession with degutting. Check what was said and remember I carefully tried to point out through the testimony of the witness what was told to them months and years before anything happened in Tucson.

But choose as you will what to do with that evidence, if you are convinced that the defendant told you the truth. . . . But ask yourself these questions, what sort of a loving father would send the letter that you saw? Are you satisfied with that explanation? Because that explanation, "I wanted to jolt her," and look what he used as an example to jolt her. The swamp. "I wanted to jolt her."

Is he a loving father or is there some truth in what Christina told you?

There are the things that will be up to you to decide.

Glaser came out swinging. His voice boomed loudly as he went on the attack. Christina Henry and her parents were fabricating, he said, in order to get the child away from his client. And we were helping them, he implied, by giving them information so they could get their stories straight. Repeatedly he called the state's evidence ridiculous. "I can't use that word enough," he told the jury.

But Glaser was clever. Whenever he made an accusation he couched it in the form of a question, as in this volley about the capsule of chlordiazepoxide found in the schoolhouse sweepings:

This pill they had had since December 16 until February the ninth. And they have known all along, here's this dog, got sleepy, that threw up, was never mentioned before.

What do they do with this one pill? They put it in the sweepings so it could be found? Does that makes sense? Does that make sense?

Over and over he repeated that we could not prove anything Christina Henry was saying. Her story was not supported by any other evidence—or if it was, it was just her family's. He pointed out that everything Janis Tyler knew had been told to her by Christina, who had been lying then just as she was now.

The prosecution had contended that the contents of the briefcase corresponded to Dr. Henry's torture fantasy. To

explain this away, Glaser suggested that Mrs. Henry had bee
informed of the case's contents, and had then dreamed u
stories to fit the items. Karen, who had testified to hearin
her brother-in-law discuss this fantasy at the dinner table, wa
just going along with her sister. The same theory was ac
vanced to explain the testimony she had given us unde
hypnosis. He did have the good grace to say that we mig
have given her all this information inadvertently rather tha
intentionally.

With a great deal of emotion, Glaser moved rapidly fro
one subject to another:

> Janis Tyler. Were you ever present when he wer
> into any of these rages? No.
>
> Living next door could you hear any of them? No.
>
> You have heard Nancy Henry testify. You have
> judge all the testimony. She has two little girls from
> former marriage. They get married in 1975 or so. The
> live together ever since. He adopted her two children.
> that somebody who is evil toward children? Did yo
> hear her testify about their marriage, how he is to he
> and how he is to the children? Does that coincide wit
> the testimony? I would suggest it doesn't. I strongl
> suggest that it doesn't.
>
> She's got him stroking his camera like it's a livin
> thing. She has this man who is a doctor forgetting
> shave, coming home and bawling her out for forgetting
> tell him to shave.
>
> You reach a point, really, where you can overd
> something, overkill it to the point where it's nonsensica

Glaser had a harder time trying to explain the vomitu
Having implied that Mrs. Henry and her family had perjure
themselves, he went on to insinuate that they could hav
doctored their dog's vomit as well. He also pointed out tha
not one chemist had reported finding meat in the vomitu
Since Dr. Henry's plan called for feeding the dog meat, tha
was more proof that he hadn't gone ahead with what he'
intended.

Glaser then presented a string of facts that we, th
prosecution, had developed: the distance from the house
the airport, the time Randall Butler saw him leave the termina

the delayed luggage claim, the notation on it that the bag had been located in El Paso. All of this, contended Glaser, was proof that Dr. Henry couldn't have done what he was accused of doing. And the prosecution's own investigation had revealed these things.

He was ignoring, of course, my entire cross-examination of his client. Nor was he about to mention Janes's testimony as to how the delayed luggage claim could have been created. Instead he argued furiously that the claim proved unquestionably that his client was innocent.

I have spoken to you, it's been approximately an hour and 50 minutes. Maybe a few minutes short.

Frankly, one of the things, or two of the things they always talk about when they talk about lawyers is maybe we're hams at heart and we like to hear our own voices. I could speak to you two hours more, three hours more. I didn't cover anywhere near what I wanted to cover with you, but what I covered— what I covered should certainly indicate to you reasonable doubt.

Yes, he went there with the intent to murder. Couldn't carry it out. He changes his mind. Not after an intervening cause or after he started, he changed his mind because he couldn't do it and he was running away from Tucson.

Can you understand why he was there, the type of person? . . They want to show that he is a total lunatic to have done it. Of course, it's out of his character to do it and he couldn't do it.

Each and every one of us somewhere along the line in our daily lives, based on relationships that we have, reach a point of so utter helplessness and frustration that we are ready to tear our hair out and think of drastic steps.

How many times have you ever thought if I could only kill this person, or that? But here's a man, and you have heard it all before, you saw his son, and he has seen the son two or three times in five years for a total of maybe an hour and a half. Anyone who is a parent can understand the feeling.

Finally, so much issue was raised, eventually, he is a dermatologist, you can afford to take trips. Can you think of flying out to Tucson and seeing your son for twenty or thirty minutes with your ex-wife, who is talking about you as being *that man*. They didn't even let the grandparents [see him] "Mr. and Mrs. Bellios, we love the child, don't take him away. He's our one and only." Did they think of [Dr. Henry's] parents? Wouldn't even let them see the child and they were living in Phoenix, and finally in '76 they were forced to. I'll never let him see his child. I'll never let him go to Baltimore. He has to fly out from Baltimore to Tucson for twenty-minute visits with the ex-wife.

Even when they went out to the park she sat there and took the child back after thirty minutes.

What do you do? Courts can rule. We can always make directions. We can make laws. There is a law that says that I can't go out and steal. It couldn't stop me from stealing if I really wanted to. I may have to pay the penalty, but I can go out and steal.

There's laws that say you have to be a resident for so many days to file a bill of particulars or a complaint for divorce. But I could lie. It's against the law, but I could do it.

She made his life with that child so miserable that it ate upon him and ate upon him and ate upon him. And when you think of Patrick Henry, Jr., whose name has been changed to Stevie from Pat or Paddy, when you think of Pat, who has his own child totally, totally taken away from him.

What was the last question I asked him that he answered from the witness stand? He has resolved in his own mind that he will probably never see his boy again. Regardless of your verdict he has lost. He is finished, regardless of your verdict.

What should the verdict be? Are there reasonable doubts? Is this lost baggage a reasonable doubt? Is Christina's testimony reasonable doubt?

I sure wish they would have kept that blue piece of foam so we could put it around the waist.

Is the fact he went back to the airport and took an earlier plane and tried to leave, is that a reasonable doubt, instead of staying until the next day?

Is the fact that he never made any overt acts toward her, is that a reasonable doubt?

Does his testimony give you a reasonable doubt?

Does the fact that all those years in hospitals without any complaints? As Dr. Burnett said, what type of a physician he was with his patients. A Yale graduate, a Harvard graduate, Dr. Burnett, one of the top dermatologists in the United States. Is that a reasonable doubt?

What about Dr. Hayden's testimony?

What about Nancy Henry's testimony of her life with him? Is that a murderous life? Is that a life consistent with what was testified to by Christina Henry?

When you look at the house, 1409, there was no entry whatsoever. Is that a reasonable doubt? Not even attempted entry.

Now, I could throw in so many things. You have the Wright Thomases saying there was an alligator in the picture. You have Mr. and Mrs. Bellios—I could read his testimony again as I did yesterday saying it was in a different slide. Is that a reasonable doubt? The fact that she had a story, a weird torture story for everything found in that briefcase or on his person, is that a reasonable doubt?

Is the fact that when the briefcase was opened by Sergeant Reagor that the box was taped shut, is that a reasonable doubt?

Is the fact that in no way was she attacked or assaulted, is that a reasonable doubt?

Ladies and gentlemen of the jury, the decision is yours. It's not mine. I have done all my work. I have spoken to you as sincerely as I can, not with platitudes, not with phoniness, not with any rote, not as a lawyer coming in and looking at Patrick Henry and seeing him as a dollar sign, another case, and tomorrow I go on to my next trial, but as a human being sitting there who is not guilty of this crime that he is charged with.

One of the things that Judge Birdsall is going to tell you is that he is guilty of no other—excuse me—you must try him and make your decision on attempted murder and no other charge. No other charge.

He said he saw her and his son and he couldn't do it. Obviously he couldn't and obviously he didn't and obviously he didn't stay around the next day and come in that door.

Regardless of what I have said, you have heard the evidence by way of listening to the testimony, looking at it, and examining it. This is your decision.

The jury began deliberating at 4:50 P.M. on the afternoon of September 19. Twenty-two months of investigation, hundreds and hundreds of man hours, but most important, Christina Henry's future—the jury had it all in their hands.

She and her parents were waiting at home for us to call with the verdict. Earlier that morning I'd phoned from outside the courtroom and learned that William had been released from the hospital. This was surprising, since only a week had passed since his heart attack, but Mrs. Bellios said the doctors had advised it. At the hospital he had been making himself crazy with worry. Lying in bed, attached to a bottle of oxygen, he had done nothing but will the telephone to ring. He was much better off recuperating at home, in the middle of what was happening.

"God is with us, Mr. Stevens," Athena Bellios told me as we said good-bye. "I'm sure he is. You'll see."

If only He was, I thought. We sure could use Him. Our office was just upstairs from the courtroom. When Carol Eley and I got back, I noticed that the hallways were empty. Although there are thirty-five prosecutors in the office, none of them were around.

"Where is everybody?" Carol asked.

"They don't want to see us right now," I told her.

"Why? What did we do?"

"We didn't do anything. It's what they think we're about to do—lose. They're embarrassed for us. They don't want to see us and have to pretend they don't know what everyone is saying and thinking."

"Are you serious?"

"Yeah. I've seen it before. The afternoon the Mincey jury began deliberations, it was the same thing. They know all the work we've put in, they feel sorry, and they're embarrassed. As their leader I'm not supposed to lose."

I told her not to worry about it; they had been wrong in the Mincey case and they were wrong now. Then I tempered my proclamation of confidence with some reality.

"It comes down to this, Carol: If the jury believed Christina, they'll convict. If they're lazy, if they don't try to figure out who's telling the truth about the marriage, then we've got problems. And, if they decide the case only on what happened the morning of the sixth, we've got *big* problems, unless they follow the law exactly. But something tells me this jury is smart, they'll do the right thing. The only one I'm worried about is the old man, the retired cowboy from Wyoming—he'll never understand that there could be an attempted murder without someone shooting or stabbing someone. I'm counting on the others to convince him."

"How sure are you of all this?"

"As sure as I can be, but you have to remember that juries are capable of anything. They're notorious for disregarding the law and just doing what they think is fair."

No matter what lawyers and judges tell them, juries know they have the power to forgive. They don't have the right, but they have the power—and they do it every day in criminal trials across the country. A jury will decide the defendant is guilty, but he's certainly learned his lesson and won't ever do it again; therefore, they pronounce him not guilty. This is especially likely if the victim wasn't hurt. The more violent the crime, the less forgiving the jury.

In our case no one was hurt, and Dr. Henry had testified that he knew how wrong he had been. He told the jury he'd begun to wish he hadn't come, and realized that he could never commit a murder. Unless they believed Christina's testimony, the jury's decision was all too predictable. Even though he had technically violated the law, he could be forgiven this single transgression in an otherwise exemplary life. If the jury thought Christina Henry was lying, they might even understand how her ex-husband could have been driven to the edge of murder.

If the jurors' sympathies had needed a stimulus, Nancy Henry might well have provided it. Her description of their loving home had been powerful. Even if the jurors found Patrick Henry a cold, unsympathetic person, aloof and even strange, his loyal, beleaguered wife might still have won them over. It only took one juror to block a conviction. After Nancy Henry testified, I'd seen several jurors with tears in their eyes.

Waiting for a verdict is never easy, at least not for me.

Besides trying to anticipate the verdict, I'm also reliving the days of testimony, thinking of all the things I should have said or done differently. We needed a way to make time pass faster.

"I'll be right back," I told Carol. "I'm going to go find Glaser."

I found him. He was waiting alone in the hallway outside the courtroom and he looked awful. Patrick and Nancy Henry were sitting further down the hall, holding hands; Nancy was crying.

"Harold, I've got a bottle of Scotch upstairs in my office. Why don't you come on up and have a drink with us?"

"I'd like that, Randy."

We went up to my office, and the three of us waited for the verdict.

Glaser's face, his eyes, even his speech were fatigued. I could only imagine what I looked like.

For the next couple of hours Harold entertained us with war stories from his long career. After a few drinks, we began telling each other why we had done certain things during the trial. We weren't really revealing anything—just confirming each other's suspicions.

Even as we talked, my mind kept returning to the jury room. Were they understanding what I'd tried so hard to point out? Had they seen through the defense? What were they discussing? No doubt Harold was wondering the same thing.

More hours went by, and more stories. Come on, jury. Come on. Neither the Scotch nor the conversation were making this any easier. Nine o'clock. Ten o'clock. Where were they? What were they hung up on?

A momentary lull in the conversation was suddenly shattered by the sound of my telephone. All three heart's stopped. The jury had a verdict. I told the bailiff we'd be there in a few minutes.

My eyes went to Glaser's; we looked at each other, but said nothing. This is the worst time in a trial, and undoubtedly unquestionably, the most exciting. This is the moment I live for, and the moment I dread most. As we waited for an elevator, Glaser and I said polite things to each other, but don't remember what they were. I'm positive we didn't wish each other good luck.

We sat down at our respective counsel tables and the jury filed back into the courtroom. Dr. Henry sat stiffly, facing straight ahead. The jurors weren't smiling, but they usually don't; they were very serious, and there was no hint of their verdict in their tired faces.

The judge came in; everyone stood until he was seated. Then he addressed the jury:

THE COURT: Mr. Smith, you are the foreman of the jury?

MR. SMITH: I am, sir.

THE COURT: Has the jury arrived at a verdict?

MR. SMITH: Yes, it has.

THE COURT: Would you hand the verdict to the bailiff, please. [Document handed to bailiff and thence to the court.]

THE COURT: I'm going to hand the verdict to the clerk and the clerk will read the verdict to the jury. Then she'll ask you a question which requires an oral answer from each juror.

You may proceed. You may omit the the caption.

THE CLERK: We, the Jury, duly impaneled and sworn in the above entitled action upon our oaths, do find the defendant, Patrick G. Henry, guilty of the crime of attempted murder, second degree, as charged in the indictment. Signed by the Foreman, Allan D. Smith.

Members of the jury, is this your verdict and the verdict of each of you? [Whereupon, each juror indicates affirmatively.]

My heart was beating almost out of my chest. I could barely wait for the judge to thank the jurors and excuse them before turning to Carol. We congratulated each other, feeling suddenly numb and drained as we did so. Over at the defense table Glaser was visibly upset. Dr. Henry showed nothing.

I stood and addressed the court, requesting that Dr. Henry be taken into custody immediately. Glaser opposed my request, but the judge had little choice. In a case where imprisonment is likely, and there is not much probability of the evidence being reversed, the law requires that the defendant be taken into custody prior to sentencing. Two uniformed deputies were summoned to take him to jail.

Nancy Henry had not been present when the verdict was read; she had waited in the hallway outside the courtroom. Someone had come out and told her the verdict. Now she came rushing in, weeping, only to see the deputies preparing to take her husband away. She cried out at the sight, then yelled, "Where's Mr. Stevens? Where is Mr. Stevens—I want to talk to him! I want to see him!"

She was out of control, yelling threats at me. I don't remember what she screamed at me; I was too busy watching Dr. Henry. And he was really scary.

He was staring at me. His anger and outrage were obvious, but his sheer hatred overshadowed both of them. He glared at me just as he had at Christina when she dared to testify against him. As I returned his stare, he said, "I back her up. I back her up."

Without responding to that, I turned to his wife. "I'll talk to you at another time, Nancy," I said, and walked out of the courtroom.

To hell with Dr. Jekyll. I went to my office and called the Bellios house immediately. Athena Bellios answered.

All I said was, "We got him. He's guilty."

Her reply: "Oh, thank God. Thank you, thank you." Then I asked her to have Christina call me. I would be waiting in my office.

Mr. and Mrs. Bellios always relay my calls to Christina now that she is married again. I don't know where she lives. I don't know how to call her. I don't even know her new name—and I don't want to know. She is hidden, and I don't want to know where. That's our agreement, and it has been since she remarried. Now that the trial was over, and she had no need to remain in Tucson, she would move again, and I would not know where. If I needed her, her parents would have her call me.

Christina called within minutes. I knew, she knew, but I told her anyway.

"We got him, Christina, we got him. The judge locked him up; he's in jail. You're safe."

Her answer I will never forget; she spoke with the fervor of someone who'd been released from a long and terrible slavery: "I'm free! I can breathe! Thank God, I can breathe."

Only the final hurdle remained—sentencing. Again, both sides went all out. Glaser had numerous doctors, psychiatrists, neighbors, ex-patients, friends, and family write to the judge asking for leniency. They all thought Dr. Henry should be released on probation, so he could return to his wife and the practice of medicine.

We, of course, pressed for the opposite. We wanted him locked up for as long as possible. Dr. Henry hadn't changed, we insisted, he was still extremely dangerous. Only months before, a psychologist had written that Patrick Henry was "obsessed with hatred and disgust" and "dangerously preoccupied with his obsessions." We knew his ability to cover up his feelings. We also knew that the trial, with its attendant humiliations, would only tend to fuel those hidden emotions.

On November 5, 1979, sixteen days after the jury verdict, Glaser and I argued for hours before the sentencing judge: Glaser first, then me, then Glaser again. In the back of the courtroom sat William Bellios, not about to miss this final step. When he'd called to tell me he was coming, he'd promised to stay calm, and not to get overly excited. "I be there, Mr. Stevens. I don't miss this."

Glaser was still insisting that everything Dr. Henry had said at the trial was true. This required that he completely disregard what I had done to his client on cross-examination, not to mention the jury's verdict. He also continued to contend that Christina Henry's testimony was ridiculous, false, and totally unbelievable. Working from these two premises, he asked the court to show mercy to the distraught father, who had almost had a nervous breakdown over the loss of his child, and who, in the final analysis, couldn't hurt anyone.

That nonsense that was said in this courtroom, I'm not talking about the facts of the day in December, December 6 and December 5, I'm talking about the collateral background material. It just—a person—he can't be Dr. Jekyll and Mr. Hyde. He can't be to such an extent. That's for the movies. That's for Spencer Tracy. That's the the magic potions. It's absolutely and totally uncorroborative evidence from the testimony of Christina Henry.

Is there—is there other corroborative evidence? Let's look at the facts of the case as it came out, again looking at it in the best light to the state.

This man, this defendant, was so frustrated and went to the point of attempting to commit an act because of his feelings for his child. I would think so, at least that's the whole testimony, that's everything you have in your presentence report.

I mean, he went strictly for broke as a result of that. At least from that testimony.

What does it mean? Does it mean that he disliked the child? Does it mean that he had no use for the child? Did the two adoptions mean he was jealous of the child, because this is the testimony? It's absurd. It's absurd, the fabrications that were made by those who testified, or if not fabrication, such distortions as to the perceptions that after the baby was born, Your Honor, the inference that was tried to be given by the prosecution through Christina Henry is that he went in the room and tied the baby up in blankets with knots and tried to strangle the baby. Can you believe it? Especially in light of his life thereafter, can you believe he walked into the baby's room and the baby's arm was blue and he said, "Oh, it's probably congenital heart problems. Nothing we can do about it." Can you believe it?

The importance of all this, the importance of all this, if the court pleases, is this: not to the actual facts of what happened on that day or proceeded that day, but to whether or not you put a man who, whether for reason or no reason, was emotionally so sick as everybody says, you put a sick person in jail. I say that you don't.

Glaser argued with all the force and sincerity of a southern preacher, never once acknowledging that the jury had found against his client on these matters.

On my side I had a powerful weapon—the Sheppard and Enoch Pratt psychologist's report, which I was free to use for the first time. When it was my turn, I went through Dr. Henry's cross-examination, a transcript of which my office had prepared for this hearing. I pointed out each lie, each denial, each memory lapse—there were more than ninety of those—and suggested possible reasons why he had answered as he did. I compared what Christina Henry had told us about him with what the psychologist had found— revealing how each confirmed the other.

Dr. Henry, I told the judge, was "one of the most dangerous individuals" to come to trial during my tenure as chief prosecutor. Since this judge had presided over many of the cases I'd prosecuted, he knew that some of the worst killers in the country were included in that description. I hoped he saw my point: Dr. Henry was capable of murder, of torture, of deceit, but he was a great deal smarter than the others who were capable of the same thing.

In closing I told the judge:

> The state contends, and feels quite certain in this; the defendant did not act to regain his son. Perhaps that was a secondary result of what he intended. He acted as he did act with the intent to murder his wife. He came out here and conducted activity that he now denies, that has been proven, beyond doubt. There is no question that he went much further than he admits he did. He came out here to court and continued to give false testimony. He was caught several places in his cross-examination.
>
> His testimony shows he is a danger. His demeanor on the stand, as he relates so coolly the "elimination," and the possibility of contending with others.
>
> I submit he is dangerous. He was in December . . . and he was in September, and he is today.
>
> I submit that Christina Henry's life will be in danger for as long as he lives, or as long as she lives. . . . He acts out of anger. He is tenacious. He will not forget and he will not forgive. He will come again.
>
> He showed this not only in what he said, what he told her he would do, but in the psychological evaluations of him. "I'll get them later or at another time." He admires himself for his tenacity.
>
> I submit that Christina's life will be in jeopardy no matter what this court does.
>
> I would ask the court to impose the maximum time possible, with the knowledge that it will be served one-third time only, and he will be released, and he will then

be in a position to carry out what he tried here, but it was impossible for him to do.

I expect the court to base sentencing on the doctrine of protection as well as retribution.

Patrick Henry was the last person to address the court. He stood and, with more emotion that I'd seen during all the hours he testified, pleaded with the judge for leniency:

> I'm deeply sorry for this entire affair, Your Honor. I would give anything in the world if I could go back in time and undo the events of 1977.
>
> However, I did prove myself incapable to commit violence before actually putting my plan into motion.
>
> In reality, I never actually attempted murder at all, Your Honor.
>
> I have continued to live an upright and law-abiding life during the past two years since that time.
>
> Now, this is my very first offense of any kind, Your Honor, and all I ask is one chance—one chance, to prove to the world that I can be a good and useful citizen and a good father and husband for my family.
>
> I would guarantee you, Your Honor, if you give me that chance, you won't be disappointed with me.

Again Glaser and I were at war. But this time we were both defeated. The judge sentenced Dr. Henry to a term from five years to fifteen years in the Arizona State Prison—a term too heavy for Glaser and too light for me.

As the judge pronounced the sentence, I felt my stomach drop. My face and neck flamed hot with disappointment. It was the first time in my career that I'd ever reacted so strongly to a sentence, and I knew why.

I could not turn my head to look at Mr. Bellios. He'd counted on me, he had shared his responsibility with me, and I had failed him. At that moment I couldn't face him.

In the days to follow, Christina and her family tried to console me, to assure me they were pleased with what had happened, but I could see their disappointment. I could only apologize to them.

Christina tried to explain that I had given her what she had never dreamed possible: I had given her some time. As long as Patrick Henry was in prison she would be free from worrying, free from expecting something awful to happen, free to live her new married life.

It wasn't enough. With everything we did—the detailed investigation, the hours of worrying, the sleepless nights, the exhaustive preparation and trial—we had won her very little time. Based on the judge's sentence, Dr. Henry would have served a maximum of only four and a half years. Now it seems likely his imprisonment will be even shorter.

Four months after Dr. Henry was sent to prison, I learned that he was fooling people again. Prison officials called to notify me that a staff psychiatrist had examined the prisoner and declared him no danger to anyone. As a result he was being transferred to a minimum security institution and would probably be released even earlier than we had anticipated.

When he is, Christina's waiting will resume. We know Dr. Henry will come again. There is no comfort for any of us.

ABOUT THE AUTHOR

William Randolph Stevens has been Chief Criminal Prosecutor for the Pima County, Arizona, Attorney's Office for ten years. He lives in Tucson.